IDYLLS & REALITIES

IDYLLS & REALITIES

Studies in Nineteenth-Century German Literature

J. P. STERN

Frederick Ungar Publishing Co.
New York

Printed in Great Britain

Library of Congress Catalog
Card Number 72-157095

ISBN 0 8044 2830 1

Contents

1690516

Acknowledgements

My thanks are due to the editors of *The Listener* (London), *Novel* (Providence, R.I.), and to Messrs. Prentice-Hall, Inc., publishers of *German Language and Literature: Seven Essays*, for permission to reprint in this book material which, in a somewhat different form, first appeared in the pages of their publications.

St John's College,
Cambridge

ONE

Palms and Odalisques

The essays assembled in this book are concerned with German literature in the period which, outside Germany, saw the efflorescence of European realism. This period spans the decades between Goethe's death in 1832 and the foundation of the German Reich in 1871. However, it seemed proper to extend it so as to include some of the writings of Theodor Fontane, the only major realist on the German scene, whose fiction was written between 1878 and his death in 1898, and the last novels of Wilhelm Raabe, written in the early 1890s; and I conclude with an account of Nietzsche's *The Birth of Tragedy*, completed in 1872, which contains both a critique of Nietzsche's own age and intimations of the age to come.

It seemed best to consider this literature not chronologically but according to its three major genres – the drama, poetry, and that most characteristic of nineteenth-century forms, the narrative prose of novels and Novellen. In an earlier book[1] I concentrated on the prose writings of this period and the problems peculiar to it. These problems, I argued, were symptomatic of a literature which was not readily accommodated within the common social certainties and *données* of its time; the world being presented (in the prose writings I then considered) not so much as a thing final and indisputably real but rather as in itself an 'interpretation'. It was thus my aim to suggest criteria, alternative to the common notion of realism, according to which the value of those writings, their especial charm and the weaknesses to which they were prone, may be more justly and fruitfully estimated. This argument is continued in the present book, a companion volume, where I have cast my net more widely.

It has not been my aim to write a comprehensive literary history, nor have I attempted full accounts of the achievement of individual writers. Instead, I have concentrated on a few major works which have seemed to me characteristic both of their authors and of the age to which they belong. The claims of literary-historical scholarship are not at odds with those of literary criticism – indeed, I don't believe that either can do without the other. Nevertheless, it may be well to confess at the outset that my emphasis throughout has been critical.

The literature of this period is only loosely and at best indirectly related to the chief events and cross-currents of contemporary German history. This is hardly surprising, seeing that it is a literature created by middle-class authors and determined by middle-class values and aspirations, yet written in a political climate in which the middle classes were virtually powerless when it came to ordering any of the large-scale aspects of their lives. Occasionally protests are registered against this state of affairs – in Büchner and Heine, and in the ephemeral writings of Jung Deutschland – yet no coherent alternative ethos is formulated.

The early part of the era is dominated by the oppressive régime of Metternich's police state and its imitations among the smaller principalities of what had until recently been parts of the Holy Roman Empire. The opposition to this oppression, articulated by the national-liberal intellectuals, reaches its climax and quick defeat in the Frankfurt Parliament of 1848 – a defeat whose shadow lies over the next seventy years of German history. The foundation of the Second Reich on the balustrade terrace of the Salle de Guerre at Versailles represents the triumph of an improbable combination of three incompatibles: the anachronistic idea of the medieval imperium and Romantic notion of '*das Volk*'; Prussian militarism and bureaucracy; and industrialism.

In terms of economic history (which Karl Marx in 1845 declared to be the only real kind of history) the period under discussion sees the belated beginning and momentous acceleration of the process of industrialisation; it is here that the Protestant states of Germany take the lead. Among the circumstances favourable to this development were: a uniquely efficient system of higher technological education; an astute competition modified by State-aid, protective tariffs and cartels; and the lessons learned from the notorious English 'Manchesterismus'. The powerful will to catch up with 'the West' manifest in this development is confined to industry and commerce. Political thinking, on the other hand, fails to keep pace. Outmoded institutions must appeal for their sanction either to out-moded values or to coercion of various kinds. The gradual enfran-chisement and parliamentary debating chambers and constitutions are wrung from the reluctant ruling princelings and heads of states, but these concessions are used lamely and ineffectually; it is in the higher echelons of the civil service that major political and economic decisions are made. The German bourgeoisie is exposed to a complex tug-of-war of ideologies which leave it paralysed; the several pressures which the English and French middle classes were able to accommodate over a period of centuries, one after another, the *Bürgertum* has to face all at once. From the right they have to contend with the hostility of a rigidly exclusive aristocracy, to which belongs the higher executive of the civil service. They have to cover their left flank against a proletariat that is growing in numbers by leaps and bounds. Behind them is the sad débâcle of 1848. Before them, industrial expansion and economic progress – power to be wielded concretely, in the factory yard and counting house, not through sham parliaments. In this predicament the conception of nation-hood emerges as the only point of positive contact with the State.

During the Wars of Liberation the German intelligentsia had been strengthened in its patriotism by the example of France, its enemy.* The tension between the democratic ideas of the French Revolution and German nationalism remains unresolved throughout the sub-sequent era. The sequence of French and English – but also of Russian and Austrian – history is reversed: the Reich is founded as a political derivative of 'the Nation', whereas 'the Nation' itself is based upon a common language and literature, not upon a common political past; which is why the Reich has constantly to be defined, why it cannot be taken for granted.

And now the characteristically German situation develops: politics comes to be regarded as an unworthy pursuit, undeserving of the attention of intellectuals, whereas literature, philosophy, and the arts generally are thought to offer an alternative to political

* Fontane explores this situation in *Vor dem Sturm* (*Before the Storm*, 1878); see below, pp. 176f.

engagement. Perhaps the best way to illustrate this curious situation
is to follow Nietzsche's advice when he tells us that 'Three anecdotes
are enough to give the picture of a man . . .';[2] a handful of characteristic quotations should suffice to give us an impression of the age.

We begin with Goethe, whose shadow lies heavily on the whole
period. His poetic drama *Die natürliche Tochter* (*The Natural Daughter*,
1803) was intended as an allegorical comment on the French
Revolution. In Act IV, the spokesman of moderate middle-class
opinion regrets the miscarriage of justice whose victim the heroine
has become:

> Ich schelte nicht das Werkzeug, rechte kaum
> Mit jenen Mächten, die sich solche Handlung
> Erlauben können. Leider sind auch sie
> Gebunden und gedrängt. Sie wirken selten
> Aus freier Überzeugung. Sorge, Furcht
> Vor grösserm Übel nöthiget Regenten
> Die nützlich ungerechten Thaten ab.
> Vollbringe was du musst, entferne dich
> Aus meiner Enge reingezogenem Kreis.

> Not for me to condemn the tool, to argue
> With those powers who permit themselves
> Such action. They too, alas,
> Are bound, hard pressed. They act
> But rarely from a free conviction. Care
> And fear of greater evil compel princes
> To act unjustly from expedience.
> Do what you must do, and leave
> The narrow, nicely drawn circle of my life.

To this anxious, almost plaintive defence of the private sphere no
other point of view is opposed – this is all the play has to say on the
relationship between State and individual. One therefore wonders
what Goethe made of that famous remark of Napoleon's at their
meeting in Erfurt in 1808:

> . . . Returning then to the subject of drama, Napoleon made
> several very weighty observations, which showed that he followed
> the tragic theatre with close attention, like a judge in a criminal

trial. Turning to the [then fashionable] tragedies of fate, he expressed strong disapproval of them. They belonged to a darker age. After all, he said, what have we nowadays to do with fate? Politics, that is fate!

'Die Politik ist das Schicksal!' – is the sentence really open to the misinterpretations it has so often received? Certain it is that 150 years later Bertolt Brecht was still berating German politicians and dramatists alike for their indulgence in 'fatalism' and 'historical inevitability'. And in so doing Brecht was echoing the voice of his master who, in 1845, was opposing his own view of history to the traditional 'concept of family' which Marx saw as dominant in German historiography. In exposing the absurdity of subordinating all social forms to that concept, Marx is of course attacking the paternalistic régimes on the contemporary scene as well as the ethos of the academic historians. History, he is saying, is neither the story of a disembodied World Spirit, nor can it be explained in terms favoured by the German paterfamilias. On the contrary,

> . . . a certain mode of production, or industrial stage, is always combined with a certain mode of co-operation, or social stage; . . . from which it follows that 'the history of mankind' must always be studied and worked out in close connection with the history of industry and exchange. But it is equally clear that in Germany no such history can be written, because the Germans lack not only the power of comprehension and the material but also the 'sensuous assurance' necessary for such a history. These are things of which you cannot have any experience on the other side of the Rhine, for there history no longer occurs.[3]

We shall see how reluctant the poets and writers of Marx's age will be to leave that area of private and familial values which Goethe had staked out for them; how unwilling to accept the data of their society as the substance of their art. Grillparzer will project the old values into a cosmic order in which all change amounts to offence. Hebbel will replace them by 'the World Idea' and 'the Absolute'. And when the young Georg Büchner pushes through the cardboard figures of idealist ideology, what he finds looks at first sight like Marx's 'real history'; but is in reality the bare, unalterable desolation of individual human existence.

The domination of private values and the disaffection with politics, coupled with an intense speculative fervour *and* rapid advances in the natural sciences and industrialisation – all this suits the aspiring politician well enough:

> As for Germany, there can be no doubt that what binds us to- gether is not that external institution, the police, but the com- munity, uniting all German lands, which has evolved in the sciences, the arts and literature – a community whose develop- ment cannot be arrested.[4]

As a definition of what, twenty years before, Karl Marx had called 'die deutsche Misere', the young Bismarck's observation of 1867 could hardly be more accurate. It sounds like an echo of that famous statement of Jacob Grimm's – at once bitter complaint and proud self-justification – in the 1854 Preface to his *Dictionary*: 'After all, what else have we [Germans] in common apart from our language and literature!'[5] The appeal from a merely 'external' institution to intellectual and artistic values, the combination of 'Kultur' and police state, provides the setting, after 1871 no less than before, for that most enduring of all the figures on the German political stage, the non-political – that is conservative – *Bürger*.

If this was the setting in which the literature of the age came to be written, the political trials of the 1830s with their draconic sentences and the wave of liberal emigration after '48 show that the ruling ideology didn't go unchallenged. There were men on whom the lesson of the betrayals and failure of the Frankfurt Parliament was not lost, men who passionately opposed the isolation of the intel- lectuals and had a very different conception of the *Bürger* and his responsibilities. In his testament of 1899, the great Roman historian, Theodor Mommsen, wrote:

> I have never held a political position, and I have never had, nor aspired to, any political influence. But in my innermost being and with the best that is in me I have always been a political animal and have always desired to be a citizen [*Bürger*]. In our nation that is not possible, for with us the individual man, even the best among us, never rises above doing his duty in the ranks [Dienst im Glied] and above political fetishism. It was this inner estrange- ment from the people to which I belong that firmly decided me to

shun the German public whenever it was possible for me to do so –
a public for which I lack respect.[6]

'With us even materialism is hardly more than an idea.'[7] Brecht's
taunt may stand as a motto to the German Naturalists' strenuous
theorising. They certainly face the social problems of the 'eighties
and 'nineties, insisting on the literary relevance of the grimmest
aspects of industrialism. Their alliance with the Social Democrats
may have its ups and downs, but it does represent the first conscious
party political *engagement* of any movement in the history of German
literature. Their literary achievement, on the other hand, is less
easily demonstrated. The only great dramatist the movement could
call its own, Gerhart Hauptmann, was never an easy bedfellow.
His long career (he died in 1946), which is not without its moments
of genuine pathos, is typical of the careers of many lesser men.
Hauptmann owes to Naturalism the first channelling of his creative resources. But even in his early plays (from 1889 onwards),
which are cast in the Naturalistic mode, he is chafing under an
increasingly uncongenial literary doctrine. Even there he is more
concerned with the inescapable because predetermined tragedy of
human suffering than with its socially demonstrable causes. Around
the turn of the century the tension from which Hauptmann drew his
inspiration lapses. And although the social realism of the early plays
is never entirely abandoned, he (like his admirer, James Joyce)
moves all too readily into a world of fairy-tale, mythology, and
symbolism.

Hauptmann's is, as I said, a typical development. Theodor Fontane, who belonged to an earlier generation and was not given to
historical generalisations, summed it up with his customary in-
formality in one of his stories:

If a man *has* something – well, of course, he can take life as it is,
he can be what they nowadays call a realist. But a man who has
nothing, and who always has to live in a Sahara desert – why he
simply can't exist without a fata morgana with palms and
odalisques and all that sort of thing.[8]

A good many personal and literary aspirations of Fontane's
century – a good many arguments of these essays – are illuminated
by this parable. The pathetic search for 'the great personality' in the

stories of Conrad Ferdinand Meyer, the jingoism and dubious missionary zeal of Gustav Freytag, the dialectic of the exotic and the frowstily-provincial in the later novels of Wilhelm Raabe, even Nietzsche's Superman himself – are they not all variations on this theme of 'a fata morgana with palms and odalisques'? But is this not (it will be asked) the age of the Ballins and Krupps, of the Baghdad Railway, of German colonies in Africa and China, of rayon and high-grade steel, of the ever-increasing importance of industrial growth and economic power . . .: an age, surely, singularly free from any sense of deprivation ('Wer aber nichts hat . . .')? Not Fontane but Nietzsche and after him Thomas Mann explain the German malaise and that discontent which, on the political level, manifests itself in an atmosphere of perpetual emergencies. To Nietzsche the ideology of the age represents 'the defeat, nay the extirpation, of the German spirit by the German Reich'; the Wilhelminian ethos represents not the resolution of the 'pathological discrepancies' between an out-moded morality and religiousness and the realities of contemporary life, but the victory of the philistines. And Thomas Mann's *Budden-brooks* is (among other things) the story of that defeat of 'the spirit' by 'life' writ large – 'the spirit' becoming ever more etiolated and esoteric, 'life' ever more coarse in the process. It is true that, from *The Birth of Tragedy* to the end of the days of his mind, Nietzsche exalts 'life', knocking down one set of moralities and erecting another all in the name of 'life's' ineffable splendour. Why then does he not see the new Reich as an embodiment, or at least as a partial expression, of his high ideal? Because it is, for him too, no more than 'an ideal'; because the utopia he creates lies beyond any possible incarnation. With the destructively critical part of his mind Nietzsche reaches beyond his age, into a well-nigh complete isolation; by the side of his critique the work of a Matthew Arnold is as milk and water. In the constructive part of his philosophising, on the other hand – that is, in his utopia – he remains a son of his age.

The excellence of the German universities as places of the highest learning remained unchallenged to the end of the nineteenth century; Harvard was built in their image, even Oxford (and to a lesser extent Cambridge) came under the influence of neo-idealist philosophy. There is no contradiction between the wretched record of the German academics after 1933 and the fact that, to the end of the Second Reich, in classical philology and jurisprudence, in philosophy, history but also in mathematics and the natural sciences, the German universities represent one of the finest achievements in the intellectual history of the West. Nor is it to be thought that the learning they pursued was exclusively 'abstract': the *Technische Hochschulen*, several of them founded as early as the 1830s, offered a higher technological and scientific education that was closely tied to the demands of industry. But underlying all this was the conviction that the great 'wissenschaftlich' achievements were made possible by a neat separation of politics from academic life and industry. It is perhaps best expressed in the words of a Berlin literary historian writing after the First World War, when most of this ethos had collapsed together with the institutions it supported. And it is significant that he unblushingly introduces his argument with the most hackneyed bits of popular wisdom (whose soporific rhymes defy this translator):

> How different was the life of that German nation in which Goethe had once seen the epitome of all the virtues: 'Modesty, content-ment, straightforwardness, loyalty, joyful acceptance of weal and woe, guilelessness', patient endurance . . . 'Let each sweep before his own door, and the whole town will be clean; let each learn his own lesson, and all will be well in the town council' – that was Goethe's proven principle, and he disliked nothing more than the sort of political dilettantism which today is found in such frighten-ing profusion everywhere, even in the highest circles. The fact is that before the Revolution [of 1918–19] we could, on the whole, put our trust in the honesty and objectivity of our Government, *and thus save ourselves the trouble of meddling with the affairs of our excellent Prussian bureaucratic state.* These are among the conditions in which is rooted Germany's *geistig* superiority throughout the nineteenth century, generally and above all in her scientific and technological development.[9]

For a hundred years and more the logic of this argument went virtually unchallenged; as far as I know only Max Weber offered a public critique of it[10] – but by that time 'der vortreffliche preus-sische Beamtenstaat' lay in ruins.

It is easy to see what, in such a situation, were the prospects for parliamentary democracy. More relevant to my theme are its consequences for the literature of realism. There is no need to postulate a rigid Marxist causality. However much leeway one allows to the nexus between a given society and its literature, a lack of interest in the ways that society works will not yield much illumination of those areas of experience which a man shares with other people: the areas in which public values predominate over private ones. Man in his solitude and ensconced in nature, man in the 'nicely-drawn narrow circle' of his family and friends, man facing the fundamental questions of his existence: these are spheres in which his social being is relatively uninvolved, and here above all lie the greatest achievements of nineteenth-century German literature. But we know that man's experience is not confined to these spheres; that there are no sharp boundary lines between 'private' and 'public'; and that his social experience, be it never so 'unauthentic', 'alienated' or contemptible, reaches to the very grounds of his being in the world. How do we know? This, precisely, is what the great realists of the nineteenth century teach us, this by definition is not indeed the message but the condition of their art:

> The serious treatment of everyday reality, the rise of more extensive and socially inferior human groups to the position of subject matter for problematic-existential representation, on the one hand; on the other, the embedding of random persons and events in the general course of contemporary history, the fluid historical background – these, we believe, are the foundations of modern realism.[11]

Many aspects of Auerbach's well-known conclusion will provide us with criteria for our analyses. The 'problematic-existential represent-ation' includes a portrayal of man in his proud or inconsolable solitude. But whether he enters his solitude of his own choice or whether other men condemn him to it, his journey there goes through the world of their social experience, not around or beyond it. Moreover, in the context of German literature it is important to add to Auerbach's conclusion a point which he would have con-sidered self-evident, namely that the realists are innocent of all epistemology. If ever a character in Dostoevsky has any doubts about the phenomenal world, that world is sure to assert its reality and to dispel those doubts. It is hardly ever a very good world (and the realists are not very good at portraying one that is a good world), but it is the only one they – the practitioners of a mimetic art – have got. Some of the writers we are about to consider offer other prospects.

TWO

Three Dramatists

Conformism is the dominant mode of society in the age of Metternich: similarly, the dramas of the age portray tragic heroes who are the victims of impersonal forces. The tragic guilt of individual characters is caused not by a single moral flaw or an act of personal hubris, but by a radical disharmony between their existence and the forces that govern the world in which they find themselves. The personal decisions and acts that determine their fate intimate a universe that makes game of their aspirations. Grillparzer in his early plays still follows the Shakespearian (and Aristotelian) pattern: what isolates the hero from the social collective is an individual act, his tragic guilt equals ethical guilt, its expiation in his death is followed by a renewal of the political order. In Grillparzer's later work the pattern changes: what now isolates the hero and leads to his tragic downfall is not a single act of hubris but a whole disposition of mind which amounts to his finest personal virtue – his wisdom and scrupulousness – which in the world of politics lead to chaos and strife. In the individual's downfall no order is affirmed, no divinity validated, the world just goes on. For Hebbel all assertion of individuality is tragic: its destruction by the State is the very law of universal history, the necessary condition of historical change and of the renewed political order that ensues. With Büchner we enter the world of the absurd. Where some of Hebbel's tragic heroes had shown a strange and chilling pride in their election for sacrifice, Büchner's anti-heroes live in a universe dominated by a meaningless determinism: the social collective to which they belong is implacably hostile; the only value they cling to is their sentient, suffering selfhood, their mere existence.

FRANZ GRILLPARZER: THE CONSERVATIVE VISION

If the political life of Germany, at all events up to the middle of the century, was under the shadow of the defunct Empire, the literary life of the era was dominated by the august cultural heritage of Weimar, which Goethe and Schiller had bequeathed to the subsequent generation. Franz Grillparzer, the oldest of the three major dramatists of the era, thus found himself trammelled by a high poetic convention of verse drama to which his own Viennese parlance rose awkwardly and with frequent signs of strain. Grillparzer's first play, *Die Ahnfrau* (1817), belongs to the school of 'fate tragedies' in the wake of Schiller's *Braut von Messina*; in *Sappho* (1817),[1] which treats of the conflict between the poetess's vatic calling and her sensuous humanity, he follows closely in the footsteps of Goethe's *Torquato Tasso*. Yet as the influence of Weimar wanes, so the isolation to which the characters of Grillparzer's dramas are exposed becomes more radical than anything we find in German classical drama. The trilogy *Das Goldene Vliess* (1821) concentrates in the third part on the fate of Jason's wife, Medea, who is brought to Greece from her native island of Colchis; betrayed by her husband, she reasserts her barbaric origins in a monstrous act of infanticide.

König Ottokars Glück und Ende (1825) draws on the early history of Bohemia (as does *Libussa*, 1848); in the figure of the ruthless and ambitious Bohemian king (reminiscent of Richard III) the themes of personal and political hubris are powerfully linked, whereas the peace-loving Rudolf I, founder of the House of Hapsburg, offers a not wholly adequate antagonist. In *Ein treuer Diener seines Herrn* (1828) Bancbanus, the Hungarian king's deputy, is involved in a series of intrigues in the course of which he loses his young wife; this figure of the deeply loyal but ineffectual servant of the State embodies one of Grillparzer's favourite themes – the dilemma between spirituality and worldliness. *Des Meeres und der Liebe Wellen* (1831) reinterprets the tale of Hero and Leander, and again the dramatic interest lies in the fact that Hero is by nature unsuited to her priestly calling (as Medea was to the culture of Greece, and Bancbanus to political office).

Der Traum ein Leben (1834, based on Calderón's *La Vida es Sueño*),
represents a dramatically successful combination of realism and
fairy-tale magic on which a homely moral lesson is imposed – a
characteristically Viennese prescription. (Schikaneder's libretto for
The Magic Flute contains the same elements in different proportions.)
As in *Ottokar*, the hero of *Life is a Dream* is driven by overweening
ambition beyond the confines of the life allotted to him; but when
disaster threatens, all his adventures are seen to have been but a
dream. The comedy *Weh dem, der lügt* (1838), a resounding failure at
the Vienna Burgtheater, is the last of Grillparzer's plays to be
published in his lifetime; its serious moral theme – 'every lie, even
the smallest, assails the foundation of the entire human condition' – is
not easily accommodated in the play's central figure, the scullion-boy
Leon. Grillparzer's last three plays were published posthumously in
1872. In the weakest of them, *Die Jüdin von Toledo* (begun in 1824),
the young and inexperienced Spanish king neglects the affairs of
state (and his frigid English wife) for the young Jewess Rahel; the
nobles solve his dilemma for him by murdering her, and the play
closes as the king, beneficiary of his ministers' crime, departs on a
holy crusade, leaving the regency in the queen's hands.

Ein Bruderzwist in Habsburg (begun in 1827, all but completed in
1848) mirrors Grillparzer's disillusionment with the popular cause of
the Revolution of 1848. The action centres on the Hapsburg
Emperor Rudolf II, his brother and successor to the throne,
Matthias, and the religious and political rebellions preceding the
Thirty Years' War; in addition, the lawlessness of the age is brought
home to Rudolf through the misdeeds of Don Caesar, his natural
son. From this complex plot the preoccupations of a lifetime emerge
with startling clarity. Questions of personal religiousness apart,
Grillparzer is an eminently Catholic writer: he sees the world as
part of a cosmic order in which man occupies a fixed station with its
divinely predetermined rights and duties; this is the Emperor
Rudolf's vision of the order, which is threatened by an age of rebel-
lion and lawlessness. Where King Ottokar exceeded his rights,
Rudolf II falls short of his duties. With a wholly static view of
society informing his every action, Rudolf is bound to regard every
change – indeed time itself – as disruptive of that order of which he is
the appointed guardian. But, being too sensitive and scrupulous to
engage in purposeful political action, Rudolf not only fails to come

to terms with the new revolutionary demands for religious toleration and middle-class rights, but equally he fails to protect and hand over to posterity the old order of things. The age is dark and rebellious, the Emperor is both heedless and vacillating in the exercise of power. Yet the cause of his guilt is his finest virtue. For his weakness is only partly due to his incapacity as a ruler – equally it derives from wisdom and a capacity to sympathise with human suffering. It is this sensibility which disables him for all purposeful political choice, that is, the choice of the lesser evil:

> RUDOLF: Yet who would venture in these troubled times
> to cut confusion's complicated knot
> With one bold stroke.[2]

His nephew, the Archduke Ferdinand, has no such scruples:

> FERDINAND: You ask who ventures?
> RUDOLF: Without consulting me?
> FERDINAND: Sir, it is done.
> At least, in Styria, Krain and Carinthia
> The seed of heresy is rooted out.
> One day alone on orders from their prince
> Some sixty thousand souls embraced the faith
> And twenty thousand fled to foreign lands.
> RUDOLF: Without consulting me?
> FERDINAND: Sir, I wrote
> Repeatedly and urgently; in vain.
> RUDOLF (*shuffles the papers on his desk*):
> There is confusion here at times among our papers.
> FERDINAND: Prompt action, then, became my best advice.
> My land is cleansed. Oh, would that yours might be!
> RUDOLF: And twenty thousand fled to foreign lands?
> With wife and child? The autumn nights are cold.

The intrusion of the colloquial 'At least, in Styria . . .' in an exchange of high pathos flaws the original as much as it does the translation, and so do the heavy topographical thumps *à la* 'What ho there, Cumberland!' The translation fails (as so often) where the text is at its simplest and most poignant:

Und zwanzigtausend wandern flüchtig aus?
Mit Weib und Kind? Die Nächte sind schon kühl.

The lines convey a moment of great elegiac beauty. The feeling they express is tragic by virtue of its irrelevance to the play's central political conflict. The inner dilemma between private person and public office is insoluble. The chaos that ensues on the accession of Rudolf's brother Matthias (a mere puppet of his ambitious chancellor), marks the total dissolution of the old order, and the outbreak of the Thirty Years' War. The curtain comes down on Matthias's 'Mea culpa, mea culpa, mea maxima culpa'.

In Grillparzer's last play, *Libussa* (1841), the unwritten matriarchal order of a pastoral community is challenged by men clamouring for a prince and the rule of written laws. Where, in the earlier play, the Protestants' demand for chartered rights was seen through Rudolf's eyes as an act of impious self-assertion and was condemned by him as a sign of the rebellious times, in *Libussa* the same demand is presented in a wholly peaceful situation. No particular self-interest motivates the dukes of Bohemia nor do they complain of Libussa's 'law of the heart' as unjust in any particular: all they want is progress, the change from a simple pastoral community to a more highly organised society and civilisation. A new order is born, symbolised by the founding of a city, Prague; but Libussa falls a victim to the change. The future she foretells in her last speech will be an age bereft of all those personal and intimate values which she and her forefathers had upheld from time immemorial. The rule of custom is dead, the rule of law and impersonal justice, like the life of the new city, is inevitable. Politics begin where the pastoral idyll ends. What to the dukes is progress, to Libussa is a fall from natural grace. The play's elegiac tone no less than the fact of its posthumous publication suggest that Grillparzer knew that its meaning was lost to the contemporary public, yet we can readily see it as an idealised tribute to the paternalist rule of the House of Hapsburg. It lacks the dramatic tension which makes of *Ein Bruderzwist* one of the greatest political tragedies in German, a play which comes all too close to the reality of that rule.

Grillparzer's dramatic talent is not well served by the iambic pentameters or the high poetic imagery and didactic sententiousness of classical Weimar. His acute sense of the theatre is manifest not in the language of his verse but in a rich and apt use of props, in powerful characterisation, and superb scenic groupings; he thinks not in words, even less in ideas, but in situations expressing conflicts of characters. The alien influence of Weimar gives way to an indigenous tradition – that of the Viennese Baroque drama with its emphasis on concrete, even spectacular stage effects, although the stable Catholic morality of that drama (a morality of stark black-and-white contrasts) is no longer available to him. He too, like his contemporary German dramatists and philosophers, is informed by an acute historical consciousness. However, history is for him not a store-house of wisdom, let alone a 'progressive self-realisation of Spirit' (as it was for his contemporary Hegel). History is a stage, a setting for changes, and each change is for the worse: ancient pieties, fealties and pledges are betrayed for the sake (again and again) of self-assertion which leads to anarchy. The God-given, cosmic scheme of things according to which rights and duties are apportioned is always either threatened or already destroyed, and the task of re-establishing the traditional 'order' against the anarchy of 'time' is both imperative and hopeless. The tragedy of Grillparzer's heroes doesn't consist in their isolation from a valid order (as in Greek tragedy), an order the very validity of which is threatened by their isolation. And yet their isolation is not absolute. What saves the protagonists of his plays, spiritually though not materially, is their human dignity; but the source of that dignity is insight, not action. Critics have spoken of Grillparzer's quietism. Yet the characteristic thing about his dramas (in this they resemble Shakespeare's and are sharply distinguished from Hebbel's) is that they are not *pièces à thèse*, they conform to no premeditated philosophy. The outlook they illumine we may describe as Catholic, Austrian and conservative. However, in describing it thus we are pointing to the family likeness of living characters and situations, not to a detachable ideology. 'Change there must be, but woe to him from whom change cometh' might well stand as the motto to most of his plays. The greatness of Grillparzer's tragic art derives from the dignity he is able to bestow on his characters in this predicament; this is the source of the compassion their fall evokes in us. The value that has been salvaged is a private value – the State lies in ruins, no Fortinbras enters.

FRIEDRICH HEBBEL: IN SEARCH OF THE ABSOLUTE

The nineteenth century has been called the Age of Ideologies. The ideological monoliths that dominate Europe are German in origin, obsessively systematic, pessimistic, and antinomian – that is, concerned with a reinterpretation and revaluation of the tenets of traditional morality. This description fits the philosophies of Fichte, Hegel and Schopenhauer, and the dramas of Friedrich Hebbel. The exact extent of Hebbel's indebtedness to the philosophers of his age remains a bone of much scholarly contention and may well prove impossible to determine, yet there is some evidence to suggest that he owes to Hegel the overall scheme within which his plays are located and their plots resolved. The personalities that dominate Hebbel's plays – unbending and stern, often inner-directed – are the sort of men that make up the world of Schopenhauer's philosophy; they belong to a world viewed as a product and objectivisation of the Will. Of these embattled tyrants of the Protestant parlour more will be said when we consider their rôle in contemporary prose fiction. In Hebbel's dramas they are the rulers and thus in a sense the creators of their world. They form the rigid, immovable part of a dialectic of development, and this dialectic is for Hebbel the essence of human history. Their function is to assert themselves and thus the *status quo* they represent. The protagonists of his plays are inevitably doomed, yet in their suffering and death they become (or at least are said to become) the heralds of a new order. This relentless and fully determined process is what Hebbel has in mind when (in the abstruse commentaries on his plays) he speaks of 'the Universal Law' and 'the Idea' as the sole concern of the great tragedies of all times; when, with a contempt reminiscent of the characters of his own dramas, he brushes aside all humbler and less universal themes as trivial and arbitrary. Only a cosmically determined 'necessity' is tragedy's proper concern, he argues. Now, it is true that the requirement of a 'necessary' connection between the different parts of tragedy had been important at several points in the history of European drama. However, Hebbel's notion of 'necessity' – inevitable assertion on the one side and inevitable doom on the other – is postulated with a deterministic rigour it had never possessed before.

Obviously in such an a-prioristic scheme there is little room for the display of human freedom. The interests of plot and characterisation too are limited, since both are above all the means to a predetermined end. The complex interplay of human motives, the nuances and disharmonies – as opposed to head-on collisions – of different temperaments are present in these plays as concessions to *vraisemblance* rather than as centres of dramatic interest. The traditional notions of good and evil are revalued: good is that which furthers the great 'historical process of development', evil is that which hinders it. Yet with characters so single-mindedly bent on destroying or being destroyed, that revaluation is apt to seem too easily accomplished.

What this grandiose scheme betrays is an inordinate appetite for the unconditioned. Is the inspiration behind it dramatic or ideological? What does Hebbel ultimately care for – people or ideas? His dramas often fail to reach the point where the distinction between 'people' and 'ideas' is shown up for the misapprehension it is. The heedless self-assertion and high, occasionally hollow, rhetoric of his dramatic figures suggest that Hebbel is struggling with an impossibility: his ultimate aim is to represent 'the Absolute' on the stage, no less. His greatest success as a dramatist lies where he is content to intimate the Absolute in a psychological light, presenting it as the object of a character's beliefs. Where he sets out on the impossible task of representing that Absolute in some more direct way, as a transcendental necessity, there rhetoric takes over from drama, and strange incoherences ensue. To say all this is to admit the adventitious nature of the metaphysics, and to suggest that the dramatist gains where the philosopher ceases to press his scheme on him.

But this is not the whole story. We notice in Hebbel's plays an interesting pattern which is only loosely connected with his doubtful cosmic theories. The static part of the dialectic, representing the *status quo*, is almost invariably played by men, whereas the victims of the process of 'historical change' are almost invariably women. This being so, a Freudian interpretation would argue for the derivative and compensatory origin of Hebbel's metaphysical beliefs, and see in them a rationalisation of a more fundamental experience, the war of the sexes. And it is in terms of such an interpretation that Hebbel's first play, *Judith* (1842), yields its fullest sense.

The play follows roughly the Apocryphal story of Judith and Holofernes, but adds a historical meaning and psychological motivation of its own. Its protagonists become the representatives of Jewish monotheism and paganism respectively. In seeking out, yielding to and eventually killing Holofernes, Judith believes herself to be carrying out God's plan for the Jews – she is freeing His own people from the arbitrary rule of a foreign heathen tyrant. (In this sense the play illustrates what Hebbel regards as one of the 'turning points' in the history of mankind.) Judith believes herself to be the vessel of God's will because she alone among all the citizens of Bethulia has the strength of purpose and the courage required for the task of liberation. She is surrounded by cowards: with Holofernes' forces outside the city gates (Act III, scene 11), the atmosphere of panic among the Jews is comparable, for sheer intensity, with the chorus scenes of ancient tragedy. She alone is the worthy opponent of a Holofernes who, intended as a representative of absolute might, ends up as a caricature of bathos and grandiloquence. (Johann Nestroy, Hebbel's Austrian contemporary, wrote a splendid comic parody of the heathen general.)

Why then, in carrying out God's will, does Judith fail – what makes the play 'a tragedy'? Hebbel's intention, disclosed after the murder of Holofernes in Judith's dialogue with Mirza, her confidante, is clear enough. Not the divine command was her motive (she tells Mirza), not the desire to free her people from the threat of extinction, but personal revenge – '. . . what drove me was only thought for myself'. She has taken revenge (she confesses) for the violation of her womanhood and individuality, to which she submitted before she did the bloody deed. This revenge, in her own view, makes her guilty of hubris, even though the Jews acclaim her as their saviour. And in this personally motivated excess she appears to be fulfilling Hebbel's scheme for tragedy: her strength is the cause of both her election and her undoing, yet through her undoing an example is set and a historical change accomplished.

However, another motive runs through the play, making it at once more interesting and more opaque. Judith is introduced to us as the widow of Manasses, whose marriage was not consummated.

The words (Act I, scene 11) in which she describes the fiasco of her wedding night to Mirza are free from the exclamatoriness which mars most of her other speeches:

> Manasses called: I see you as clear as daylight, and he came towards me. Suddenly he stopped. It was as if the black earth had stretched out her hand and held him down. A ghostly feeling seized me. Come, come, I called, and I was not ashamed. I cannot, his answer came dark and leaden, I cannot. . . .

Just as there is no one in the Jewish camp who dares face Holofernes, so there is no one who can assuage her sexual passion; Ephraim, who woos her, is as inadequate as the rest. Her virgin-widowhood is related to her courage and spiritual strength, through it she becomes the vessel of the divine will. And the imagery in which she speaks of Holofernes –

> If a giant's head points so high into the sky that you cannot reach it, why then, you must throw a jewel at his feet – he will stoop to pick it up, and then you will easily overpower him.

– makes it fairly clear that, consciously or not, she sees in him the means for fulfilling her unsatisfied erotic passion. Her encounter with Holofernes (we must conclude) brings her the consummation she failed to find among her own kind. And this in turn makes her confession to Mirza incomplete. To the motive of a divine mission betrayed by personal revenge we must add her realisation that her people's enemy was her lover; and only with this realisation is the full complexity and the full tragedy of her situation encompassed.

However, much of this must remain conjecture. Hebbel introduces the erotic motive, he does something to maintain it (Judith speaks of Holofernes in images that intimate it), but in the moment of disclosure in Act V it remains unexpressed. Did he fail to see how deeply he had committed the character of his heroine to the motive of erotic fulfilment? Hebbel's characters overwhelm the spectator with self-accusations and abundant disclosures of motive. His dramatic argument never moves by intimation. Our final impression therefore is one of incompleteness, of a mind whose complexity and grounds of division are not, after all, fully realised.

Agnes Bernauer (1851) displays more clearly and more chillingly than any other play Hebbel's strange notion of cosmic 'morality'. Its

central conflict involves the complete annihilation of personal
interests in the name of political expediency, just as the resulting
historical 'turning point' involves a recasting of traditional morality.
The time of the action is the early fifteenth century, the tragic
heroine is the daughter of the Mayor of Würzburg. Agnes's only
transgression is that, of middle-class origin and 'excessively' beautiful, she is betrothed to Albrecht, only son and heir of the ruling
Duke of Bavaria, and refuses to agree either to a morganatic marriage or a divorce. When the prospect of Albrecht's succession
threatens to disrupt the State by civil war, the Duke orders her
judicial murder. In the final scene the disrupted 'moral' equilibrium
is restored by the old Duke who, by abdicating and placing the
symbol of sovereignty in his son's hands, forces Albrecht to assent
to Agnes's death in the name of a superior *raison d'état*. Thesis (the
feudal *status quo*), antithesis (Agnes's innocent challenge to the existing
order), synthesis (Albrecht's new sense of political responsibility) –
all are here set out in a dramatic calculation remarkable above all
for its cold inhumanity.

The theme of the war of the sexes yields no valid interpretation of
the play. If we think of tragedy as a genre that evokes pity in the
spectator (it is hardly a very restrictive definition), then clearly
Hebbel's drama is only marginally tragic; his very insistence on the
'necessity' of the events leading to Agnes's death impairs this kind of
tragic effect. He endows Agnes not only with an absolute devotion to
her husband but also with a heedless pride in her sacrifice. This
pride of the victim in being chosen by fate for annihilation the philosopher F. W. J. Schelling had singled out as the chief element in
modern tragedy. It is an idea of tragedy all too readily available to
dramatists writing in a language which in the single word 'Opfer'
obliterates the distinction between 'victim' and 'sacrifice'.

Agnes faces the conspiracy that will smother her life as an all but
unresisting victim, in her passivity there is even an insinuation of
compliance with the dastardly act. This passivity is met on the other
side of the dramatic equation by a good deal of cold-blooded
casuistry, of which the abstruse language of Duke Ernst is typical, as
when he describes Agnes as 'the purest victim [das reinste Opfer]
claimed by Necessity in all centuries'. And when, finally, he explains
this 'necessity' to his chancellor, who has undertaken to 'liquidate'
the innocent victim –

There are things that must be done as though in one's sleep. This is one of them. The great wheel passed over her, now she is with him who turns it

— we seem to be watching an ideological charade. The deed too easily done; the alternatives too easily disposed of; the reasons too neatly expounded; expiation too readily available and consciences too easily cleared – these are the flaws of *Agnes Bernauer*. There is here little occasion for that simple and undivided feeling that tragedies evoke on both sides of the footlights, the feeling of 'What a fall was here!'

Maria Magdalene (1843) affords the pleasure of reporting on a masterpiece. It is a play that belongs integrally to the tradition of 'bürgerliches Trauerspiel' ('domestic tragedy') from Lessing to Gerhart Hauptmann; it enriches this tradition by single-mindedly exploiting the social world to which it is confined. (The play is ill served by its author's theoretical introduction, in which excellent insights are buried under an extravagant syntax.)

The chief flaws of Hebbel's dramas can be traced back to his ever-repeated attempts at conveying 'the Absolute' on the stage. This he hopes to achieve by invoking historical and hence dramatic 'necessity'. The practice of establishing necessary (rather than arbitrary) connections between the individual parts of a play has its origin in Aristotle. Drama, for Aristotle, is the purposeful imitation of an action, and necessity is merely one of the means of making the imitation convincing. In Hebbel's more rigorous scheme it leads to excessively calculated dramatic structures, occasionally to melodrama and lifelessness – to a feeling in the spectator that the dramatic ends are so much more than achieved. Now this 'necessity' is certainly present in *Maria Magdalene*; indeed, it is to this that the play owes its taut structure and economy of dramatic means. But here for once the social and personal determinism which motivates the action is not imposed from the outside. The chain of causes and effects doesn't take its origin in a cosmic ideology, nor do its conclusions appear to contribute to that idea of historical progress which that ideology is meant to exemplify – necessity is in the very air surrounding the characters. It is an objective social condition, yet implanted (as Hegel would say) in the most intimate subjectivity of their souls. Thus the setting of the play merges with its plot, form with content, social pressure with moral responsibility, yet not completely: there is no 'synthesis', facile or otherwise.

The play's setting and theme is that 'terrible constriction in one-sidedness' and social bigotry characteristic of life among the petit bourgeoisie of mid-nineteenth-century Europe. From this constriction, and the social conformity it exacts, no one is wholly free – it informs all the characters and impels the action of the protagonists. This is the concrete social circumstance in which their imaginations are imprisoned and their lives all but completely determined; it merges with and dominates their moral qualities. For all we know the preface to the play may be right: this lethal constriction and conformism may well be the 'Universal Law' under its temporal aspect, showing 'the very age and body of the Time, his form and pressure'. However that may be, to the drama itself the invoking of an Eternal Law behind the social conflict is irrelevant; where the temporal is so fully realised, the Absolute is mercifully dispensable.

The hiatus between the preface and the play is not without its peculiar interest. It is not merely the kind of incongruity one might expect to arise between theory or ideology and dramatic practice: here the theory, in its very terminology and assertions, repudiates a good part of the realism that is the play's strength. In method and intention alike, Hebbel's preface is the opposite of Aristotle's *Poetics*. Aristotle proceeds inductively, moving from an assortment of aesthetic insights and descriptions of actual dramatic devices to an informal statement of rules on how to construct successful tragedies. The *Poetics* implies a coherent view of the destiny of man, certainly – the precise nature of that view has been argued over for twenty-four centuries – but it no more than implies such a view. Hebbel proceeds deductively. His view of the destiny of man is central to the intention of the preface, the importance he gives it is never in doubt. Here he is quite prepared to exclude a whole range of realistic motifs (motifs reflecting social and material conditions) from serious drama for no other reason than that they are said to be irrelevant to 'the Idea' (the dialectic of history). The subtle contempt for such motifs expressed here and elsewhere in the theoretical writings is character-istic of the literary temper of the age – the play itself, on the other hand, is free from any such egregiousness: *its* dramatic argument as well as the circumstances in which it is placed are firmly realistic.

But why this hiatus between theory and practice? The play's realism leads its characters to defeat – defeat as individuals and also as members of a social class. Their personal protest is accompanied in the play by social acquiescence. The theoretician moves one step further, to the point where the dramatist cannot follow: to the point where the personal defeat and social acquiescence are evaluated metaphysically, where they are glorified as a 'necessary' and thus in some esoteric way 'positive' fulfilment of a cosmic principle of change and progress. The author of *Maria Magdalene* no longer allows himself the chilling and dramatically unconvincing 'positive' synthesis of several earlier plays. The author of the preface on the other hand cannot let go. The defeat must not be allowed to 'dissipate' into anything so mundane as a political reform or social protest. Instead, he turns it into a vindication of a cosmic scheme of things, which by definition must leave the actual state of affairs, the circumstances realistically depicted in the play, unaffected and unchanged. The theoretical synthesis, which justifies social defeat in cosmic terms, is made possible only by being removed from the realistic sphere of Hebbel's play. But it is this removal that makes the synthesis effective as ideology outside the play, in the sphere of contemporary reality, where it gives a metaphysical blessing – something much like a religious sanction – to acquiescence and acceptance. The defeat of 'Bürgertum' is metaphysically validated.

It was, I suspect, Hebbel rather than Aristotle that Bertolt Brecht had in mind when, in his plea for 'an anti-Aristotelian theatre of the scientific age', he attacked the idea of dramatic necessity. Certainly he would have had nothing but scorn for the Hebbelian acquiescence in catastrophe, and for his scheme of cosmic justification. And yet, one wonders whether there isn't something like an overlap between the two theorisers. After all, the social utopia that is said to lie behind the conflicts and suffering of his characters is almost as remote and unrealised by Brecht the honest dramatist (which he isn't always) as it is by Hebbel the author of *Maria Magdalene*. And in both cases one can only be thankful that the two dramatists' pursuit of ideology (one cosmic, the other utopian, both equally unrealistic) does not encroach on their finest plays.

Seduction and the dread of illegitimacy are the traditional motifs of middle-class drama; in *Maria Magdalene* they are set in a small-town environment that is at once narrow, inward-turned, and ferocious. The coffin-maker Meister Anton, tyrannical father of Klara (the seduced girl), is the representative of this ethos of conformity and moral uprightness. As a tradesman he is unbendingly honest, as a citizen he is rigidly class-conscious, as an artisan he sees in hard work (but not, incidentally, in money, the product of work) the only hall-mark of morality. And the severity and self-determination of the man are at their most patent in his relationship with his daughter, whose dishonour he suspects long before it is confirmed. Hounded from scornful seducer to reluctant childhood friend, Klara anticipates by her own death Meister Anton's threat of suicide. Yet what makes the conflict between them so poignant is that it is based on a sense of values common to both.

Nineteenth-century German literature is not rich in the variety of women it depicts. Klara belongs to its most characteristic type, the Gretchen figure. The only escape she knows from the world that encompasses her is the escape into death. Her journey leads from fear to despair and ends in frenzied suicide, and her various attempts to avoid her fate constitute the main line of the action. Yet her fate is in no sense imposed from the outside. Each step, except perhaps the initial seduction, is taken in strict accordance with her character, and her character is above all that of a dutiful daughter who must expiate her single lapse from virtue. She is incapable of a life outside the family circle and its taboos. Much the same is true of her childhood friend who, in the crucial moment when he is faced with the fact of her pregnancy, falls back on the conventional judgement. When, a short while later, he recovers his love for her, it is too late, his brief hesitation proves fatal. The strength he has gained leads him to revenge her death by killing her seducer, but it leads to no new life. Only Klara's brother, suspected of theft, pilloried, and at last proved innocent, makes an escape of sorts.

Obloquy is the hostile deity that rules this world. The morality that informs Meister Anton's every reaction is not really 'inner-directed'. Nor is his attitude determined by care for his family. These are certainly important motifs in the play, but both his moral righteousness and his family relationships are subordinated to his anxious concern for a good name. Yet again, this is not a genuinely social care – he cares for the collective only in order to protect himself against it: the foundation of his tyranny, like the foundation of his pew-renter's piety, is fear.

Meister Anton's is a hybrid morality. He regards his son's guilt as proven and suspects his daughter's loss of innocence on the strength of rumours and suspicion only. In other words, the judgements he applies to his family derive from the small-town social collective. Conversely, the morality by which that collective is ruled is as arbitrary and subjective as though it were imposed by one of Kafka's father-figures. Appeal to an objective authority there is none (small wonder that elsewhere Hebbel turns to a quasi-religious Absolute for justification). This confusion – or rather negative conflation – of public and private values is part of the familial ethos that Marx and Engels satirised and attacked in their early writings. Hebbel's *Maria Magdalene* is its unsparing critique and its finest dramatic portrayal.

GEORG BÜCHNER: POTSHERDS OF EXPERIENCE

The students of the Johann Wolfgang von Goethe University of Frankfurt have re-named it the Georg Büchner University.

(Newspaper report, May 1968)

Georg Büchner (1813–1837), the third major dramatist of the age, is a discovery of the early twentieth century. In spite of the efforts of his friends Gutzkow and Franzos in the decades following his death, his work remained unknown to a wider public. Yet the passionate, feverish intensity that informs the twenty-three years of his life endows it with a symbolical quality. He belongs to the revolutionary generation of the 1830s, which in Germany was silenced by violent police measures and long-drawn-out oppression – a combination remarkably effective for its time. But his literary genius, and the pace at which he absorbs and abandons the ideological attitudes of his contemporaries, distinguish him from all of them except Heine.

He was in no obvious sense a literary man. Born near Darmstadt, the son of a doctor who, as a field surgeon, had served in Napoleon's Old Guard, Georg Büchner intended to follow in his father's

C

footsteps. He studied medicine at the universities of Strasbourg and Giessen, graduating as a physiologist at Zürich where, in the last year of his life, he was appointed *Privatdozent* on the strength of his work on the nervous system of fish. In the summer of 1834 he was involved in subversive political activities in the Principality of Hesse. These culminated in the clandestine publication of a revolutionary pamphlet and its distribution among the wholly unresponsive peasantry; the pamphlet is clearly pre-Marxist in its argument, its biblical trimmings were added by a clerical fellow-conspirator. The complete fiasco of these activities, ending with the denunciation of the conspiratorial group (probably by one of its student members), led to the disillusionment with political activism which is reflected in Büchner's first major play, *Dantons Tod*, written in the first five weeks of 1835, whilst he was in constant fear of arrest by the authorities and of detection by his hostile father. Büchner fled to Strasbourg in March 1835, where he resumed contact with the family of Minna Jaeglé, to whom he had become secretly engaged during his first stay there in November 1831. (A warrant for his arrest was issued in June 1835, but no extradition from France seems to have been requested.) That summer he translated two of Victor Hugo's plays and wrote *Lenz*, his only Novelle, based on a memoir of the life of the poet J. M. R. Lenz (1751–92), which was made available to Büchner through Pastor Jaeglé. In the late spring of 1836 he wrote his only extant comedy, *Leonce und Lena*, which failed to win a competition set by Cotta, the Weimar publishers. At that time too he wrote three papers, in French, on the nervous system of the barbel, and a number of letters to his parents and friends, which contain brief but important observations on his aims as a dramatist. In October 1836 he moved from Strasbourg to Zürich where, towards the end of that year, he wrote *Woyzeck*. At Christmas he received a letter ('more in sorrow than in anger') from his father, the first since his flight. He died in Zürich of typhoid fever on 19 February 1837, after an illness lasting seventeen days. We are told by the wife of a liberal deserter from the Hessian Army with whom he lodged that his last words were, 'We do not suffer too much pain but too little, for through pain we enter the Kingdom of God.' The first part of the sentence, that certainly, may stand as a motto to Georg Büchner's extant writings.

The elements of Büchner's life cohere in our minds into a strange yet familiar picture. Its ambience is one of hectic intellectual exertion through philosophical studies and of political enlightenment through radical pamphlets; his arrogance and aloofness are paired with a capacity for intense friendship; his conspiratorial activities and utopian plans go hand in hand with naïveté in practical political matters and an annihilating sense of disillusionment; early attacks of meningitis are followed by suicidal moods; the medical student's shock-tactics and youthful cynicism deepen into a sustained rejection of accepted bourgeois values; the consolations of conventional religion and of enlightened teleology alike are sarcastically rejected; the somewhat unreal, certainly tortuous love-affair fails to sustain him at the crucial moments; never abandoning his work in physiology, he hopes to repair the shattered fabric of experience – a scientifically based philosophy of nature is to be the nostrum; and the final intervention of disease and death comes suddenly yet not unexpectedly in a life pitted throughout against a father's inescapable authority – in fine, the young man stands before us as one of the anarchist or 'nihilist' characters of a Dostoevsky novel. What distinguishes him from such a character is his literary achievement. But to his contemporaries, and especially to his father, only the ruins of his life were discernible, not the brief triumphs of his art.[3] **1690516**

In several important senses Büchner's work is fragmentary, exploring questions rather than offering answers. It could hardly be otherwise, seeing that the theme on which it centres is that of suffering. The rudimentary and episodic movement that characterises his plays is never explicitly stated. This movement is the very opposite of a system, cosmic or otherwise. It is simply a retracing, in dramatic and (in *Lenz*) narrative form, of his experience of life. The poles of this movement are boredom and accidie on the one hand, and the conquest of these by feeling on the other. It is a movement from unreality, intimated as the reign of solipsism, unfeeling and isolation, to reality, which is experienced above all as encroachment, violation and ravage of the self by another. The grim fact of pain is seen initially as 'the bedrock of atheism', the irrefutable proof that a just and loving omnipotent God does not exist: 'But I, if I were almighty [says the poet Lenz, on the verge of insanity, to his host, Pastor Oberlin], you know, if I were almighty, I could not tolerate suffering – I would save, save. . . .' Yet the recognition that 'the last twinge of pain, if it stirs only an atom, rends creation from top to bottom'[4] does not lead Büchner to the Hobbesian view that a man should put himself in a position where he may avoid pain, or to the Schopenhauerian view that he should regard it as illusory. On the contrary, in Büchner's plays a man's capacity for suffering is his bedrock of reality, his one and only proof that he *is* and that the world *is*. Thus Büchner's anti-hero is like a man waking from an anaesthetic or a condition of total shock; the life and feeling that flow back into his limbs and flood his consciousness are the life and feeling of pain: 'the sentient vein is the same in almost all men – only the hull through which it must break varies in its thickness' (*Lenz*). The breaking of this hull is a man's only ontological proof, yet it is also more than he can endure; a man's proof of existence is also his undoing. The laconic detachment and ribald humour of Büchner the medical student contributes to this vision of men as specimens which are being 'prepared' – their every spasm is watched – by a demiurge whose intentions remain hidden in sinister obscurity. The dialectic into which Büchner's 'heroes' are pinned is thus not between good and evil, or hatred and love, or fate and will, but between feeling and unfeeling. Existence is manifest not yet in positive action but in sentient endurance, not yet in pleasure but in pain. This far Büchner's writings take us, but no further. The 'not yet' belongs to our logic, not to his vision.

> Mardi. Rien. Existé.
>
> (J.-P. Sartre, *La Nausée*)

A play on the life of *Pietro Aretino*, possibly completed, was destroyed by Büchner's fiancée. *Leonce und Lena*, his only extant comedy, is concerned with the first half of the dialectic. The hero, prince of an imaginary kingdom *à la* de Musset, is one of those 'who are incurably unhappy merely because they are' (Act II, scene 2). His escape from a well-nigh suicidal boredom is effected by a fairy-tale device of coincidences. So long as they know each other as the world knows them, Prince and Princess frustrate the silly King's matchmaking. Intended for him by a royal Polonius (whose mind is filled with Kantian maxims), Ophelia is the object of Hamlet's scorn. But once they don the masks of the marionettes they 'really' are, thus becoming ignorant of each other's identity, Prince and Princess fall in love and marry. The curtain comes down on a happy Lena, and a caustic Leonce wryly reconciled to their union.

All the trimmings of comedy are here – absurd courtiers, a sly Leporello, disguises and intrigues – yet the intensity of the Prince's emotion casts an uncomic chill on the harlequinade. Leonce recognises the 'happy end' as one more proof that an inescapable determinism governs his every action, that freedom is wholly illusory. This determinism – the rationalisation of arbitrary actions – is here the intellectual correlative of boredom, where boredom is the soul's response to the void that encompasses it. Some of the most powerful speeches in the play describe this emotion on the border-line of *Angst*. Just as boredom is interest without an object, an encounter with 'nothing in particular', so *Angst*, a negative boredom, is fear without an object, fear of 'nothing in particular' and thus of everything – of existence itself as well as its end. Portraying the Prince's boredom not as an unimportant interlude between mean-ingful actions but as a mode of life, Büchner is writing out the experience of the post-Byronic, post-Napoleonic generation in Europe everywhere. Writers whose work he did not know – Chateau-briand, Lermontov and Stendhal, K. H. Mácha, Leopardi, Heine and Schopenhauer – as well as de Musset (whom he knew well) speak of the atrophy of the heart and the dulling of the senses in a world where conformism and commerce, the civil service and bourgeois taboos, have taken the place of heroism and adventure. This theme Büchner draws out to its extreme point, the point of anguish of soul:

Komm, Leonce, halte mir einen Monolog, ich will zuhören. Mein Leben gähnt mich an wie ein großer weißer Bogen Papier, den ich vollschreiben soll, aber ich bringe keinen Buchstaben heraus. Mein Kopf ist ein leerer Tanzsaal, einige verwelkte Rosen und zerknitterte Bänder auf dem Boden, geborstene Violinen in der Ecke, die letzten Tänzer haben die Masken abgenommen und sehen mit todmüden Augen einander an. Ich stülpe mich jeden Tag vierundzwanzigmal herum wie einen Handschuh. O, ich kenne mich, ich weiß, was ich in einer Viertelstunde, was ich in acht Tagen, was ich in einem Jahre denken und träumen werde. Gott, was habe ich denn verbrochen, daß du mich wie einen Schul-buben meine Lektion so oft hersagen läßt?

LEONCE: Come, Leonce, let's have a monologue, and I will listen. My life yawns at me like a big white sheet of paper that I should fill with writing, but I can't produce a single letter. My head is an empty ballroom, a few withered roses and crumpled ribbons on the floor, broken violins in the corner, the last dancers have taken off their masks and are looking at each other with eyes weary to death. I turn myself inside out like a glove twenty-four times a day. Oh, I know myself, I know what I shall be thinking and dreaming in a quarter of an hour, in a week's, a year's time. God, what have I done that you should make me recite my lesson over and over again, like a schoolboy? . . . (Act I, scene 3).

In what follows, the Prince's anguish ('merely because he is') is only stifled, not assuaged.

Dans les salons d'Arras, un jeune avocat froid et minaudier porte sa tête sous son bras parce qu'il est feu Robespierre, cette tête dégoutte de sang mais ne tache pas le tapis; pas un des convives ne la remarque et nous ne voyons qu'elle. . . .

(J.-P. Sartre, *La Nausée*)

In *Dantons Tod* the encompassing emotions are substantially similar. But their proximate causes are fully intimated, and the dramatic situation is more commensurate with their intensity than it was in Büchner's romantic comedy. The drama opens on 24 March 1794; Danton has reached the point of complete disillusionment with the cause and development of the Revolution. He now knows the trivial concerns, the greed and corruptness of the 'People' on whose behalf he conducted the September massacres. He also knows the cynicism and the hypocrisy (so strong as to be self-delusive) of his fellow-revolutionaries, chief among them St Just and Robespierre. He has all but exhausted the round of physical pleasures – his occasional obscenities in the early part of the play are a desolate echo of past excesses. He is like a man imprisoned in a maze, who knows the mechanism of every lock and of every guard's mind, yet who also knows that unlocking the next door and outwitting the next guard is not worth the effort since it will only take him into another part of the same maze. His awareness of his own and of the Revolution's predicament is as complete as it is paralysing. This determinism is reflected in almost suicidal *nausea vitae*, but it is also projected on to a wide historical plane: almost every other scene in the play presents some aspect of the 'revolutionary' mood of '*la canaille*', whose actions are either wholly arbitrary, or else fearful, self-seeking, and corrupt. In this initial situation Danton is incapable of any meaningful contact:

Was weiß ich! Wir wissen wenig voneinander. Wir sind Dick-häuter, wir strecken die Hände nacheinander aus, aber es ist vergebliche Mühe, wir reiben nur das grobe Leder aneinander ab, – wir sind sehr einsam. . . . Einander kennen? Wir müßten uns die Schädeldecken aufbrechen und die Gedanken einander aus den Hirnfasern zerren.

We know little of each other [he says to Julie, his wife]. We are thick-skinned creatures, we stretch out our hands to each other but it is wasted effort, we are only rubbing our coarse hides together – we are very solitary. . . . Know each other? We should have to break open each other's skulls and drag the thoughts out of each other's brain-coils (Act I, scene 1).

The play is divided into four acts of between six and ten episodic scenes each. Since Danton's and his friends' execution is, from fairly early on, a foregone conclusion, the interest of the play does not lie in the overt action but in the dialectic of emotions which the action throws into relief. Thus Danton's brilliant rhetorical defence before the Revolutionary Tribunal (Act III, scene 5) serves not to avert or even delay his fate, but to demonstrate its arbitrariness: all rational argument and all personal and political action appear overshadowed by the irrational imperative of history – '*das Muss*' – from which there is no escape. The moment Danton recognises his own guilt in the September massacres (Act II, scene 5), he recognises that Robespierre, his puritanical adversary, is, like himself, merely another link in the chain of historical causes. When St Just asserts that the Revolution is governed by natural laws as strict as the laws governing physical actions (Act II, scene 7), he echoes Danton's own recognition that 'the Revolution devours its own children' (Act I, Scene 5). And when Danton recognises that his own flagrant immorality has 'been turned into a political crime' (Act I, scene 3), and that all moral considerations too have thus become subject to the rule of political success, which in turn is subject to historical inevitability, it becomes clear that the area of meaningful *action* the playwright leaves to his characters is severely restricted. Once Robespierre and St Just have succeeded in branding Danton and his friends as traitors to the popular cause, the way to the guillotine is clear; and Danton's contempt for his rivals, coupled with his fatalism ('they will not dare', is his repeated answer to the warnings of his friends), makes Robespierre's brief victory easy.

This is essentially epic theatre, though not in the sense intended by Bertolt Brecht, its theoretician and practitioner. Brecht envisaged a theatre of loosely connected episodic scenes and open endings as a challenge to the traditional 'well-made play' with its tragic or 'inevitable' conclusion. To Brecht such conclusions were not at all 'inevitable' but on the contrary manifestations of a bourgeois morality which enjoins passivity where it should propagate active resistance leading to meaningful social change. Brecht writes as though the epic theatre were indissolubly tied to a left-wing progressive ideology. The facts are more unsettling – the forms of literature are indifferent to extraneous intentions, political or other. With similar means Büchner attains the opposite end: whatever aspect or episode of the political (that is, revolutionary) situation is presented, all lead to the same nihilistic conclusion. From the world of politics no change for the better can come. All men (Danton proclaims in Act I and again in Act IV) are Epicureans, the only thing they seek is the fullest enjoyment of pleasure and the greatest avoidance of pain. Yet this is not the maxim according to which Danton acts out his part. And it is not he but Laflotte, a fellow-prisoner in the Luxembourg, who says, 'Pain is the only sin and suffering the only vice – I shall remain virtuous' (Act III, scene 5): this is not the conclusion towards which the play leads us.

Its greatness, it seems to me, springs from two sources. The first, remarkable in a literature singularly poor in political themes, is Büchner's exploration of a variety of revolutionary attitudes. Of course, all political action in the play is *eventually* shown up as predetermined and meaningless. But this conclusion is not allowed to foreshorten the detailed exploring: a whole spectrum of reactions to the rule of terror, among the rulers and the ruled, among the temporary victors and permanent victims, is presented before the devastating conclusions are drawn. Take Danton's great defence speech before the Tribunal. We know it is bound to fail. But its reception has been carefully prepared by a discussion of his prospects (Act III, scene 2), its splendid rhetoric is fully reproduced (Act III, scene 4), and so are its effects (scenes 5 and 6; like several others, these scenes are partly based on verbatim transcripts of revolutionary documents). *Coriolanus* is not less of a political play because Shakespeare shows up tribunes and plebs to be governed by self-seeking, corruption and vacillation; nor is *Dantons Tod*, because Büchner shows up the Revolution as a juggernaut. But each turning of its lethal wheels is the result of a calculated action, and each calculation is dramatically conveyed.

At the same time *Dantons Tod* (like *Coriolanus*) is also a personal drama, the episodic portrayal of Büchner's dialectic of pain. The first two acts present a hero who is wholly heedless of his fate, who is so disillusioned that he refuses to fight for his life. The climax of the personal drama lies very near the climax of the political, but it does not quite coincide with it. It is reached at the point (Act III, scene 7) where the 'vein of feeling' breaks through Danton's accidie, cynicism and surfeit. And the end comes upon a Danton who, having become conscious of the irreducible reality of his own existence, at last fears death *and* cares for his friends, and looks for peace not in Nothingness but in the sacrificial love of his wife.

The climactic scene of the personal drama takes place in the Conciergerie, before Danton's second and final address to the Revolutionary Tribunal. He has fought his rhetorical battle well, but his friends protest that now it is too late – what is there to hope for?

PHILIPPEAU: Was willst du denn?
DANTON: Ruhe.
PHILIPPEAU: Die ist in Gott.
DANTON: Im Nichts. Versenke dich in was Ruhigers als das Nichts, und wenn die höchste Ruhe Gott ist, ist nicht das Nichts Gott? Aber ich bin ein Atheist. Der verfluchte Satz: Etwas kann nicht zu nichts werden! Und ich bin etwas, das ist der Jammer! – Die Schöpfung hat sich so breit gemacht, da ist nichts leer, alles voll Gewimmels. Das Nichts hat sich ermordet, die Schöpfung ist seine Wunde, wir sind seine Blutstropfen, die Welt ist das Grab, worin es fault.

PHILIPPEAU : What is it you want?
DANTON : Peace.
PHILIPPEAU : Peace is in God.
DANTON : In Nothing. Immerse yourself in something more peaceful than Nothing, and if the greatest peace is God, then isn't Nothing God?

This is the credo, the ontological argument of nihilism. And Danton himself demolishes it in the next breath: *'But I am an atheist.'* Here is no statement of fact but a cry of despair: a piece of irrefutable logic *and* a violent assertion of the truth of his experience – and thus the sentence implies the opposite of its overt meaning. He goes on:

Oh, that accursed sentence, 'Something cannot become Nothing!' And I am that something, that's the pity of it! Creation has spread itself everywhere, nothing is empty, everything is crawling with it. Nothingness has murdered itself. Creation is its wound, we are the drops of its blood, the world is the grave where it lies rotting.

All of which, as Danton adds, 'sounds mad'. Yet what has here been asserted is the opposite of that nihilism with which Danton began: what is asserted is the irreducible reality of existence. Now, this irreducible Being is not anything positive. On the contrary, it is Being filled out with pain, sensate and throbbing with painful life; but it *is*. Danton takes up the argument once more (Act IV, scene 5): of course peace (=Nothing) would be desirable enough: 'Das Nichts ist der zu gebärende Weltgott': 'Nothingness – *that* is the world's god that should be born.' But (he now knows) peace *is* not, has no place in creation. Consequently (here again the astonishing combination of cold logic and cry of despair) absolute solitude too does not exist, solitude is always breached by another. Danton's love for Julie is love in the face of death (as, in Büchner's last play, Woyzeck's love for Marie will be sealed by murder) – an emotion as irreducible as was the assertion of existence: 'O Julie, if I were to go alone! If she were to leave me solitary! And even if I were to fall asunder utterly, dissolve entirely – yet would I be a handful of tormented dust, and every atom of me could find peace only in her.'

It is this changed Danton that goes to the guillotine. His last words are addressed to the executioner who tries to separate him from Hérault, his last remaining friend: 'Will you be more cruel than death itself? Can you prevent our heads kissing each other in the bottom of the basket?' Danton's old bravado is in these words, and his newly-found loving care.

> ... *pitié, au secours, au secours donc j'existe.*
>
> (J.-P. Sartre, *La Nausée*)

From *Dantons Tod* through *Lenz* to *Woyzeck* Büchner is attempting to find ever more adequate media for expressing the central experience of his life. Gradually discarding all that, from *its* vantage-point, appears as contingent, he is intent upon grasping the dialectic of feeling in its barest form. The complex political circumstances in which Danton was involved are discarded in *Woyzeck*.* Instead of Danton's highly articulate consciousness we are presented with a central character who is victim pure and simple – of his own birth and circumstances, of society, and of his own dark nature. Or rather, Woyzeck is as nearly a mere victim as it is possible – that is, dramatically convincing – for a living man to be; perhaps the greatest of the dramatist's achievements is that he gives us the imaginative measure of that state. Once again Büchner bases himself on documentary evidence (the legal and psychiatric reports on the trial for murder, in 1823–4, of a wig-maker of that name; the case seems to have been the first at which psychiatric evidence supporting a plea of diminished responsibility was admitted by a German court of law). Yet in creating Woyzeck as the embodiment of a *ne plus infra* of the human condition Büchner is wholly original. For the figure of this down-trodden simple soldier there are no literary precedents anywhere, not even in Shakespeare, whose influence upon many details in the rhetoric of *Dantons Tod* is obvious, and once or twice overpowering. The Shakespearian parallels are here too – in Poor Tom, in Private Feeble's 'I'll ne'er bear a base mind: an't be my destiny, so; an't be not, so' (*Henry IV* Part II, Act iii, scene 2). But these, for Shakespeare, remain minor and peripheral figures, whereas Büchner, in moving Woyzeck into the centre of the stage, makes him the protagonist of a whole vision of life. Erich Auerbach might have had

---

* The play was written in Zürich in the winter months of 1836 and published by Büchner's friend Karl Emil Franzos in *Sämtliche Werke* . . . (Frankfurt 1879). The MS. of Büchner's final version is lost.

Woyzeck in mind when, in his definition of realism (see above, p. 16), he spoke of 'the rise . . . of socially inferior human groups to the position of subject-matter for problematic-existential treatment'.

Woyzeck is as solitary as any man can be in our world. The people round him rise up from the cracks in the earth's thin crust (an image which Büchner employs in all his works) as in a dream or delirium. They stand in certain simple social relations to the 'hero', yet they involve him in nothing like a substantial plot. He earns the barest of livings as a private soldier, batman, and military barber. He has a mistress, Marie, and a child – it is for them he works and endures the humiliation of his service. The Captain (a sketch of hypocrisy and defective sympathy) taunts him with accusations of immorality and insinuations of Marie's unfaithfulness. The Doctor (a harsh satire on inhuman scientific curiosity, perhaps on Büchner's father) rewards Woyzeck with a pittance for experimenting with his digestive system in order to observe his mental reactions. And the Drum-Major, all virile sexuality and brute strength, seduces Marie. Yet these three, outlined in the briefest possible way and with unparalleled dramatic energy, are not Woyzeck's antagonists so much as the inescapable facts of his existence.

Woyzeck's relationship with his world is not one of conflict. The facts of his existence are hostile for no other reason than that he is defenceless, delivered to hostile existence without hope of mercy or redress. He is thus the very *a priori* of man: not, that is, a philosophical abstraction but the embodiment of Lear's anguished cry to Poor Tom, 'Is man no more than this. . . . Thou art the thing itself. Unaccommodated man is no more but such a poor, bare, forked animal.'

Does love belong to the irreducible being of such a man? Marie, a victim of degrading indigence but also of her deprived Eros, is not so much the object of Woyzeck's love as rather the one hold he has on existence: the only thing, in the threatening void outside his tormented mind, that tells him that he *is*. Hardening her heart against him, Marie returns the Drum-Major's embraces; and Woyzeck, a good man and a good father to their child, murders her. The deed is done in a passion of jealousy, yet its true source lies even deeper, at the barest level of self-assertion. It is the act of a man who must 'make a bruise or break an exit for his life': who must carve a notch upon the tree of experience before he is himself crucified on it: who must do *this* deed since no other, more positive, lies within his power.

Although Woyzeck is presented in a state of all but complete deprivation, he is an individual, sharply outlined against all others; not so much by virtue of a distinct consciousness as by the capacity for suffering that echoes through his wayward, somnambulistic consciousness. Even more succinctly, but also more powerfully than in *Dantons Tod*, Büchner again conveys his feeling for the fragmentariness and discontinuity of experience by resorting to episodic scenes. In both plays (but more successfully in *Woyzeck*) these scenes are made up of strange patterns of words arranged in contrasting mosaics of greys and violent crimsons, which trace out his anti-hero's movement towards the reality of pain. Unfeeling and boredom are presented by an imagery, occasionally obscene, related to the digestive and sexual functions. The repetitious tedium of the daily chores of dressing – eating – sleeping; the 'symbols of exhaustion' – discarded clothes, mechanical dolls and marionettes, frozen ground and arid wastes and the smell of the grave, ashen skies and marshy landscapes – these are the images that give poetic form and dramatic substance to one side of the dialectic:

WOYZECK: Ich geh. Es is viel möglich. Der Mensch! Es is viel möglich. – Wir haben schön Wetter, Herr Hauptmann. Sehn Sie, so ein schöner, fester, grauer Himmel; man könnte Lust bekommen, ein' Kloben hineinzuschlagen und sich daran zu hängen, nur wegen des Gedankenstrichels zwischen Ja und wieder Ja – und Nein. Herr Hauptmann, Ja und Nein? Ist das Nein am Ja oder das Ja am Nein schuld? Ich will drüber nachdenken.

WOYZECK [when taunted with Marie's unfaithfulness]: I must go. Many things are possible. A human being! Many things are possible. – Fine weather we're having, Captain, Sir. Look you now, such a fine sky, all grey and hard. It almost makes you want to knock a hook in it and hang yourself on it, merely because of the little dash between Yes and again Yes – and No. – Well, Captain, Sir: Yes and No? Is the No to blame for the Yes, or the Yes for the No? I will think about that.

In intense dramatic contrast with this is the imagery of flesh and blood, of suffering and of the crucifixion, the language of violence:

Das Messer? Wo is das Messer? Ich hab es da gelassen. Es verrät
mich! Näher, noch näher! Was is das für ein Platz? Was hör ich?
Es rührt sich was. Still. – Da in der Nähe. Marie? Ha, Marie! Still.
Alles still! Was bist du so bleich, Marie? Was hast du eine rote
Schnur um den Hals? Bei wem hast du das Halsband verdient mit
deinen Sünden? Du warst schwarz davon, schwarz! Hab ich dich
gebleicht? Was hängen deine Haare so wild? Hast du deine
Zöpfe heut nicht geflochten? . . . – Das Messer, das Messer! Hab
ich's? So! Leute – dort! (*Er läuft zum Wasser.*)[5]

WOYZECK: [after the murder, alone on the edge of the forest,
near the pond]: The knife? Where is the knife? This is where I
left it. It will hang me! Closer, still closer! What's that noise?
Something moved. Sh!... close at hand. Marie? Ha, Marie. Hush.
It's so quiet. Why are you so pale, Marie? Why have you got that
red cord round your neck? Who paid you with that necklace for
your sins? You were black with sins, black! Have I made you
white now? Why does your hair hang down so wild? Didn't you
plait it this morning? . . . The knife, the knife! Have I got it?
There now. People! I hear them coming – there! (*Runs to the
water.*)

Words, everywhere in Büchner's writings, are such strange,
isolated objects: now like gaudy phials of poison, now again like
knives quivering in the target, now like scalpels dissecting limbs, now
like gory wounds, now again like muffling gags of cotton wool.
Woyzeck speaks without expectation of being understood or hope of
being spared. Yet his all but incoherent language, rent by doubts,
sign of his utter isolation, is also the hallmark of Woyzeck's authenticity. In contrast to this, all coherent speeches in the play are cast as
satirical diatribes on the hypocrisy of the hostile world that engulfs
him. The Doctor's learned disquisitions on Woyzeck's physical
reactions to his Pavlovian experiments, the Boothkeeper's exhibition
of a calculating horse –

Ja, das ist kein viehdummes Individuum, das ist ein Person, ein
Mensch, ein tierischer Mensch –, und doch ein Vieh, ein Bête.
(*Das Pferd führt sich ungebührlich auf.*)

Yes indeed, ladies and gentlemen, here's no stupid beast, here is a person, a human being, an animal human being – and yet (*the horse misbehaves* [*as Woyzeck had done earlier*]) an animal, a beast. . . .

– or the parody of a teleological sermon Büchner had heard, put into the mouth of a drunken journeyman –

Warum ist der Mensch? Warum ist der Mensch? – Aber wahrlich, ich sage euch: Von was hätte der Landmann, der Weissbinder, der Schuster, der Arzt leben sollen, wenn Gott den Menschen nicht geschaffen hätte?

Why is man? Ah, why is man? Verily, verily I say unto you: what should the ploughman live on, the pargeter, the cobbler and the physician, if God had not created man?

strikingly resembling Lucky's monologue in *Waiting for Godot* – all these relentlessly coherent speeches contain not an ounce of truth or sympathy or insight: they are wordy lies against Woyzeck's inchoate truth. Their very rhetoric – the world's coherent discourse itself – is the harbinger of chaos, pain and death. A number of figures pass hurriedly before our eyes: Andres, his fellow-soldier, a mere human vegetable, who provides a contrast to Woyzeck's sentient soul; Marie, whose last words before she succumbs to the Drum-Major are words of dead indifference; the Grandmother, with her fairy tale about the earth void of life, the moon a piece of rotten wood, and the stars 'that were little golden gnats stuck on pins just as the shrike sticks them on blackthorns' (quoted in full below, p. 105); the Jew who sells Woyzeck the fateful knife; the Policeman who sums up Woyzeck's passion, 'A good murder, a good honest murder, a lovely case. As nice a case as you could wish to see' – they are all only shadows in that icy void which Woyzeck must somehow breach, even if all that is left to him is a deed of violence.

Insisting on the proletarian status of Woyzeck and on the indigence of his circumstances, Marxist criticism offers a useful corrective to the disembodied assertions of some existentialist metaphysics with its egregious contempt for social fact. But that criticism is wrong in suggesting that material deprivation is the sole source of Woyzeck's anguish, and that therefore his condition is remediable. What if his circumstances were different? They are not detachable. One has only to ask the question to see its absurdity. Woyzeck is what he is: 'the thing itself', the very *a priori* of man. 'The poor you have always with you' is not a statement in defence of the capitalist system.

A NOTE ON JOHANN NESTROY

The few comic passages which are woven into Büchner's plays don't really lighten the atmosphere of desolation that hangs over them; on the contrary, the ribald and occasionally coarse humour underlines the grim absurdity of a man's effort to assert himself against the demiurges of history and blind instinct. And yet . . . viewed in another light, there is something comic about the divided characters and minds he portrays; the fragmented experience is the stuff of tragedy, yet in its inconsequentiality it may provide the material of high comedy. The originality of Büchner's dramatic form is undoubted; the dialectic of suffering and boredom, on the other hand, belongs to the spirit of his age.

The sad monoliths *à la* Meister Anton are a sport of the chilly parlours of the Protestant North. In the South, however, cheerfulness keeps breaking in: it is hard to think of an Austrian playwright who could take these embattled personalities seriously. Parody and farce are an essential part of the Austrian popular theatre – the only popular stage in all Europe that has an unbroken tradition of three centuries, from the Baroque to the end of the Austrian Empire. And Johann Nestroy (1801–1862) in his comedies, parodies both kinds of character – Büchner's distraught anti-heroes as well as Hebbel's aggressive monoliths.

> JOAB: Ich hab' gebeten, daß man mich melden möcht'. Den Herrn von Holofernes such' ich – geh' ich recht?
> HOLOFERNES: Wär' mir nicht lieb, wenn's außer mir noch einen gäbet. Ich hab' die Spiegeln abg'schafft, weil sie die Frechheit haben, mein Gesicht, was einzig in seiner Art is, zu verdoppeln . . .

> JOAB [in drag, as Judith]: I've asked to be announced. I'm looking for Lord Holofernes – am I in the right place?

HOLOFERNES: I wouldn't fancy it if there was another one beside me! I've had all mirrors abolished, because they have the cheek to reduplicate my face, which is quite unique in its way.[6]

But then, parody is built into the linguistic situation of Austrian literature, which is what makes it so unsuitable for export. We must leave aside the vexed problem whether Austrians are or are not Germans, the answer to which has in the recent past depended on unemployment statistics and the state of the Austrian currency rather than on high cultural considerations. The question is, do they have a language of their own? It is difficult to think of another body of literature anywhere in Europe that is able to derive its comic effects from nothing more sophisticated than plain quotation of the 'correct' speech habits of its mighty neighbours. Yet when a character in a Viennese comedy is to be shown in an apparently inescapable predicament, he need only employ a few abstract nouns in '—keit', '—heit' and the like, lace his syntax with a few subsidiary clauses, place the verbs in the 'correct' order and get his pronominal case-endings right – and he has brought the house down, to the despair of any critic who has to convey this humour to a foreign audience. Take Act II, scene 9 of Nestroy's comedy *Der Zerrissene* (*Tattered and Torn*, 1835). Herr von Lips, a millionaire who doesn't know what to do with his money or his life, thinks he has drowned a jealous locksmith (who in turn thinks he has drowned the hapless Herr von Lips), and flees to one of his own farms in fear of the police, disguised as a labourer. There he is recognised, and given breakfast by his god-child:

LIPS: O du liebe Kathi, du kommst mir allweil lieber vor! (*Will sie ans Herz drücken.*)

KATHI: Aber, Göd –

LIPS: Gleich a Milich drauf, das kühlt. (*Frühstückt gierig und spricht währenddem weiter.*) Was mir ausserdem is, das kannst du gar nicht beurteilen. Nicht wahr, du hast noch niemanden umgebracht?

KATHI: Was fällt Ihnen nicht noch ein!

LIPS: Na, wenn sich zum Beispiel einer aus Lieb' zu dir was angetan hätt', wärst du seine indirekte Mörderin, Todgeberin par distance.

KATHI: Gott sei Dank, so eine grimmige Schönheit bin ich nicht.

D

LIPS: O Kathi! Du weisst gar nicht, was du für eine liebe Kathi bist! (*Umfasst sie.*)

KATHI: (*sich losmachend*): O, gehn S' doch –

LIPS: Gleich wieder a Milich drauf! (*Trinkt.*) So, jetzt bin ich wieder ein braves Bubi. – Dass ich dir also sag', ich hab' Visionen.

KATHI: Die Krankheit kennen wir nicht auf 'n Land.

LIPS: Das sind Phantasiegespinste, in den Hohlgängen des Gehirns erzeugt, die manchmal heraustreten aus uns, sich krampusartig aufstellen auf dem Niklomarkt der Einsamkeit – erloschne Augen rollen, leblose Zähne fletschen und mit drohender Knochenhand aufreiben zu modrigen Grabesohrfeigen, das is Vision.

KATHI: Nein, was die Stadtleut' für Zuständ' haben –

LIPS: Wenn's finster wird, seh' ich weisse Gestalten –

KATHI: Wie is das möglich? Bei der Nacht sind ja alle Küh' schwarz.

LIPS: Und 's is eigentlich eine Ochserei von mir, hab' ich ihn denn absichtlich ertränkt? Nein! Und doch allweil der schneeweisse Schlossergeist! – Du machst dir keine Vorstellung, wie schauerlich ein weisser Schlosser ist.

KATHI: So was müssen S' Ihnen aus 'n Sinn schlagen.

LIPS: Selbst diese Milch erinnert mich – wenn s' nur a bisserl kaffeebraun wär' – aber weiss is mein Abscheu.

LIPS: Oh my dear Kitty, I get fonder of you every moment. (*Makes to embrace her.*)

KITTY: But god-father . . .

LIPS: Quickly, a glass of milk to cool me down. (Breakfasts greedily, talking all the time.) You've no idea what else I've got on my mind. I suppose you've never killed anybody?

KITTY: How can you think such a thing!

LIPS: Well, if for instance a man did himself a mischief for love of you, that would make you into his indirect murderess, death-dealer par distance.

KITTY: Thank heavens, I'm no such cruel beauty.

LIPS: Oh Kitty! You don't know what a dear Kitty you are! (*Embraces her.*)

KITTY (*freeing herself*): Now, go away . . .

LIPS: Quick, another glass of milk! (*Drinks.*) There now, I'm a good little boy again. – I must tell you, I have visions.

KITTY: That's an illness we don't have here in the country.

LIPS: Phantasms they are, created in the hollow ducts of the brain, which sometimes step out from within us and place themselves, Mephistopheles-wise, on the Christmas Market of our solitude – extinguished eyes rolling, dead teeth gnashing – and with threatening skeleton-hand they incite to a mouldering funereal box on the ear. That's a vision.

KITTY: Why, I never knew the things city-people go through . . .

LIPS: When it gets dark I see white figures . . .

KITTY: How can that be? At night all cows are black.

LIPS: And I'm really an ass: did I drown him deliberately? No. And yet, all the time I see this snow-white ghost of a locksmith before me! You've no idea how gruesome a white locksmith is.

KITTY: But you must put him out of your mind.

LIPS: Even this milk reminds me of him – if only it had a dash of coffee-colour in it – white gives me the horrors. . . .

The farcical action turns, as so often in this theatrical tradition, on the curse of money, the double-dealings of false friends, and the hero's rescue from adversity by the poor-but-faithful lover. In many of Nestroy's comedies these stock situations are embellished by the wagers and temptations of fairies and interfering goddesses; the ambience is familiar from Johann Emmanuel Schikaneder's libretto to Mozart's *Magic Flute* (1791). In Ferdinand Raimund's *Der Bauer als Millionär* (*The Peasant Millionaire*, 1826) a plot of this kind has affinities with the story of Everyman and is used as a vehicle for a homely and serious moral lesson.

Nestroy's aim, in *Der Zerrissene*, is more sophisticated. The figure of Lips is a spoof on the *Weltschmerz*, boredom and insouciance of the late Romantic hero, his very circumstances (Lips has lots of money but little grammar) offer a farcical comment on the noble station of a Leonce. The passage I have quoted is a parody, too, on the grave-yard inanities of contemporary fate tragedies, a parallel to Peacock's *Nightmare Abbey*. Nestroy was the only actor-manager among German playwrights. The real source of his greatness lies neither in the plots (which he pilfered from several European literatures)[7] nor even in the complex and highly effective theatrical devices of his comedies. It lies in his characterisations or, more precisely, in the astonishing verbal inventiveness and virtuosity of his dialogues. His famous 'couplets' – doggerel or ballad songs, sometimes improvised before the show – are a unique mixture of the topical and the perennial, full of hidden allusions to avoid the absurd censorship of Metternich's police. They are built from puns, popular sayings turned inside out, and parodies of archness and sententiousness. In them and in the fast repartees of his characters, the German (or rather the Austrian) language is exploited for a shot-silk, silver-and-dross quality it had never displayed before.* Comparing these verbal cascades with the homely utterances of Raimund's characters, one is not surprised at Raimund's despairing remark on seeing one of Nestroy's comedies: 'Das kann i nit. Da is gar mit meine Stuck.'†

Above all it is the pun – the second look at a molecule of speech, leading to the brilliant illumination of a familiar mental landscape in an unfamiliar light – which Nestroy presses into the service of his abundant theatrical talent. Nestroy's puns, like those of Karl Kraus, his greatest admirer, raise an interesting paradox in the ethics of language. Only one who is deeply, intuitively *and* intellectually familiar with a language (and thus with the ethos of its speakers) will know where to dig below its smooth colloquial surface in order to bring up an illuminating pun; but only moments of alienation from the common concerns and 'colloquialisms' of those speakers will enable him to perform the act.

* At least not on the stage; in prose the earlier master of this mode is his fellow-Viennese, the Augustinian friar Abraham a Sancta Clara (1644–1709).

† 'That's beyond my powers. That's put paid to my plays.' Ferdinand Raimund (1790–1836) committed suicide a few days later.

THREE

Heinrich Heine's Contentious Muse

Evaluations of Heinrich Heine's poetry have been bedevilled by comparisons with Goethe. In that august company his lyrical poetry has inevitably been branded as shallow and derivative, his emotions as insincere and divided. He himself, it must be admitted, invites the comparison. Almost to the end of his life he wrote poetry which, consciously or instinctively, alludes to the tradition of the *Volkslied* that Goethe had all but initiated and immeasurably enriched. In verse-forms, range of images and sentiments alike these allusions span Heine's creative life, from *Early Sorrows* (1817) and the immensely popular *Book of Songs* of 1827 (published when Heine was thirty) to the *Last Poems* of 1852 and the posthumously published verses of his Paris exile. To speak of Heine as a *German* poet is to speak of one who continues the tradition of the *Volkslied* into the post-Romantic age, and completely modifies it to accommodate a new, un-Goethean kind of consciousness. Overall evaluation apart, the comparison with Goethe is justified when we consider the sheer variety and range of Heine's poetic *œuvre*.

Both were, emphatically, all-purpose poets. They saw in poetry not a sacerdotal activity, not an aesthetic rite or a mode of utterance reserved for high occasions and deepest feelings only, but something like their natural mode of expression, suitable for Sundays and weekdays alike. They are both blessedly prolific and generously unfussy, sometimes undiscriminating, in their productions. Their creativeness takes many and varied forms, it readily moves from poetry to easy versification and hence to prose. Their lives are devoted to their poetic and literary métier, but this devotion is in no

way exclusive and solemn. Theirs is a poetic existence in the sense
that they are instinctively driven to give meaning to all their
experiences through their poetry, to *use* them in and for their art. In
this respect as in several others Heine's self-consciousness is more
fully developed, certainly more fully and unsparingly expressed,
than Goethe's; and it is in some ways a very different, less harmonious self. There is no equivalent, in Heine, to the persona of
savant, elder statesman, and 'sage of Weimar' which Goethe so often
assumed in the last three decades of his life. Heine's highly developed
sense not of irony only but of humour, too, saw to it that whatever
attitudes he struck he was never pompous. But underlying these
differences is their confidence that the self and all its most private
joys and sorrows, its loves and hates, its trusts and betrayals and its
changing beliefs, are worthy of being made the subject of poetry –
that their self is *interesting* to contemporary and future generations;
and in this confidence, together with the not unimportant fact that
it is justified, they are unique.

Furthermore, neither of them is an intellectual. Instead, they are
possessed of a bright, worldly intelligence, they use ideas but are
hardly ever interested in them for their own sake. 'I have never
thought about thinking', Goethe writes in one of his epigrams;
Heine sums up his 'doctrine' as follows:[1]

> Schlage die Trommel und fürchte dich nicht,
> Und küsse die Marketenderin!
> Das ist die ganze Wissenschaft
> Das ist der Bücher tiefster Sinn.
>
> Trommle die Leute aus dem Schlaf,
> Trommle Reveille mit Jugendkraft
> Marschiere trommelnd immer voran,
> Das ist die ganze Wissenschaft.
>
> Das ist die Hegelsche Philosophie,
> Das ist der Bücher tiefster Sinn!
> Ich hab sie begriffen, weil ich gescheit,
> Und weil ich ein guter Tambour bin.
>
> Beat the drum and be not afraid
> And kiss the cantinière!
> That is the sum of all sciences,
> That's what all books are about!

Wake all people from their sleep with your drum,
Drum their reveille with youthful might
March with your drum at their head,
That is the sum of all sciences.

That is old Hegel's philosophy,
That's what all books are about!
I've grasped its meaning because I am clever,
And because I can drum so well.

And twenty years later: 'I haven't played hide-and-seek with symbolical riddles, nor have I denied my powers of reasoning.'

Both were critical, sometimes scathingly so, of the overwhelmingly intellectual and philosophically informed culture of their ages. Goethe made a few concessions to it, which take the form of a high moral seriousness and occasional sententiousness; in this respect Heine learns much but concedes nothing – his critical response to the *furor philosophicus* ranges all the way from banter and jokes to cutting sarcasm. Unlike Goethe he is interested in finding out the historical and social causes behind the philosophical passion, which he sees as an integral part of Germany's past and present – a present to which he does not attempt to set up a rival cultural kingdom as Goethe had done in Weimar. The coherent and even to some extent autonomous 'Geist der Goethezeit' has no equivalent in Heine's age. The direction of his creative intelligence is incomparably more social and political.

Time and again Heine's detractors (they are many and they come from very diverse quarters) have denied him the highest title in the German cultural vocabulary, that of 'Dichter', calling him a superior journalist. What is certain is that the prose he wrote is (as Nietzsche acknowledged) an unparalleled liberation – his eye for the telling metaphor, his quick wit and sharp tongue, his regard for the limpid phrase and variation of pace, has few if any precedents in German prose, and makes him the grandfather of German journalism. He does not, when an argument bores him, go on to bore the reader with it, but is only too pleased to move on to other matters. He has, more than any German author before him, an eye on his public. Occasionally his style curries favour with his public at the very point where he is tearing that public to shreds. Nothing, almost nothing is sacred to him, certainly not his own lyrical poetry, a levity which many German critics have found unforgivable. He wrote for the day – so runs the hostile argument – and his writings have perished with the day, except for a few deeply-felt lyrical poems in the Goethean tradition. (Such judgements are like solemn skids on slippery ground; Hugo von Hofmannsthal's 'vindication' of Heine, which manages to be both arrogant and lugubrious at the same time, is a case in point.)[2] It seems to me that precisely the opposite is true. Where it is serious and 'deep', consciously 'immortal', Heine's poetry no longer speaks to us in the authentic voice of uncontentious lyricism; there indeed his ease of utterance becomes fatal. Some of his early verse, even some of the confessionary poems of his last years, unrelieved by irony, strike a note of bathos. And it may well be admitted that he has occasionally perpetrated some of the ghastliest rhymes in the language, which no reference to irony, parody, or spoof can salvage. His unique, and permanent, achievement lies where his writing is fully committed, or rather exposed, to the moods and concerns of his day, where any hankering after poetic immortality is blown up into an ironical bravado. The anecdotal extravagance and mock rhetoric; the romanticism of 'deep' moods alternating with easy colloquialisms; the double-take and the joke (sometimes a little off, occasionally obscene); and the multi-levelled sententiousness – rarely serious, mostly ironical, ribald, sarcastic, using pastiche, persiflage, and shock-effects – these are the devices of his greatest poetry, whether its themes be social or personal, or a characteristic mixture of both. His unique achievement lies where his poetry, filtered through a rich and divided selfconsciousness and irony, reaches truth and depth and *Germany*, and where the poetic forms bequeathed to him by Goethe and the Romantics are no longer explored but exploded. A superior journalist? The best of his poetry was written for his day, and the more fully it encompassed it the more it lives in ours. What divides him from the journalist is his fatal inability to forgive the evil and forget the misery in the world. Many are the political and philosophical ideas he shortcircuits by means of a joke. The feelings of his outraged humanity, on the other hand, are never appeased. As he grew older he, like Marx, certainly did not grow more tolerant.

Karl Kraus, whose essay 'Heine and his Consequences' contains the most powerful attack on the posthumous poet laureate of the Wilhelminian era, has said all that is to be said about the sentimentality, the slipshod versification, the lame ironies, the journalese, and the facile effects that disfigure some of Heine's writings. That demolition anticipates all other critical objections and makes them redundant. But what Karl Kraus has demolished is not Heine. It is above all the Heine *cult* and the egregiousness of critics who, in praising Heine, were sentimentalising the memory of their own and his public's adolescent response to his poetry. No German poetry has ever evoked self-indulgence as a substitute for criticism so readily as Heine's – nor has this *ersatz*-situation ever been more splendidly refuted than in Kraus's attack. (And, as always with Kraus, the significance of the attack exceeds its occasion, and it is this excess that keeps it alive.) But when Kraus concludes his essay –

> Heine was a Moses who struck the rock of the German language with his staff. But dexterity is no witchcraft, the water did not gush from the rock – he had it hidden in his other hand, and it was eau-de-cologne.*

– he is quite wrong. It was vitriol.

Parody, Thomas Mann once observed, is the expression of love for a form that is no longer viable. Some of the greatest poems in Heine's first collection, *The Book of Songs*, are parodistic in this sense, being informed by a tension between the traditional form and the divided self. The third poem in the group, *Homecoming*, calls up, conventionally enough, the German countryside in the month of May, with its river and busy mill; a boy is fishing from a boat; girls are dancing on the lawn and bleaching the linen; 'and oxen and meadows and woods' are all included in this charming landscape that Caspar David Friedrich might have painted. The pastoral fairy-tale quality of the scene is underlined by its being surveyed by the poet from some far-off old ramparts; the shapes he sees are 'friendly' and 'tiny, full of colour'. Why then does the poem begin, 'My heart, my heart is heavy'? This too is a traditional opening: it raises in the reader the expectation of a contrast between the happy idyllic scene and a tale of unrequited or betrayed love – this is how Heine achieved

* Karl Kraus, 'Heine und die Folgen' in *Die Fackel*, vol. xiii, 31 August 1911, nos. 329/330, 33. Meno Spann (*Heine*, London 1966) justly writes of Kraus as 'the first who was not motivated in his condemnation of the poet by anti-Semitism, petty bourgeois morality or religious bigotry'.

some of those predictable effects which thrill us a good deal less than they did his contemporary public. But here the expectation of the obvious is disappointed, the reader is in for a grotesque surprise. The penultimate stanza still belongs to the landscape idyll:

> Am alten grauen Turme
> Ein Schilderhäuschen steht;
> Ein rotgeröckter Bursche
> Dort auf und nieder geht.

> Beside the old grey tower
> There stands a sentry box;
> A lad in a bright-red tunic
> Is marching to and fro.

But in the last stanza the idyll has been shattered:

> Er spielt mit seiner Flinte
> Die funkelt im Sonnenrot,
> Er präsentiert und schultert –
> Ich wollt, er schösse mich tot.

> He is playing with his musket,
> The sun makes it shine red,
> Presenting arms and shouldering,
> I wish he would shoot me dead.

No word of explanation or expatiation follows. It is pure caprice, that last line, yet it is also a stark omen of violence, an achieved contrast, and thus meaningful. The conscious alienation of a traditional form has come to express the chasm that opens up between the poet and a landscape that was, and is suddenly no longer, idyllic and harmless. It may well be that not many of his contemporaries appreciated the full effect of these poetic shock tactics. At all events, it is ironical that so good a reader and sympathetic a critic as Theodor Fontane (writing in 1892), while praising much of Heine's work for its realism, singled out this poem as a regrettable Romantic aberration.* But then, unlike Heine, Fontane was spared the torture of being a good prophet of the bad.

* 'Realism doesn't want to be "shot dead", as does Heine in one of his most famous little poems.' (*Sämtliche Werke*, München 1964, vol. XXI/i, 14.)

I have spoken of the close rapport, attested by the huge profits of his Hamburg publisher, that existed between Heine and his public. Certainly this rapport extended to his ironies, even if perhaps not to the more violent ones – after all his admirers included such sophisticated political enemies as Metternich and his secretary, Gentz. There is a good deal of the licensed clown, the court Jew, in Heine's attitude to the German philistines. He deeply despised their 'sated virtues' and 'cash-on-the-spot morality' – deeply but not quite consistently. Much has been written on the harmful, trivialising effect all this had on his art. But what this complicated love-hate relationship vouchsafed him – not as a man but as an artist – was the substance of his freedom and the source of his insight.

He had his first dose of German anti-Semitism as a little boy, it was with him throughout his turbulent life, it followed him fifty years later into that slow death in 'the mattress grave' in Paris: he never bore his Jewishness meekly, vaunting it like a yellow star on his coat or again clattering it along like a dog with an empty tin tied to his tail. (Among his own tribe he fared hardly better, as may be seen from his observation about Baruch Spinoza, who 'was solemnly expelled from the community of Israel and declared unworthy henceforth to bear the name of a Jew. His Christian enemies were magnanimous enough to leave him that name.') He knew sordid poverty, and from his millionaire uncle experienced the very opposite of that solidarity and charity which is supposed to be characteristic of Jewish family life. Money or rather the prospect of money made him fawn on its possessors, including the fabulous Rothschilds, turned him into an informer, cost him untold hours of fruitless bargaining with skinflint publishers. Baptised into the Lutheran Church, he anticipated by self-mockery the public derision and the futility of the act. He hated his fatherland with the fervour of a betrayed lover, and (like James Joyce, like Karl Kraus) neither in his emotions nor in his thinking ever moved far from its innermost concerns. He was the first of that long line of spiritual exiles who consoled themselves for the reality of life in Germany by hypostatising the German language and making of it his very own unassailable citadel. He railed against the Jewish and Christian God, and in his *Last Poems* cursed his fate and enemies more terribly than any German poet since Johann Christian Günther, yet that collection, too, contains a poem, 'Ich war, o Lamm, als Hirt bestellt', of surpassing tenderness and (nothing came harder to him) Christian humility, among the most moving in the German language. He wrote of love: of its happiness and enchantments, more often of its betrayals and bondage, rehearsing in his poems love's every colour and hue; if anyone after Goethe could have significantly added to that theme, it was he. And when death came, after eight years of progressive paralysis, he certainly did 'not go gentle into that good night' but, now wholly paralysed and almost blind, retained his poetic creativeness and bright intelligence to the end. Yet where, in all this, are there signs of freedom and insight?

Not in the travails of the man but in the products of the creative mind. The circumstances of his life, with which he never made his peace, are the vital substance from which he gained his freedom; his writings are the realm in which that freedom and insight are manifest. There is, after all, a strange truthfulness about his work. The man who suffers is not healed in the mind that creates. It is a divided self – his 'Zerrissenheit' – that speaks to us from his pages. The struggle never ceases; the strife between love and hate, trust and betrayal, the beauty of art and the ugly truth of life, between Germany and France, between the aristocrat and the rabble-rouser, is never appeased. It is Heine's creative selfconsciousness, his ability not to smother or assuage but to express these many conflicts, which makes for the delight of his poetry. His selfconsciousness is vast but rarely excessive and unnerving, for it almost always finds an adequate image or fiction to contain it; when it fails, he will turn even a comment on the failure into a wry story.

His overt political sympathies apart, he was the least democratic of poets, quickly bored with expatiation, caring nothing for smooth explanatory transitions. A surprisingly large number of his poems end abruptly, almost inadvertently, their arguments left hanging in mid-air. These laconic endings are signs not of a creative flaw, nor of a gnostic fragmentariness, but of an aristocratic impatience. They express a sudden contempt for that rapport from which the poem has been sustained. But the capriciousness is made meaningful because in the abrupt ending he still retains his firm hold on the reader's sensibility, only now the poet's rapport with the reader is no longer accommodating but critical, even derisive. Heine's imagination could not function in those aerial spaces of unconditioned freedom towards which the German Romantics had aspired, it worked at its finest when fully enmeshed in, even enslaved by, social and personal circumstances, in the *données* of the real world. He was, in this sense, the first and the greatest German realist of the nineteenth century. Yet much of his work, taking the form of romances and extravaganzas and fairy tales, is quite unlike the realism of a Balzac or Dickens or Tolstoy. But so is the reality he describes, the substance from which he frees himself. No one understood better than he that yearning for the cosmic spaces of 'pure spirit', for that dream of freedom from the actual and humiliating circumstances of German life, which informs the poetry as well as the political and philosophical writings of the German Romantics. Heine wrote not in this tradition but about it: he wrote its history, he ridiculed its hold on the contemporary scene, he warned of its future transformation.[3]

A sophisticated Marxist critic has treated Heine's work by standing Freud on his head. Heine's love poems (he has suggested),[4] especially those in which the loved one is indicted of cold caprice and betrayal, in which her beauty and physical charms are contrasted with her crude, or frivolous, or deceitful mind, are not 'really' about women at all, but about Germany, or at any rate about the contemporary world. This method of interpretation is more helpful than its bare summary suggests. Clearly it cannot be applied to much of his early poetry. Few of the poems in *Lyrical Intermezzo* for instance, too well-known to need even listing, can reasonably be seen in this way. (Though it should be added that Schubert's and Schumann's settings of these poems are magnificent in their own right rather than as consistently faithful renderings of Heine: they only rarely retrace the ironical or comic twist of some of the originals.) But from the time Heine settled in Paris (1831), more especially from *New Poems* (1844) onwards, the poetic traffic between Eros and the world – the world of politics and culture, of philosophy and religion, as well as of Germany – comes more and more to dominate his poems, until, in his last poems, the correspondence between Eros and 'the reality principle' becomes the characteristic mode of his unsolemn muse. At the bidding of his creative self-conciousness, the ironical division within the poet's mind is now perceived and expressed as a reality in the contemporary world at large.

Sometimes this double preoccupation leads to incongruous results, as in the longer *Tannhäuser* poem of 1836 (from which incidentally, derives Wagner's interest in the theme). The first two sections of the poem are given over to a retelling of the legend, in which the noble knight tires of Lady Venus after seven (obviously strenuous) years of life in her mountain: the bliss, the fulfilment, her ageless immortality have proved too much:

> Frau Venus, meine schöne Frau,
> Von süssem Wein und Küssen
> Ist meine Seele geworden krank;
> Ich schmachte nach Bitternissen.

> My soul is sick, O Lady Venus,
> Of sweet wine and kisses,
> My soul has come to yearn, sweet wife,
> For thorns and bitterness.

She may chide him for being 'an ungrateful, cold Christian', the heavy-hearted German knight must leave her to confess and, if possible, expiate his sinful life with the heathen goddess. Both here and in the next section the contrast has a wider, national meaning, which at this stage forms merely an unemphatic background. Tannhäuser now leaves for Rome, but the very words in which he makes his confession to Pope Urban conjure up Lady Venus' physical presence, and it is clear that his contrition is fighting something of a losing battle with his yearning for her embraces. It hardly surprises us that the Pope cannot absolve him (all he can do is 'wretchedly' raise his hands), and that he must pronounce sentence of eternal damnation. What is poor Tannhäuser to do? He returns to his lady, who is only too happy to welcome him back and who, after a passionate reception, 'goes into the kitchen to cook him a broth', of which he is much in need. He tells her of his journey through the world, confining his observations about Rome to discreetly remarking that he 'had business there' and . . . – now the poem as good as collapses, Tannhäuser's spiritual conflict is left hanging in the air.

Spiritual conflict? It sounds as though the critic is spoiling a funny story by heavy-handed commentary. And yet, it is there, for all the banter and mockery: the losing battle our Tannhäuser is fighting is Luther's old *Busskampf* and the *pugna fidei* of Northern spirituality against the temptations of the sensual South, it is the conflict of mortality and consciousness of sin against eternal or at any rate

unageing innocence – what Heine movingly presents *is* a profound
spiritual conflict, no less. Movingly? In spite of the ribaldry, the
comic turns? It is the prerogative of every great artist that he should
challenge the distinctions inherent in our critical vocabulary, and
Heine exploits this prerogative to the full. The spiritual conflict is
established, and in a poignant manner, not in spite of but through
the divided action, whose charm lies precisely in its inimitable
(though often imitated) mixture of the serious and the comic and
ribald. A little more can be said about this mixed mode. It is fatally
vulnerable to vulgarity and to the 'clever-clever' line, both of which
are here avoided. Above all, it is achieved by a wholly concrete,
sensuous vocabulary (elsewhere Heine will use even philosophical
vocabulary as though it designated things and people living a real
life in the world). When Tannhäuser returns to the mountain.

> Frau Venus erwachte aus dem Schlaf,
> Ist schnell aus dem Bette gesprungen;

> Lady Venus awoke from her sleep,
> Swiftly she jumped out of her bed;

and when she embraces him (one thinks of Yeats's 'Crazy Jane'),

> Aus ihrer Nase rann das Blut,
> Den Augen die Tränen entflossen;
> Sie hat mit Tränen und Blut das Gesicht
> Des geliebten Mannes begossen.

> The blood, it ran from her nose,
> The tears, they ran from her eyes;
> With blood and tears did she drench
> The face of her beloved.

Whereas:

> Der Ritter legte sich ins Bett,
> Er hat kein Wort gesprochen.

> The knight he laid himself down,
> And never a word did he speak.

And the point about this sensuous-erotic vocabulary – the reason
why it can express the spiritual conflict – is that it is morally and

spiritually neutral, being equally appropriate to the serious and even tragic as well as to the comic and even ribald side of poor Tannhäuser's predicament.

However, as I have said, some thirteen stanzas from the end the poem collapses. Instead of either stopping at Tannhäuser's perfunctory mention of the 'business in Rome', or proceeding somehow to resolve his spiritual dilemma, the knight (who at first 'never a word did speak') now produces a catalogue of all the German cities through which he made his way and a list of all the idiocies, bigotries and hypocrisies he found in them. True, these verses in their turn are funny and biting, good political satire; only Heine and once or twice Gottfried Keller could write such controlled venom in the nineteenth century, and only Karl Kraus in the twentieth. But not the faintest attempt is made to relate them to the powerful erotic theme. Heine himself knew how vital to him was that nexus between Eros and the contemporary scene when he spoke of 'the two passions to which I dedicated my life: the love of beautiful women and the love of the French Revolution, that modern *furor francese* which drew me into the fight against the medieval mercenaries'. But here no connection is established, the satirical last section is glaringly (one can't even say contemptuously) irrelevant to the body of the poem, there is no integrated whole.

The prerogative of the comic muse is to leave an argument uncompleted, a situation unexplored, to whip away the serious, possibly tragic conclusion from under our eyes, to create an integrated whole from a combination of omissions and exaggerations. The tricks which the humorist plays with our everyday world do not 'fundamentally' challenge its reality, for he merely plays with parts of it, and cares nothing for what such play implies for the whole. The attitude that makes his playing possible is not doubt and deprivation, not criticism even, but abundant assurance that the world is what it is. This is why neither 'profound humour' nor 'deep jokes' (nor, incidentally, revolutionaries) are likely to be very funny; and this is also the reason why the areas of humour and satire do not, alas, overlap. In a culture where profundity is identified with a 'fundamental' questioning of the order of things, a writer like Heine is bound to be condemned as unserious, and his humour as shallow; the Marxist alternative, which is no better, is to appropriate him to a humourless political line by imputing to him an 'underlying' revolutionary intention a good deal more alien than the philistinism he challenged.

The story of Heine's political opinions (it will hardly be surprising) is as complex and perplexing as most other aspects of his life and writings. The general drift of his sympathies after 1830 is attested in an exchange of letters with Karl Marx in 1844–5[5] and it is clear that even before the fiasco of 1848 Heine had moved far to the left, from republicanism to communism. The remarkable document which testifies to his sympathies is the 1855 Preface to a collection of articles he had written in the years 1840 to 1843 for a German newspaper.[6] It is no exaggeration to say that this preface contains the classical defence of the literary man's allegiance to the communist cause; indeed, in the hundred years that follow few if any ideas have been added to that much-discussed topic which are not contained in Heine's declaration. Of course, here too (it is well to recall) he writes not as a doctrinaire intellectual but as a poet and a brightly intelligent contemporary; not, certainly, as a party man but as a political freelance. But hasn't recent history taught us that the position of the freelance more than almost any other is incompatible with the communist ideology? This, precisely, is what the preface of 1855 is about (hence my claim that little has been added to the debate it initiates).

The poet in him (he tells us) looks forward 'with dread and fear to the time when these sinister iconoclasts [the communists] will seize power and with their brutal fists will destroy all the marble images of my beloved world of art', when 'the lilies in the field which toil not nor spin and yet are arrayed as beautifully as King Solomon, will be ripped out of the soil of society', and when

> Alas! the grocers will be making paper bags out of my *Book of Songs* and will wrap in them the coffee or snuff of the old women of the future. Alas, all this I foresee, and an inexpressible sadness fills me when I think of the decline with which communism threatens my poems and the entire old order of the world. And yet, I confess it freely, this very communism works like a charm on my mind, a charm I cannot resist.

Not because he is a trimmer, but because logic and emotion alike appear to make it irresistible. Logic, which is based on the premise 'that all men have the right to eat', and which he feels compelled to follow even if *fiat iustitia, pereat mundus* (and not only the world of art) should be the conclusion to which it leads. We can see that, like Brecht the author of *Die Massnahme*, Heine in his candour would have made a disconcerting party member. But the second, the emotional reason is even more powerful than the first. It is hatred – and Heine was a magnificent hater –

> The hatred that I bestow on our common enemy, who forms the sharpest contrast to Communism . . – I speak of the party of the self-styled representatives of nationalism in Germany, of those false patriots whose love of country consists in nothing but an imbecile dislike of everything foreign and especially of the neighbouring countries . . . the remnants or successors of the Teutonomanes of 1815. . . . And now that the sword slips from the dying man's hand he is revived by the conviction that communism will assuredly dispatch them, not with a blow, no, with a mere kick, as one squashes a toad, even so will the giant squash them. It is because I hate the nationalists that I would fain love the communists.[7]

And one wonders whether Karl Kraus knew this preface when, after the murder of Rosa Luxemburg, he wrote:

> Communism as a reality is nothing but the antithesis of the life-despoiling ideology of [the ruling classes]; deriving its origin at all events from a purer set of ideas, it is a perverse [vertrackt] means toward a purer intellectual end. The devil take its practice, but may God preserve it for us to hang as an everlasting menace above the heads of those who own the goods and lands of this earth and, in order to cling to what they own, would let others starve or dispatch them into battle, all for patriotic honour's sake and with the consolation that 'there are greater things than life'. May God preserve Communism so that this evil brood, whose impudence knows no limit, may be prevented from becoming more brazen still; so that the gang of consumer-drones, who believe that mankind's need for love is adequately met if they give it their pox, shall at least go to bed with a nightmare, lose all taste for preaching morality to their victims, and choke on their sense of humour.[8]

> *Where all is rotten it is a man's work to cry stinking fish.*
>
> (F. H. Bradley, *Appearance and Reality*)

There *are* points in Heine's later work where the divided self is united, where the irony lets up; in the portrayals of the devil he knew he is quite single-minded. No poem of his contains an affirmation of the communist cause. He was, after all, a realist – the world yielded him no substance for such a poem. The division of his mind is resolved in the depiction of that which outraged the sense of compassion of the man and (the phrase is Matthew Arnold's) 'the intemperate susceptibility' of the poet. *The Silesian Weavers* (published in 1844 in Karl Marx's revolutionary journal *Vorwärts*), is perhaps the greatest poem ever written on behalf of the proletarian cause:[9]

DIE SCHLESISCHEN WEBER

Im düstern Auge keine Träne,
Sie sitzen am Webstuhl und fletschen die Zähne:
'Deutschland, wir weben dein Leichentuch,
Wir weben hinein den dreifachen Fluch –
  Wir weben, wir weben!

Ein Fluch dem Gotte, zu dem wir gebeten
In Winterskälte und Hungersnöten;
Wir haben vergebens gehofft und geharrt,
Er hat uns geäfft und gefoppt und genarrt –
  Wir weben, wir weben!

Ein Fluch dem König, dem König der Reichen,
Den unser Elend nicht konnte erweichen,
Der den letzten Groschen von uns erpreßt,
Und uns wie Hunde erschießen läßt –
  Wir weben, wir weben!

Ein Fluch dem falschen Vaterlande,
Wo nur gedeihen Schmach und Schande,
Wo jede Blume früh geknickt,

Wo Fäulnis und Moder Wurm erquickt –
  Wir weben, wir weben!

Das Schiffchen fliegt, der Webstuhl kracht,
Wir weben emsig Tag and Nacht –
Altdeutschland, wir weben dein Leichentuch.
Wir weben hinein den dreifachen Fluch,
  Wir weben, wir weben!'

Here is Friedrich Engels's incomplete English version:

Without a tear in their grim eyes,
They sit at the loom, the rage of despair in their faces:
'We have suffered and hunger'd long enough;
Old Germany, we are weaving a shroud for thee
And weaving it with a triple curse.
  We are weaving, weaving!

The first curse to the God, the blind and deaf god,
Upon whom we relied, as children on their father;
In whom we hoped and trusted withal,
He has mocked us, he has cheated us nevertheless,
  We are weaving, weaving!

The second curse for the King of the rich,
Whom our distress could not soften nor touch;
The King, who extorts the last penny from us,
And sends his soldiers, to shoot us like dogs.
  We are weaving, weaving!

A curse to the false fatherland,
That has nothing for us but distress and shame,
Where we suffered hunger and misery –
We are weaving thy shroud, Old Germany;
  We are weaving, weaving!'

AN OLD FRIEND OF YOURS IN GERMANY

Inspired by their abortive revolt of June 1844, the poem doesn't
set out to render the feelings of the starving weavers in a direct,
mimetic way; it is, emphatically, not a naturalistic poem. Instead,
it is informed by the highest rhetoric. The tense, melodramatic tone
is struck in the first lines –

Im düstern Auge keine Träne,
Sie sitzen am Webstuhl und fletschen die Zähne.

They shed no tears from eyes of doom
Gnashing their teeth they sit at the loom.

– and maintained throughout. The effects are harsh, even lurid. The usual devices of Heine the ironical lyricist are abandoned. The poem is not interrupted by picturesque asides, it is unalleviated by irony or joke, unburdened by any personal or poetic selfconsciousness, and unabridged by a contemptuous ending. It is a paean of hate in the same single-minded way as so many of Goethe's poems are paeans of happiness and joy. Its central image of deprivation and misery, raised from concrete circumstances to a rhetorical fortissimo, is the loom and the winding sheet which the weavers are working on it:

Deutschland, wir weben dein Leichentuch,
Wir weben hinein den dreifachen Fluch –
Wir weben, wir weben!

A threefold curse we work,
Germany, into thy shroud,
We are weaving, we are weaving.

There is a classical, exemplary quality about the poem which makes it unnecessary to do more than sketch in the critically obvious. The argument is entirely accommodated within the central image (e.g. 'the shuttle flies in the creaking loom/All day and all night we weave thy doom') and in the emotions of the weavers; the rhythm, related to the rhythm of work,[10] is heightened into the monotonous beat of a choral refrain that is both poignant (never melancholy) and threatening. The weavers' threefold curse of 'God, King and Fatherland'; the superb craftsmanship of the poem's five stanzas, each of five lines, containing two pairs of four-foot iambics with alternating feminine and masculine rhymes and the over-riding iambic refrain; and its structure, which frames the three stanzas of the searing indictment in the opening stanza whose third line reappears in the concluding stanza, heightened from the original 'Deutschland, wir weben dein Leichentuch', to the chilling and momentous 'Altdeutschland, wir weben dein Leichentuch' – it is this classical quality that makes of *Die schlesischen Weber* one of the greatest poems in a language most of whose articulate speakers have been only too ready to pour scorn on 'A nasty song, fie, a political song!', and to look on the poem and its author with a jaundiced eye.

Analysis of Heine's poetry of the kind favoured by the ancient 'New Critics' tends not only to elaborate the obvious, it can also be peculiarly misleading. A pike plays havoc among elderly trout – to evaluate Heine's poetic shock-tactics according to the criteria established for 'pure' lyrical poetry leaves the critic with tatters in his hands. Like Schiller – only more successfully – he is above all a rhetorical poet. (And his liberal sympathies, again like Schiller's, are those of an aristocrat.) Words to him are not mysterious, let alone mystical, icons. To regard his poetry as an intimation of the unsayable, of Being behind or beyond language, is a deplorable mystification.[11] His images are not 'seen', or 'lived', or 'fully experienced'. His poetry abounds in romantic clichés, and these clichés are often exploded, though not always. Metaphors and epithetic phrases which, in a lyrical context, look like empty gestures are pressed into the service of powerful feelings, but these are not the feelings of uncontentious lyricism. Heine's aim as a poet is not the exploring of an idea, the solving of a problem, or the creation of a 'heterocosmic' world of the imagination, though on occasion he can do all these things; even the conveying of an intimate personal experience is to him a means rather than an end. His poetry makes its way through countless extravaganzas and 'oases with palms and odalisques'. There is hardly a poem of his in which the divided self is not asserted. But the poem always comes back at the reader, to induce moral feelings in him and impatiently, unashamedly to manipulate them – I mean feelings which belong to the totality of our persons, including our public and social self. Hence his rhetoric (e.g. the weavers' 'eyes of doom' and 'gnashing teeth') is not a failure of the lyrical vein, but an essential means to his poetic undertaking.

We don't like rhetorical verse – or at best are baffled by it – because we lack the firm and comprehensive moral scheme on which rhetoric relies for a full meaning. Heine does not provide us with such a scheme, and yet his rhetoric is not empty. For what he does give us, at all events, is the negative half of a moral framework. Unlike Nietzsche (whom he resembles in many other ways), he had no stomach for 'positive' solutions. His predicament is the predicament of modernity: it lies precisely in his refusal to allow his critical, sardonic consciousness to be appeased and arrested by assent. And his predicament is as inseparable from his greatest virtue as is his rhetoric from his poetry. This is the leap-frog game of value-giving that Nietzsche knew so well (see below, p. 208). No sooner has Heine put an object of value before us – the love of a woman, of Germany, of Nature or of God – than his critical consciousness overtakes it. His vision is neither tearful nor jaundiced: its organ is 'the evil eye' of which Nietzsche boasted and which he admired in Heine. He cannot tell us what to admire, and moments of absurdity interrupt even his most intimate love poems. But he leaves us in no doubt where to direct our contempt, our hatred, and our pity – in *that* area of experience certainly he is a reliable guide.

> *Almost every one of his poems ends with such a suicide.*
>
> (Joseph von Eichendorff)

All the same, it would be misleading to end with *The Silesian Weavers*. Heine has written no more than three or four poems of this kind, none as accomplished. The division of mind and muse goes on, all the way to the end. His great Judaic fling ends as wryly as the rest, the creative energy never ebbs, there is no death-bed conversion. He hurls his imprecations into the dark night. I have stressed the anti-naturalistic, rhetorical mode of *Die schlesichen Weber* as I have stressed the anti-naïve, 'sentimentalisch' mode of the best of his earlier love poetry. The language of art – of masks and carnivals, of music, sculpture, and painting, of poetry within poetry, of emblems and mementoes[12] – came to him naturally, whereas Nature herself enters his poetry only in terms of its human significance, as a pathetic fallacy consciously explored. All these elements are present in the poem which many regard as his last, *Für die Mouche* (1856), dedicated to Elise Krinitz, a young German woman living in Paris who, in the last year of Heine's life, fell under the spell of his personality and engaged him, paralysed and blind and suffering almost constant pain, for a last time in that ambience of intelligent Eros which was the ruling passion of his life.

The poem recounts a dream of death. Its central artifice is a

Renaissance marble sarcophagus, whose bas-relief portrays all the emblems, the archetypes – 'Fabelzeitfiguren' – of man's history and creative imagination: the shameless heathen gods disport themselves next to Adam and Eve 'each in the fig-leaf apron chastely clad', Paris and Helena next to Moses and Aaron, Phoebus Apollo, Frau Venus and Balaam's ass as well as Lot 'who with his daughters drank and merry made', Mount Sinai and young Jesus in the temple. The round of archetypes is also a list of the poet's themes; he is the dead man in the coffin. As in several earlier poems, the divided mind is bodied forth in an eerie *doppelgänger* theme. A similar division runs through the images assembled in the bas-relief. The Greek figures are sharply ('grell') contrasted with the Judaic ones, the spiritual with the natural, the pagan with the Christian, the harmony of the marble composition hides a strife of contrasts. A yellow-and-mauve passion flower – an allegory of the loved one – inclines over the poet's grave, each detail of its blossom expressing (as in the legend that gives the flower its name) an aspect of the passion of Christ. An inconsolable silence reigns in the moonlit night. Then a conversation begins between the poet and the loved one,[13] but it too is silent, beyond the indication of human language. Is this really, as some have claimed, the silence that ensues when all that poetry can say has been said – the mysterious silence of the ineffable? No imagery could be 'higher', more luscious, than that in which the wordy intimations of that silence are enshrined. This surely, we feel, is artifice carried beyond the point of poetic redemption.

It is a bewildering poem, bewildering above all in the variety of its themes: death and a highly peculiar resurrection, *musée imaginaire* and cultural history, Eros and the passion of Christ, Dionysos and Apollo, all held together – but how precariously! – by an allegorical first-person tale. And as for the central image, that sarcophagus, we feel, belongs to the nineteenth-century Baroque of Père Lachaise rather than the Renaissance, it is an imitation of an imitation, con-temporaneity with a vengeance. If in the first fifteen stanzas (the 'cultural history') the statuary was relieved by a few touches of humour, the next fourteen (the passion flower and its communion with the poet) are cast almost entirely in the language of high pathos and deep feeling. But this is the language which (as we have seen) Heine can wield only in the space of a short poem; he is unable to sustain the note of lyricism undistracted (as Goethe does in *Marien-*

bader Elegie,) and one wishes he didn't try. The bathos is redeemed by the contrast that follows. Towards the end of the second section (stanza 29), where the wordiness of that wordless communion begins to pall, Death is apostrophised as the only source of Eros ('Nur du kannst uns die beste Wollust geben'); it is contrasted with the restlessness of 'stupid, brutal life', and then:

Doch wehe mir! Es schwand die Seligkeit,
Als draussen plötzlich sich ein Lärm erhoben:
Es war ein scheltend, stampfend wüster Streit,
Ach, meine Blum, verscheuchte dieses wüste Toben.

Ah, woe is me! A tumult rose without,
And chased all calm and happiness away.
I heard them arguing with stamp and shout,
My gentle flower drooped with sore dismay.*

The break – the famous 'Stimmungsbruch' – comes not a moment too soon. The images on the bas-relief begin a violent quarrel, the frantic call of Pan vies with the anathemas of Moses, the Barbarians berate the Greeks, the old battle between Truth and Beauty is resumed, there is no quietus even beyond the grave. Instead, the hideous braying of Balaam's ass drowns the contending voices of gods, saints and heroes. Is it the voice of bigotry and stupidity that wakes the dead man from his grave, the poet from his nightmare? But then, the braying of his ass made Balaam turn his curses into blessings, it saved the people of Israel and put them, at least for a while, on the path of righteousness. Is simple asinine piety the answer to it all? And is the poet's awakening to the wretched sound of heehaw a resurrection, as some have declared? On the contrary: it is the intimation of an eternal recurrence, the wretched eternal recurrence of all that Heine regarded as vulgar and opinionated in his age. 'Once I saw both naked, the greatest of men and the least – all-too-like one another they were, all-too-human even the greatest! – this was my disgust of man', wrote Nietzsche, Heine's most perceptive admirer, three decades later.

* It is touching to note that 'la Mouche', Elise Krinitz, disclaimed any identification with the flower: it was, she said, Heine's way of conveying his communion with his 'patrie lointaine'; see S. S. Prawer, *German Lyric Poetry* (London 1952), 261.

The poem, even this very last poem, ends with invective and bitter sarcasm – not even in his grave is the poet safe from the hideous strife. But there is a fuller reading of those last stanzas. Does he *want* to be safe? For Heine, to be safe would be to be dead. Beyond their sarcasm the lines and the whole poem convey an unabating care, concern with the world of our common indication even in the hour of death. Many are the indulgences Heine allowed himself, but retreat into the comfort of an exclusive private feeling was not among them. And so the divisions of a lifetime are unhealed, the battle is unfinished. As Heine wrote a little earlier in one of the *Lazarus* poems:

> Woran liegt die Schuld? Ist etwa
> Unser Herr nicht ganz allmächtig?
> Oder treibt er selbst den Unfug?
> Ach, das wäre niederträchtig.
>
> Also fragen wir beständig,
> Bis man uns mit einer Handvoll
> Erde endlich stopft die Mäuler –
> Aber ist das eine Antwort?

> What's to blame? Is it perchance
> That our Lord's not quite almighty?
> Or himself plays all those tricks?
> Ah, *that* would be base indeed.
>
> So we go on, asking questions,
> Till with a handful of earth
> They stop our mouths at last –
> But is that an answer?

We have come a long way from Heine the ironically playful lyricist, from the purple patches of *Das Buch der Lieder*. The strained enjambement and broken lines of that last stanza defy the dominion of lyricism over poetry. Death-bed conversion? In the ironically disdainful 'perchance' and 'not quite almighty' ['etwa', 'nicht ganz allmächtig'], in the sardonic, chillingly impersonal 'they' ['man'], all theodicy as well as all existential blather about death wither away. And what is asserted (what else remains for us to assert, Christian and Jew alike?) is the sheer indignation at the scandal of death. Another poem in that group ends:

Impotent curses! The worst of them
Will not kill a fly.
Bear your fate and try
To cry a bit, to pray.

But the German text is better than that:

Gelinde zu flennen, zu beten.

FOUR

Eduard Mörike:
Recollection and Inwardness

*... like a Greek bowl: inwardness that has sprung open, the weight of existence
lightened in the created thing.*

(Romano Guardini)

The area of experience charted by the lyrical poetry of Eduard
Mörike (1804–1875) is not difficult to delimit. Its settings are rural,
provincial, uncontaminated by contact with the great world. At its
most memorable it is concerned with intimate personal encounters
and their evanescence. Its tranquillity and its deep emotions are
those of a solitary soul; only the ineluctable passage of time, not
faction and strife, intimates the common lot of man. Mörike excels at
showing man in contact with the natural world; Nature often acts as
a consoler, a giver of meaning to human relations; sometimes she
echoes and confirms man's essential solitude. Those readers in
Germany and abroad who, until a generation ago, saw the finest
achievement of nineteenth-century German literature in its lyrical
poetry, justly recognised in Mörike its finest representative. But even
if, as one suspects, this view has now become something of a cliché,
his achievement remains assured. Among the critics Mörike has no
enemies. He has been subjected to the mystagogic treatment[1] with
its all-too-ready appeal to 'demonic powers', for no better reason
than that much of his poetry issues from unhappy emotional tangles.
As against that, there is his warm yet not uncritical humanity, laced
with a dose of Swabian humour;[2] or again his considerable influence
as a craftsman and as a quiet guardian of intimate personal values.[3]
His spirituality is uncontentious, wholly undogmatic and free from
all strenuous antitheses, yet it has a reassuring strength all its own.[4]

In the word 'Erinnerung' the German language underlines the
inwardness of memory or recollection, its re-creative intimation, and
critics have often pointed to the special place that lyrical poetry has

in this inward re-creation of the past.[5] In this sense Mörike is a German lyrical poet *par excellence*. What makes him into a modern European poet is the fact that in many of his poems such a re-creation no longer takes the form of a story or fable but of an extended image transfixed in a moment of time.

The freshness and apparent simplicity of his poetic utterance gives one the impression that several decades of strenuous aesthetic debate have left no trace on his verse, that idealism, industrialism, and the social movements of his time have passed him by, unconsidered. Thus one of the most famous of his poems, *Verborgenheit* (*Withdrawal*, 1832) expresses a gentle resignation, a contentment with that which the heart has already experienced, and a renunciation and apprehension of further turbulent emotions; yet its first and last stanza begin with the line 'Laß o Welt, o laß mich sein!', and it is as a renunciation of the *world* that this poem has commonly been read. We know from Mörike's lively correspondence with writers fully involved in contemporary controversies that he knew that world, vicariously perhaps, but well enough. But we also know that, for all his personal vacillations and unresolved conflicts, he firmly exercised his choice as a poet, and consciously resisted being drawn into the arena. In this as in most other ways he was the opposite of Heine.

Such a consciousness of withdrawal, it is clear, is hardly compatible with that simplicity of diction for which Mörike is often praised. He is not the 'naïve' poet of Schiller's definition. His poetry is an artifact that neither vaunts nor hides its essential character. The consciousness that enters his poetry is mainly confined to personal feelings. It expresses not so much a deliberate withdrawal from the issues of the contemporary world as an apprehension of and a withdrawal from the things around him, from some of the *données* of private experience, in order to portray a subtle state of mind in which joy and sorrow combine; yet the themes of parting and solitude predominate. The apparent simplicity of his finest poem is a measure of his success in conveying the consciousness of loss by converting it fully into poetic story and image – the result, it may be, of a complex creative process; but we have no means of telling as the process of transformation leaves little or no trace in the poems.[6] They do not readily lend themselves to a reconstruction of his inner biography. Therefore, instead of attempting to establish his or their 'Entwicklungsgeschichte', I shall confine myself to a discussion of five of his finest poems, occasionally disregarding chronology and leaving out his ballads, narratives and miniature epics.

Mörike began writing in the age of Goethe and in the heyday of German Romanticism. Yet he was a contemporary of Baudelaire, and his last poems overlap the poetry of Verlaine and the Symbolists. His work intimates some of the changes that lyrical poetry underwent during his lifetime; and it does so more clearly than his retired existence in a Swabian backwater would lead one to expect. Implicitly challenging the traditional notion of poetry as an 'Nacheinander' (which Lessing had contrasted with the 'Nebeneinander' of painting), Mörike's poetry turns from story to meaningful image for its most characteristic effects. He wrote no theoretical statement of his aims, and only a reader who saw his work through anachronistic preconceptions could persuade himself that Mörike wrote poems about the writing of poems. (Such a reader is notoriously hard put to it not to see all poetry in this light.) He has extended the area of German poetry, both in the direction of emotional depth and also by placing imaged artifacts, including works of art, at the centre of some of his finest poems. But his discoveries seem to have been largely intuitive: the consciousness that informs his poems is not a literary selfconsciousness. The artifact is, for him, not a symbol of the aesthetic experience but, being itself an object hallowed by human use, it becomes a repository of deep, nonliterary emotions. As for his art, he might well have repeated his fellow-countryman Albrecht Dürer's modest paradox, 'Was aber die Schönheit sei, das weiss ich nit.' ('As to what Beauty be, I wot not'.)

The tradition in German literature which recent criticism has dwelt on contains no traces of Mörike's serenity. Fragmentariness, visions of the extremes of the human condition, exposure to the daemonic forces of Being, and an unnerving search for the roots of that Being accompanied by dread and *Angst*, a longing for the unconditioned and a lack of accommodation in the real world – these make up our current image of German poets. Having few of these traits, Mörike's poetry questions our assumption that depth is always the depth of despair, or that the depth of despair must always resort to the fragmentary or visionary manner for its expression. He has fully considered the dark side of the world, he too knows that the world of the unhappy man is different from the world of the happy. Yet his creativeness bears him on, all the way to the completed form, to the point where discord is transmuted into the harmony beyond. Yet again, this is no aestheticism, no triumph of perfect form over base, irredeemable matter. On the contrary, underlying his poetry and occasionally made explicit in it is a belief in the connectedness of the human and the divine. Art for him is not an expression of the ineffable. It is an expression of the world (or at least of a small, intimate part of the world) as a creation of God, *'pulcher horologium Dei'*.

Only occasionally – once or twice in his poetry; more often, though not always successfully, in his prose – he allows desolateness itself to speak. The cycle of his five short *Peregrina* poems (1824) relates to the most painful of his love affairs; the subject is a girl, half vagrant, half dévote, whom he met during his years as a student at Tübingen. Here if anywhere in Mörike is a direct evocation of the daemonic, destructive forces of love; but here too is its containment.

From Wilhelm Meister's Mignon and Eduard's Ottilie to Peregrina (first conceived by Mörike in the context of a not wholly successful 'Bildungsroman'), to the gipsy girl of one of Stifter's stories, even to Hans Castorp's Clavdia Chauchat and Josef K.'s Leni, there runs a line of mysterious girlish figures who, by their untoward appearance, disrupt the placid, often staid lives of their lovers and would-be protectors. They are the pagan counterparts of the Christian Gretchen figures. Whence they come and whither they go we are not told. The threat they represent to the virtues of the 'biedermeier' or 'bürgerlich' world in which they alight is symbolised in the erotic challenge they offer (this part of the theme is isolated in the orgiastic Lulu figure of Frank Wedekind's *fin-de-siècle* plays). But the erotic is only one aspect (and often a deeply hidden one) of their powerful instinctual lives. They are free from qualms of conscience, from ordinary consciousness itself even. They seem to lead an existence beyond good and evil, to which those who briefly harbour them respond with bewilderment and anguish.

The Peregrina of Mörike's poems, that *'anima naturaliter pagana'*, knows nothing of the Pauline 'It is better to marry than to burn', nothing of the fire of conscience that consumes her lover. The poet calls her 'an unknowing child', smilingly she hands him 'death in the cup of sin'. (We must wait for the third section to allay our suspicion that this line is mere bathos.) The second section contains the attempted accommodation. It describes the poet's solemn wedding to the girl, the graceful, airy bower in which it takes place, and the garden, faintly echoing the noise and music of the feast, in which they spend their night of love. But even now, in the fervour of his embraces, the union is not, and cannot be complete, for in *this* setting and under *this* solemn dispensation it would have to be entirely on the lover's terms. The failure of sexual fulfilment ('too soon for my desire, tired too soon/the lovely head lay lightly in my lap'/) is but part of her strangeness that lies beyond all possible appropriation; it is a butterfly, not a mistress, not a wife, that he holds in his arms; and when he wakes her, it is into '*his* house' that he takes 'the wondrous child'.

Never again will desolation speak so directly in Mörike's verses as it does in the third, free-verse section of this elegy of passion. The word that opens these lines, 'Ein Irrsal . . .' (so much more than 'A madness . . .'), has the full force of tragic conflict behind it: what else than a thing of unreason can he call his shattering discovery of her 'long-standing betrayal'? What else is there left for him to do but, 'with weeping eyes but cruel', send her away for ever? The discovery of her betrayal side by side with the sure knowledge of her love; the silence with which she accepts his verdict and leaves; the sick heart and the inconsolable longing to which her departure condemns him – these are the simple elements from which this scene is created, they yield a poignancy that may be compared to Troilus' discovery of Cressida's betrayal (though, unlike drama, the lyrical structure doesn't require the events leading up to it – 'verjährter Betrug' – to be specified). The aesthetic effect of all such scenes in literature derives alike from a full expression of the horror of the betrayal committed and a full expression of the beauty of the passion now so absolutely condemned. The poet's horror at the 'madness' and his severe judgement would be mere moralising were they not contrasted with, and thus given living substance by, the beauty that they must destroy. Must? The ordinance here is that of an unquestioning Christian morality. He obeys it, but his heart will know no peace.

The final two sections are given over to the unabating sorrow that follows Peregrina's departure. This cycle of poems is an early work – the bare, direct invocations of grief exceed, once or twice, Mörike's poetic gifts. (In the lives of poets, does their expressiveness sharpen or their capacity for suffering blunt?) Again and again the poet's imagination returns to the beloved figure of the 'unknowing child', but each of the scenes it conjures up ends in a recollection of the betrayal. Nor can the form-giving imagination encroach upon the raw reality: it expresses but doesn't assuage: the last poem, a sonnet, ends on a note of despair.

Into this narrative line are woven three scenes which have the static quality of pictures. The first is that of the wedding bower, a tented garden folly with serpentine pillars and latticed roof; its curious and elaborate design seems to suggest the unreality of the solemn ritual that takes place in it. (Mörike will return to this image in a later poem.) It contrasts strongly with the second picture, which is directly inspired by the wayward girl, Maria Meyer, who was found unconscious and destitute in the streets of Tübingen some days before Mörike met her, and who later turned up under similar circumstances in Heidelberg, begging for his help. The third section of the cycle ends:

> – Wie? wenn ich eines Tags auf meiner Schwelle
> Sie sitzen fände, wie einst, im Morgen-Zwielicht.
> Das Wanderbündel neben ihr,
> Und ihr Auge, treuherzig zu mir aufschauend,
> Sagte, da bin ich wieder
> Hergekommen aus weiter Welt!

> What if one day I found her sitting
> Upon my threshold in early dawn, as once she did,
> The wanderer's bundle by her side,
> Her eyes trustingly looking up to me,
> Saying, Here I am again
> I am come back again, back from the world!

This image is repeated in the final sonnet,

> Die Liebe, sagt man, steht am Pfahl gebunden,
> Geht endlich arm, zerrüttet, unbeschuht;

> At the cruel stake, they tell us, love stands bound,
> Ends barefoot and deranged, in tatters dressed. . . .

And there is the third scene: 'yesterday, in the children's room/By the bright flicker of their pretty candles . . .' ('Ach, gestern in den

F

hellen Kindersaal,/Beim Flimmer zierlich aufgesteckter Kerzen . . .'),
when Peregrina appears before him, 'tormented image, piteous and
beautiful' ('Bildnis mitleid-schöner Qual'). Each of these scenes
contributes to the action of the cycle, to the story told. Yet each is
also an arrest, a picture reminiscent of the 'Genrebilder' of the
Romantic school of painting.

The main lyrical elements of the *Peregrina* poem should now be
clear. Once or twice the emotion that informs it is expressed with a
rawness, a directness which exceeds Mörike's poetic means; and
since there is no escape into irony, this excess is apt to turn into
bathos. Significantly, it is in pictures – moments of arrest in the flow
of 'Erinnerung', of recollected experience – that Mörike instinctively
seeks an 'objective correlative' for his feelings; they – the pictures –
in turn contribute at least as much to the structure of the poem as
does the action, and they are the more memorable of the two. In
Mörike's later poetry each of the two elements will tend to go its own
way: action and story will expand into ballad and epic verse-tale,
the picture will more nearly fill out the framework of a lyrical poem.
Here in the *Peregrina* poem they achieve a felicitous whole.

Mörike's most famous poems exemplify a curious paradox: that
lyrical poetry, which is concerned with the most fundamental and
thus the most universal, human emotions, should also be the least
translatable. The paradox is resolved once we realise that the translator's problem is less a problem of content than of form, and that
the more extended the form – the more elbowroom it leaves him –
the fewer are his unrecorded frustrations. This is why the great
narrative novels of the nineteenth century lose less in translation, and
thus become more readily common European property, than the
taut structures of small lyrical poems. The fundamental and therefore universal nature of the feelings expressed recedes behind the
particular configuration into which these feelings have been
organised; and the translator's difficulties increase to the extent that
such a configuration is determined by the physical properties of the
words that shape it, by their sounds and their connotative and associative features within the language to which they belong. However,
in lyrical poetry the language is used, not exploited. It is used
unselfconsciously, without drawing attention to itself in word-play
and special emphasis on those characteristic features: it is the

merest grain of its surface that is hardest to re-create in another medium. And again, the more taut the structure – the less play between the words – the less room there is for the interplay of synonyms, substitution, expatiation and all the other devices that are apt to turn translation into something like a commentary on the original poem. In narrative prose the translator may well hope to gain on the swings, etc.; in lyrical poetry there is no room for comment, there is only the luck of elective affinities.

Mörike's poem *Früh im Wagen* (1843–6) (*Early morning. In the carriage*), set to music by Hugo Wolf, is a case in point:

Es graut vom Morgenreif
In Dämmerung das Feld,
Da schon ein blasser Streif
Den fernen Ost erhellt;

Man sieht im Lichte bald
Den Morgenstern vergehn,
Und doch am Fichtenwald
Den vollen Mond noch stehn:

So ist mein scheuer Blick,
Den schon die Ferne drängt,
Noch in das Schmerzensglück
Der Abschiedsnacht versenkt.

Dein blaues Auge steht,
Ein dunkler See, vor mir,
Dein Kuss, dein Hauch umweht,
Dein Flüstern mich noch hier.

An deinem Hals begräbt
Sich weinend mein Gesicht,
Und Purpurschwärze webt
mir vor dem Auge dicht.

Die Sonne kommt; – sie scheucht
Den Traum hinweg im Nu,
Und von den Bergen streicht
Ein Schauer auf mich zu.

It is, as so many other poems of Mörike's, an *aubade* on the theme of parting, only the title (which is integral to the poem) contains an

indication of a setting beyond that of Nature and of the narrator's
emotions. The contrast that traditionally informs the dawn-song –
between the departing night and the rising day – is retraced in the
contrasting imagery of the natural landscape as it is seen, and of the
inner landscape as it is felt, by the departing traveller. The pre-
dominant emotion is one of regret and loss; the analogy between the
natural sphere and the emotions is neither made into an issue nor is
it in any way hidden (the third stanza opens with an explicit but
unstressed 'So . . .'). The poem opens and concludes with the dawn –
the coming of the day is seen with apprehension, as a threat even. Its
first and last lines centre on two of those onomatopoeic words – 'Es
graut' and 'Ein Schauer' – in which the emotive vocabulary of
German is so rich, words which even today carry into the sphere of
feeling something of their original physical connotations (the greying
of the early hoar-frost; the shudder that comes with the breath of
chill mountain air). The contrasting states of Nature are accompanied by an ambivalence of contrasting feelings: the morning star
is waning, and yet a full moon still stands above the pine forest; the
poet's gaze is drawn into the distance, and yet it would still rest in
the blissful sorrow of the night of parting. But the ambivalence of
these feelings is not maintained, it soon resolves itself into pure
sorrow. Night, the lover's eyes, a dark lake, the purple-and-black of
Eros, of the last embrace, are all assembled to convey a sorrow and a
fear – to convey, that is, a past which is all but lost and a future
which is braved unwillingly. Not only the images, but the very
particles of the poem's language – those 'schon', 'doch', and 'noch'
which are the translator's despair – speak of the evanescence of that
night of love which the imperious light of the sun is even now turning
into an insubstantial dream. Here the poem ends. It doesn't speak of
'the world', it doesn't say what the day will bring. The mood it
creates derives its poignancy from a tension between past and
future. At the same time we notice that the particles of time are
stressed by the fall of the iambic beat; these stresses don't quite
break up the flow of the poem, yet they are clearly marked. In this
way there emerges something like a second structure in which the
mood of evanescence is established; the lingering, arresting images
of the natural and inward landscapes are explicitly connected into a
sequence, into the 'Nacheinander' of the poem as a story. But the
subtle tension between images and story, like that between past and

future, is not left unresolved. The consciousness and apprehension of loss goes entire into the poem, and no fragment is left over.

Among the many poems that Mörike devoted to this mood of the *aubade* it may be well to choose one whose elements are more varied, and whose effect is more complex. (It is for this reason neither a better poem nor a worse one; description throws no bridges to judgement.) *An einem Wintermorgen, vor Sonnenaufgang* (*On a Winter Morning, before Sunrise*, 1825) opens with a line – 'O flaumenleichte Zeit der dunklen Frühe' – which for subtlety of evocation through image and sound has few to equal it in German poetry. These first words intimate the lightness of snowflakes and feathers, and this lightness of touch and expression is maintained throughout. There is almost no story. The poem conveys that most fleeting of moments between the dream of night and the reality of day, striking in its last stanza a subtle erotic note ('The lips of purple, closed, now gently part,/sending forth breaths of sweetest air'); these last lines contain the only indication we have of the presence of another human being, for the rest the poem is confined to the experiencing, sentient 'ich'. The line of argument is richer than in our previous poem: the decision to abandon the fleeting moment for the day is taken, then again forgotten in the contemplation of a wayward happiness, and resolutely taken again in a final upsurge of energy. Yet there is no personal event (like the imminent departure of our previous poem) to serve as a poetic guide-line. The poem closes with an apotheosis of the new day. No fable, no episode or experience extended in time, only the rising sun – almost the sheer passage of time – is the source of the poem's movement. Similarly, what detains the self is not an event but the complex, semi-allegorical vision which forms the core of the poem.

The soul, as yet undisturbed by the 'false' light of day, itself colourless like a crystal, is the vessel of this vision. Into it crowd images, thoughts, and impressions, shot through with many colours like golden fishes. Earthly and spiritual elements are harmoniously united in this vision, sounds of shepherds' flutes round the Jesus Child's crib alternate with the joyful songs of Bacchus' young attendants. The Christian and the pagan Greek, those two sources of poetic and spiritual inspiration which created the all but disabling tension of Hölderlin's last poems, appear here to be united in the most natural and unemphatic way. Yet how natural is this or indeed any such vision? It is, and has quite explicitly the traces of, an artifact, a work of the imagination. A suggestion is thus present in the poem that the imagination offers a transient refuge, or at least a little time of respite; indeed, it is its function as a moment of arrest before the coming of day that relates the vision to the rest of the poem and justifies it. But again, this is not elaborated – even though Rubens may have inspired the Bacchic scene, this is not a poem about the consolations of art. The antithesis between art and life – the stock-in-trade of mid-nineteenth-century aesthetics – is no more Mörike's creative concern than is the antithesis between Greece and Judea (hence, too, my interpretation below, p. 93). His muse is more concerned with creating and tracing out the fleeting moments of happiness or sorrow than it is with exploring the chilling divisions of the *Zeitgeist*. Yet this is a modern poem, at least in the sense that it no longer seeks to maintain a balance between images and narrative. The diction that bodies forth the dream-like vision has a certain simplicity, a naïveté, quite unlike the diction of the symbolist and imagist poetry of a later era. In these qualities lies much of the charm of the poem. Furthermore, the vision is open, almost allegorical, it has no mystical depths and complex correspondences. But it is no mere simile or rococo ornament. It not only intimates an emotional state, but endows that state with an imaginative value which becomes inseparable from it, making of it almost a thing self-contained. The poem's central image lives half way between classicistic allegory and modern symbol.

Little more need here be said about Mörike's life[7] than that he was a reluctant pursuer of the humblest of clerical and pedagogic careers in various rural parishes and schools in Swabia; and of his faith, that he was the least indefatigable of homilists. To his considerable classical learning we owe a large number of translations from Latin and Greek poetry, as well as several original poems with classical subjects, including the remarkable presage of death, *Erinna an Sappho* (1863). Mörike was ordained into the Lutheran Church in 1826 but did not receive his living until 1834, and retired from pastoral work nine years later. His Christian faith, at least as it enters into his poetry, was largely indifferent to any -ism or -ology, being rather akin to a natural piety; and the only liturgical elements he uses belong to the popular piety of the people among whom he lived. His poetry expresses no 'religious problems'. Of a discussion with his friend David Friedrich Strauss (notorious author of *The Life of Jesus*) he reports in 1843: 'I told him . . . of the firm distinction I draw between . . . the use I am able to make of Christianity for my own person and my task as a preacher. . . .'; and, he continues, 'Not until I have once again made a clear way for myself in matters of faith and am entirely content with myself can I hope to establish a pure and fruitful relationship with my art.' His try-outs are consigned to oblivion; there is nothing sketchy or half-finished about his poetry – no unresolved doubts importune the reader.

Only rarely did he touch on the mysteries of faith. The finest of his religious poems, *Göttliche Reminiszenz* (1856), is composed in unrhymed iambic trimeters, handled however quite freely. In German this verse form has traditionally been used in philosophical poetry – it has a stateliness reminiscent of the alexandrine. Here it forms a poem of thirty lines, lightened by caesurae and occasional breaks of rhythm (at the end of the lines the iambic is more regularly maintained). The theme of the poem is indicated in its motto from St John, 1:3, 'All things come from that same Word'. The poem sets out to portray the presence of Christian Divinity in all created things, no less; and it does so without falling back on that pantheism which the *Sturm und Drang* and Goethe had made fashionable, and which, in the hands of later writers – among them some of Mörike's friends – had become completely severed from its vaguely Christian foundations. The poem contains not a line of explicit philosophical or theological argument, for its entire thought-content is absorbed and transmuted into image.

And its image is a picture and the reminiscence of a picture. The first five lines make a conventional, unemphatic opening. On a solitary walk in the mountains the poet recalls 'a wondrous picture' which he has often seen during his visits to a Carthusian monastery:

> Vorlängst sah ich ein wundersames Bild gemalt,
> Im Kloster der Kartäuser, das ich oft besucht.

The personal experience from which the poem issues is thus made more explicit than it is in *Früh im Wagen*, but it does not become part of the image, as in that poem; here it remains unintegrated, at all events it is never mentioned again, it remains the merest intimation of the poet's modest presence. The opening thus places the poem at the double remove of a recollection of a picture which seems to have only a tenuous connection with reality outside pictures and poems.

The narrative manner, determined throughout by the stately metre, is leisurely though not loose, it only once or twice contracts into the taut language of latter-day symbolism. The poem is undivided, yet its sections are quite clearly marked by its changes in perspective. Lines 6 to 16 contain the first part of the description of a picture in which the boy Jesus is sitting in a rocky wilderness, above the edge of a thinly growing strip of grass on which goats are grazing. He is sitting comfortably on a white fleece, his presence is introduced with a touch of serene humour, 'Not all that childlike did I think the beautiful child',* and then described with a wealth of living sensuous detail. The boy wears a yellow tunic with purple hem, 'the hot summer – it must be his fifth –/has gently browned his cheeks and limbs', 'from his black eyes, silent and powerful, a fire shines',† and round his mouth plays not quite a smile but a strange charm. Here ends the first perspective in which the picture is recollected. The last line of this section – it is perhaps the most powerful in the poem – is set in deliberate contrast with the preceding ones, '*But* round his mouth . . .'. The strangeness of the 'inexpressible charm' is conveyed in a verbal invention of surpassing conciseness and power:

> Den Mund jedoch umfremdet unnennbarer Reiz.

Mörike is not, I have said, a poet of the ineffable; the message the poem conveys is, as we shall see, something like the opposite, it has to do with the giving of earthly substance to the divine. Those two words, 'umfremdet unnennbarer', belong to a mode of oblique intimation he hardly ever uses, we might not be surprised to find them in Rilke's *Duino Elegies*. For the first time in the poem the central Christian mystery is briefly pointed to: all the wealth of

---

*'Nicht allzu kindlich deuchte mir das schöne Kind'.

† 'Der heisse Sommer, sicherlich sein fünfter schon,
Hat seine Glieder, welche bis zum Knie herab
Das gelbe Röckchen decket mit dem Purpursaum,
Hat die gesunden, zarten Wangen sanft gebräunt,
Aus schwarzen Augen leuchtet stille Feuerkraft . . .'.

physical detail that precedes this mention of the boy's 'mouth estranged by inexpressible charm', is needed to anchor the expression of his face in the realm of human experience, to make the intimation 'expressible'.

Now the perspective changes into the brief description of an action, which however is placed in the past. A friendly old shepherd, bending down to the child, has just given him a plaything, which the boy has examined and now holds in his hand. It is not a man-made toy but a strangely-shaped petrifact from the sea: 'ein versteinert Meergewächs,/seltsam gestaltet . . .'. The boy's 'wide gaze' is no longer directed at the object but at you, the beholder of the scene, yet not at you either but past you, 'really at no object,/moving through eternal distances of time, unbounded.' The word 'wirklich', in the lines

> . . . und jetzt,
> Gleichsam betroffen, spannet sich der weite Blick,
> Entgegen dir, doch wirklich ohne Gegenstand,

commentators have pointed out, is Swabian use for an unemphatic 'actually'; yet its metaphysical meaning, 'gazing . . . at no object, yet a part of reality', is apposite. The boy's glance is serious, 'as in a momentary apprehension', as if the lightning of the Divinity had moved across his clouded brow – though again the glance is only as the briefest memory, instantly extinguished. The final impression the boy's face leaves with us is serene: 'The Word that was in the beginning, become a playing earthly child,/Shows you, with a smile, unknowing, its own creation's work.'

The central Christian mystery is presented in the Gospels in several forms. On the rare occasions when it is concerned with it, the literature of our age speaks of its tragic aspect: how could the Son of God become man and yet suffer crucifixion? How could His agony remain undiminished by His Divinity? (It is because we find this article of faith hard that we speak egregiously of 'the impossibility of Christian tragedy'.) Mörike chooses to speak of that same mystery in its positive aspect: how could God become man, a human child, and yet be the source of all creation? The answer is intimated in the boy's smile, in his gaze that encompasses all earthly things: which includes the strange natural object in his hand; which includes you the beholder; and moves beyond all this into eternity. It is intimated, finally, in that simple word, 'unwissend', of the last line. Peregrina too, we recall, was described thus. Hers was a negative 'unknowing'. a daemonic ignorance of sin and its tragic consequences. What the boy Jesus does not know is his own omnipotence as creator of all things. Briefly, like a flash of metempsychosis, that knowledge has passed through him. As a cloud it has overshadowed his brow. (Guardini, in his analysis of the poem,[8] refers the reader to St Mark 9:7; seeing that Mörike felt no antithesis between classical and Christian, the image of 'Jupiter fulgens' may perhaps be more apposite.) Perhaps the boy's memory encompassed the dark side of creation also. But what remains with us is His smile which is now, in the brief moment of time when we behold it, an unknowing smile.

So much – is so much to be drawn out of the recollection of a picture, of a smile? Are we still disturbed, as we were at the beginning, that it should be through *a picture*, rather than through a more directly personal experience, that Mörike speaks to us of his innermost faith? Is it faith at all, and not some aesthetic empathy, some painterly susceptibility (Mörike himself was an amateur draughtsman) that informs the poem? A certain shyness and fine poetic tact characterise Mörike's mature poetry, and these we (who are so readily embarrassed by a direct affirmation of faith) understand perhaps better than previous ages. He chooses a painting to contain his intimation of the Divine not only because his art knows how to make it poetically appropriate, but also because the painting renders his own more immediate presence unnecessary. Like ourselves, the poet is a beholder of this scene, not a participant. (It may be that, retrospectively, even that awkward opening of the poem was justified.) The poetic gift he brings to it is not separate from the spiritual sympathy that enables him to 'read' the picture and to intimate the mystery he divines in it. His art is not a substitute but a vessel of his faith.

At the same time we remain aware of a certain disproportion between the smile and its meaning. But this is not, I think, the disproportion that is one of the characteristics of modern art. Mörike is not writing in the age of George, Hofmannsthal, and Rilke. What that smile, that scene are meant to intimate is a belief not of Mörike's making, is not a new 'religion' or ideology of feeling. It is the ancient piety of the Christian faith; only the vessel that is to carry it is new, and a little less seaworthy than the vessels of old had been.

Mörike's *Auf eine Lampe* (1846) has been more often interpreted than any other poem of his: because it seems to anticipate the Rilkean 'Dinggedicht'; because the perfection it achieves is peculiarly accessible to us; because it is enigmatic and is said to contain a major 'poetic ambiguity'; because we feel that it has, and speaks of, the sort of aesthetic timelessness that we are apt to identify with immortality – the only kind of immortality we contemplate without too much discomfort.

Yet the greatness of the poem is in no way diminished by the suggestion that it is very much of its own time: the time when Karl Marx wrote of the alienation of the products of labour into profit-making commodities of the capitalist market economy, evaluated not in relation to their use but as 'fetish objects', that is, status symbols; the time when Stifter wrote in celebration of 'Geräthe', of the well-made things of yesteryear, products of devoted labour which his contemporary world passed by heedlessly; when Mörike's friend Theodor Vischer wrote that exquisitely boring, maniacal, humorous novel, *Auch Einer*, concerned wholly with the conspiracy of objects against man, their maker and victim, and Carlyle wrote his equally maniacal and equally humorous *Sartor Resartus*. The object, or rather its recollection, its 'Er-innerung', now comes to serve as a symbol of arrest in the ineluctable flux of events. As objects-of-use the heavy secrétaires, the antimacassars and mullion windows of the age proclaim respectability and moral probity; as objects-of-art its historical paintings and allegorising statuary express a longing for the values of a bygone era. Among such objects belongs 'the beautiful lamp' which Mörike re-creates and apostrophises in the poem:

Auf eine Lampe

Noch unverrückt, o schöne Lampe, schmückest du,
An leichten Ketten zierlich aufgehangen hier,
Die Decke des nun fast vergessnen Lustgemachs.
Auf deiner weissen Marmorschale, deren Rand
Der Efeukranz von goldengrünem Erz umflicht,
Schlingt fröhlich eine Kinderschar den Ringelreihn.

Wie reizend alles! lachend, und ein sanfter Geist
Des Ernstes doch ergossen um die ganze Form –
Ein Kunstgebild der echten Art. Wer achtet sein?
Was aber schön ist, selig scheint es in ihm selbst.

On a lamp

Yet undisturbed, O beautiful lamp, you still adorn,
On fine-wrought chains suspended gracefully,
The ceiling of this near-forgotten festal room.
On your white marble bowl, about whose rim
Entwines an ivy garland of gold-green ore
A ring of children dances gaily hand in hand.
What charm is in all this! Laughter, yet a gentle spirit
Of gravity suffuses the entire form.
Wrought from the genuine order is this art. Who pays heed
    to it?
But what is beautiful shines blissfully within itself.[9]

The poem opens on a nostalgic, almost defensive note: the festive
room, recalling that garden folly in which Peregrina's wedding was
celebrated, lies now abandoned; the lamp that once illuminated and
now only adorns it may soon be moved and disposed of. It lives its
own life, heeded by none but – the poet? He is not named, it is as
though the spirit of creative art itself were speaking through the
silent beholder, as if all vestige of a personal story has disappeared.
'Who pays heed to it?' Yet the nostalgia is not all-pervading, it
provides a framework in which the poem's dominant argument is
set. For it *is* an argument which the poem develops – not in the least
abstruse or abstract (as perhaps all interpretations of the poem are
apt unhelpfully to suggest), but filled out by an image and the
emotions and reflections that image engenders.

Yesterday's beautiful object-of-use is the object-of-art of today.
This process, with which we are only too familiar from the higher
reaches of the antique trade, is not dwelt on in the poem, it is merely
implied. The object has become and is now a work of art, and the
poem is concerned to show that what has resulted from this process is
not an impoverishment. The lamp is not, we can see, a creation of
classical times but rather (like the vision of *An einem Wintermorgen*) a
work of classicistic re-creation. (Just so the title of the poem, 'On a

lamp', is reminiscent of the many poems from *The Greek Anthology* from which Mörike copiously translated, poems dedicated to objects of sacred or emotional value.) The figures of the composition are expressive of laughter and joy. The 'gentle spirit of gravity' is distinct from but encompasses the spirit of gaiety, it is allegorised (as in Keats) in the 'leaf-fringed legend' of the bronze relief. This 'gravity suffuses the entire form'. The lamp is a man-made thing, a repository and emblem of human endeavour, and thus possessed of a *pesanteur* all its own. It is 'a wrought thing of art of the *genuine* order' – a word we find hard to take in any poetic context (the German '*echter* Art' fares not much better) because it has become a cliché, and in this context, because it has a connotation of the defensive about it. Yet the word merely sums up what has already been intimated. The combination, in the finely-wrought thing, of joy, charm, and gentle seriousness – the integrity of the work-of-art – is what makes it 'genuine'. This work-of-art is not unique – and only today is it isolated – but it is part of an order, 'supremely good of its own kind' (as Aristotle would say).

The lamp is no longer an object-of-use: the light it now sheds is therefore of a different kind. The illumination it offers is that of a work of art, which 'shines, full of bliss, within itself.'* The harmony inherent in the object displays the '*consonantia*' of St Thomas's

* The last line, 'Was aber schön ist, selig scheint es in ihm selbst', has been the subject of a learned controversy between the literary historian, Professor E. Staiger, and the philosopher, Martin Heidegger. The former offers the interpretation that 'that which is beautiful seems blissful (i.e. has the semblance of bliss) in itself', while the latter reads, 'that which is beautiful shines blissfully within itself'. Characteristically, neither interpreter gives a thought to the actual social and historical circumstances to which the poem belongs and from which it issues – I mean the lamp's present status as an object-of-art. They confine their placing of the poem to evidence from the aesthetic arguments of Mörike's contemporaries: Staiger quotes Theodor Vischer in support of 'videtur', Heidegger Hegel in support of 'lucet'; the linguistic difficulty of (Swabian?) 'ihm', where 'sich' would have been expected, remains unresolved in both cases. I have accepted Heidegger's reading, because I know of no poem of Mörike's containing the antithesis 'art – reality' which Staiger's reading would imply, but above all because Heidegger's 'lucet' is relevant to the central image of the lamp and thus to the integrity of the poem, whereas Staiger's 'videtur' is not. (Cf. E. Staiger, *Die Kunst der Interpretation* (Zürich 1955), pp. 24–49.)

threefold definition of a work of art; the last line shows forth its inward, self-contained luminosity, its '*claritas*'; while its '*integritas*' is expressed in line 7 through 'the gentle spirit of gravity' that 'suffuses the entire form'.

It is this 'sanfter Geist des Ernstes' which contains our greatest interpretative difficulty, because the poem at this point attributes to the work of art a quality we don't readily associate with it; the mention of that quality, like the mention of 'the genuine order', makes us feel uneasy. Gravity, weight of experience is what distinguishes the man-made from the natural, King Solomon's raiment in all its glory from the lilies of the field. The poem doesn't speak of this contrast, it is only concerned with one side of it. It tells us that the world pays no heed to 'the work of the genuine order'. We may the more readily understand this order if we bear in mind that for Mörike's contemporaries the weightiness and seriousness of a man's persona and of the products of his labour indicate and indeed guarantee a *moral* quality, that this is an age when gravity is seen as the hallmark of the ethical worth of a man's work.* Sometimes this weightiness had disconcerting results: hence Schopenhauer's invective against German 'ponderousness'.† Mörike is aware of this danger. This is why he speaks of the '*gentle* spirit of gravity', why 'laughter' ('lachend') is both joined ('*und* ein . . .') and subtly contrasted ('des Ernstes *doch* . . .') with that spirit.

This notion of gravity as the integrating mode of a work of art is, as I have said, alien to us, it doesn't belong to our scheme of fashionable aesthetic emotions. Yet it is not inaccessible to us, if only we allow the poem to extend our horizon. (And why read this poem, or

---

* This identification of weightiness with value is present in the central figures of Theodor Storm's later Novellen, in the father-figure and in the fraternal conflict of Otto Ludwig's *Zwischen Himmel und Erde* (1856); it takes a comic form in Wilhelm Raabe's *Der Stopfkuchen* (1891); we shall see it in Keller, even more clearly in Stifter; but we also find it in the anti-Semitism of Gustav Freytag's *Soll und Haben* (1854), where the Germans have 'Ernst', the Jews don't. Heine doesn't share this ethos but knows it intimately, e.g. in the contrast he draws between Germany and Paris; by the time Heine had done with it, the contrast had become a cliché.

† 'Schwerfälligkeit', 'manifest in the way [the Germans] walk, in their conversation, in their language, in everything they do.' See *Über Schriftstellerei und Stil* in *Parerga und Paralipomena* (1851), para. 287.

any, if we don't?) We mustn't confuse it with Rilke's image of 'weighty inwardness', which is indifferent to the notions of ordinary morality. In Mörike's poem it reflects above all a moral quality because it connects the object with our ordinary, non-literary experience. Similarly, the *'integritas'* of *'the entire form* [which this] gentle spirit suffuses' is not designed to exclude us. It is not an hermetic or 'aestheticist' self-containedness, but a perfection that manifests at once a moral and an aeshetic value; and again, through the moral it is connected with all men, or at least with those who will heed it. The more the object – the lamp and also the poem – achieves its own perfection, the more meaningful it is to us. The more serenely it shines forth within itself, the more perfectly it illumines the world of which it is a part. 'Beauty is truth, truth beauty' has ceased to be a vexing paradox. The beautiful is now made manifest in the beautiful work of art – at least, for the few who will pay heed; at least, for a little while longer: 'Noch unverrückt, o schöne Lampe, schmückest du . . .'.

The historical situation the poem retraces is delicately balanced. The lamp is not simply – as is Keats's Grecian urn – a surviving memento of a past glory, part of a *musée imaginaire*. It is very different from the sort of objects we find in Dickens or Keller or Flaubert (one thinks of Miss Faversham's wedding cake, or Züs Bünzli's trinket box in the shape of a papier mâché temple, or Charles Bovary's famous cap). For these are essentially arbitrary things, pointing to a meaning they themselves don't contain. These objects have what Marx would call a 'surplus value' (and what we would call their value as symbols of status or emotions), which is unrelated to their value as objects-of-use. On the other hand the lamp isn't a symbol of pure feeling either – it isn't an inward substitute for a publicly valid object in the external world. Nor is it made sacred in the strict sense of the word (the world in which room and lamp exist presumably no longer contains sacred things). It belongs to a world of which art is no longer an integral part, yet in which the memory of art as an integral part of the world is still a living memory, though not for long. It is an object of art to which clings its history of the beautiful object of use it once was. What the poem gently stresses is the harmonious adequacy of the lamp to its present function, is the fact that it has no unused 'surplus value'. It is not a passive object. Having once been made as a thing of beauty, it still shows for its past, and in so doing achieves its present meaning, which is different from its past meaning but remains valid as long as men recognise, and acknowledge as valuable, the virtues and values that have gone into its making and therefore 'shine forth' from it. The lamp *reminds* men of these virtues and values and thus keeps them alive, there 'in the deserted festal room', away from the common world. In this sense *the lamp* is an emblem of all that Mörike's readers hoped to find in the contemporary artifact and work of art. *The poem's* historicity, on the other hand, is its virtue, not its predicament. It doesn't date since it is (among other things) about dating.

FIVE

Adalbert Stifter: 'Erhebung *without Motion*'

. . . and that we could have pure beauty, unadulterated by anything that is beautiful.

(Ludwig Wittgenstein)

Adalbert Stifter's writings belong to the German literature of the mid-nineteenth century. Like a great many of his literary contemporaries, especially the lyrical poets of the age, chief among them Mörike, he confines his work to the private sphere of experience. The settings these writers choose are rural and natural; the values they praise are those inherent in intimate human relations and in the soul of the solitary man. So strong is the emphasis on the human soul in its state of solitude that we may see in this exploration German literature's major contribution, not only in the nineteenth century, to world literature. And so strong is this preoccupation with solitariness as somehow the natural condition of man that his *social* condition comes to be seen as derivative and his everyday world as provisional.

The writings of the mid-nineteenth century are characterised by a unique mixture of two preoccupations: the parochial and the existential. The notion of man as a political animal is largely alien to them (to Stifter after 1848 it is increasingly distasteful); it is certainly never a positive inspiration of their muse. In lyrical poetry, we have seen, such a limitation of themes can remain uncontentious and intuitive. Stifter wrote almost exclusively narrative prose – a form, or rather a variety of forms, which is less easily accommodated to such a limited range of themes. There are two reasons for this difficulty.

The writing of verse implies a number of obvious formal restrictions unknown to prose. But it also implies a certain freedom – the poet's freedom to choose his own restriction. Of course, the choice is not unlimited; Mörike *is* a poet of his time. But in a distinct sense

G

his chosen form is his world – at least in the sense that the form will dictate his inclusions and omissions, his scale of what is or is not important and appropriate. And only then, when he has explored his chosen form, will the relevance of the poem to his contemporary world, and to ours, become apparent – or it may even then remain hidden and opaque. Similarly, the language he uses will be related to the language of the market place in a variety of ways, but it will not be a simple relationship, it will not be simply identical with it. 'The cause of the people', Hazlitt observes ruefully, 'is indeed but little calculated as a subject for poetry'; and the poetic programme of the German Romantics aims at endowing 'the People' and their language with a grandeur and a set of pristine or 'chthonic' values that would make it a fit 'subject for poetry'.

Prose, on the other hand – narrative prose no less than expository – is the social and democratic form *par excellence*. It is uniquely involved in the historical and social circumstances, the living customs and moral standards of its readers who are also its speakers; and nine-teenth-century realistic prose is a singularly direct expression of this involvement. Therefore, the less compatible their pre-occupations and standards are with the artist's conscience, the more problematic will be his attitude towards the whole enterprise of conveying 'to his readers also', 'in *their* language', *his* vision of what the world is and what it ought to be. There are various ways out of this impasse. Grillparzer regards prose as an unworthy vehicle of his creative inspiration – the occasional solecisms and hollow metaphors of his dramatic verse are the price he pays for this strange opinion. Yet Grillparzer can write a critical prose whose supreme good sense, close reasoning and fine ironies give it a most welcome sobriety at a time when, as he says, it is the common assumption of critics that 'whatever is unintelligible must therefore be sublime and profound'. His 'Reminiscence of Beethoven' is one of the most moving tributes of one artist to another to be found in the language, perhaps in any language. And in *Der arme Spielmann* (begun in 1830, completed in 1847) the humble subject matter is transformed into a tale of unique poignancy and beauty – a tale in which the pure heart and the good will celebrate a triumph beyond, though only just beyond, the con-fines of a realistically evoked life of the Viennese poor.

Stifter's solution is quite different, though he too is among that long line of German writers who have experienced and been unsettled by this quandary well before it disturbed English or even French writers. Where the social condition of men is seen as derivative and their common everyday world as somehow provisional, the prose writer will be faced with problems of composition quite different from those of the realistic tradition of nineteenth-century Europe.

The other difficulty Stifter's prose has to contend with relates more directly to the comparison with which I began. We have seen something of the predominance, in Mörike's poetry but also in Heine's, of image over story, and took it to be a characteristic trait of their work. The same is true of Stifter, only the shift occurs in a genre in which we don't expect it, and it is more radical. Stifter wrote two long novels and some thirty Novellen. Are these then stories without a story? Not quite. Certainly his early work, into the early 1840s, is full of palpable events and adventures, sometimes of a weird and wonderful kind, often inspired by Jean Paul. But even these early Novellen have not much by way of plot, the chief carrier of story in narrative prose. 'You can only create if you care', George Orwell wrote about Dickens. Care – what about? Dickens cared about Mr Dombey in his counting house; Stifter about the wanderer in the green forest. To invest creative energy in plot and story is to accept as meaningful, to care for, the social sphere in which alone the convolutions and proliferations of a plot are enacted. It is to accept the actual world, which is the world of man's social experience first and foremost, as a reality, hard or otherwise. It is to see 'the world' as capable of yielding the profoundest interests, spiritual and moral as well as aesthetic. It is to acknowledge it as a creation not wholly alienated from its creator. These are the unchallenged certainties, the *données* of realistic prose. Stifter seems to have had few of these certainties when he began writing, and none when, thirty years later, he ended his labours and his life.

It is not my suggestion that what is valuable in mid-nineteenth-century lyrical poetry becomes invalid in Stifter's prose; or that he was a *poète manqué*. To say that he writes 'poetic prose' would be to beg many questions and answer none. The comparison should merely make clear something of the nature of the task Stifter set himself, and to suggest that he needed narrative means of a very special kind to accomplish it. To understand and appreciate his work we must abandon as far as possible the expectations with which we approach the realistic novelists of his age. He is at the opposite pole from a writer like Tolstoy, who has often been praised for having something to say to every kind of reader, and to each reader in almost every one of his moods. The reader to whom Stifter speaks is one who is willing to bypass the complexities of the actual world in order to gain a view of the bare lineaments of existence.

The bare lineaments of existence? To explain these dark words I had better take the bull by the horns: Adalbert Stifter has the reputation of being a boring author. Obviously this is not a view I share. All the same, it has a plausibility that is worth exploring. It is the prerogative of the work of every major author (I have claimed more than once before) that it should challenge our literary preconceptions and cause us to revise our critical vocabulary. Boredom – like its opposite, liveliness (Aristotle's *energeia*) – is, among other things, a term in the language of literary criticism. It arises where my interest as a reader is not challenged or arrested by a definite object in front of me.

Speaking of the feeling of *Angst*, Kierkegaard, Freud and Heidegger have defined it as fear without a definite object, fear of 'nothing in particular', of the whole impalpable web of all that is – fear of existence itself. On the analogy with this definition of *Angst* we may see boredom as interest without a definite object; or again, an interest in the whole impalpable web of all that is – an interest in existence undivided, in and by itself.

Now, it will be readily agreed that literature is incapable of conveying anything so universal and disembodied as existence in and by itself. Literature is committed, through language, to evocations of specific and discrete objects; it is committed to particulars. Ludwig Wittgenstein speaks ironically of our vain hope 'that we could have pure beauty, unadulterated by anything beautiful'.[1] A literary undertaking that is concerned with the evocation of pure existence, or pure beauty, aims at an impossibility. In a great many of his stories this is, as I hope to show, Stifter's aim. Yet even though he undertakes the impossible and can never fully achieve it, his aim colours and determines his narrative means, and it is with these means that I shall here be concerned.

Like Sartre's Roquentin, Stifter writes as one who is engulfed by existence 'in and by itself'. Like Roquentin he senses its presence 'just behind him',[2] behind the things and people of the surrounding world. Like Roquentin he finds the actual social world bereft of a positive meaning. In this situation Roquentin tries deliberately, 'gratuitously', to wipe out the film of existence on things and people. Stifter, motivated not by a deliberate search but an intuitive compulsion, seeks to penetrate to the grounds of existence. Sartre's prose is the prose of almost any naturalistic *monologue intérieur*; it speaks of the metaphysical undertaking explicitly, in philosophical terms; furthermore, the monologue is placed in a fully realised social world. The fact that Bouville, the scene of Sartre's action, is a dreary provincial backwater is neither here nor there: its reality is never challenged. What matters is that this firm rooting in everyday reality is a necessary part of Sartre's fiction, and thus also of his philosophical quest. The two – Bouville and interior monologue; realistic fiction and philosophy – are not one, but they belong together. Stifter's prose contains neither monologue nor anything like a fully realised social setting. He employs neither naturalistic incoherence nor the vocabulary of philosophy. Instead, he fashions a language that intimates the compulsion that moves him; the compulsion to bypass everyday reality in a search for Being itself.

Are the grounds of man's existence propitious or malevolent? Can our reason span the meaning of our fate? Some of Stifter's stories suggest that it cannot. He then does his narrative utmost to build a protective wall between his characters and existence, yet it will not be walled in. The very things and landscapes, glaciers and rocks and trees, of which the wall is built, belong to existence and let it through. Its encroachment on man is not (as in Sartre) nauseous and absurd, but tragic and absurd. There are other stories, where the tragic and absurd is almost entirely avoided, where existence shows its propitious aspect. Or again, by joining the same bare lineaments of existence into a different pattern, he creates an idyll of Eden. One is left with the impression that there is something fortuitous about which aspect of existence will prevail, that the grounds of man's being are indifferent to his fate. No one who has read a single page of Stifter's mature work could say that he indulges in the irrational. He does as much as is in his creative power to string the 'golden chain of reasons'[3] from causes to effects. But the chain does not reach all the way.

What moves Stifter, I have suggested, is not a deliberate search but an intuitive compulsion. His style, a unique mixture of the disarmingly simple and the strangely – sometimes pedantically – contrived, becomes second nature to him. So much so that at times the simplest of statements –

In einer Ecke stand ein Klavier, an dem ein Mann sass, unter dessen Händen die Töne in den Saal strömten. Junge Mädchen und Männer führten Tänze auf, die ruhiger und vielleicht auch lieblicher waren, als man sie jetzt sieht. Die Mädchen waren entweder weiss oder farbig gekleidet. Die weissen hatten ein farbiges, die farbigen ein weisses Uebergewand. Sie waren mit Blumen, Schleifen, selbst auch Juwelen geschmückt. Die Männer waren Alle im schwarzen Anzuge. Es waren schöne Mädchen da, es waren sehr schöne Mädchen da, es waren ausserordentlich schöne Mädchen da. Als aber Hiltiburg in den Saal trat, sah man, dass von dem schönsten Mädchen zu ihr noch ein hoher Abstand emporging.

In a corner stood a piano; a man was sitting at it and sounds flowed into the room from under his hands. Young men and girls were performing dances that were more staid and perhaps also more pleasing than those we see now. The girls were either in white dresses or in coloured ones. The white had a coloured tunic, the coloured ones a white tunic worn over them. They were decked with flowers, bows, and even with jewellery. The men were all in black suits. There were lovely girls there, there were very lovely girls there, there were exceptionally lovely girls there. But when Hiltiburg entered the hall, it became apparent that a great distance separated her from the loveliest of them.[4]

– takes on the most elephantine, or balenological, of forms. The vision Herman Melville seeks to convey in *Moby Dick* is as heavily weighed down by expatiation, enumeration and circumstantiality, and of both authors it can be said that their work displays an unnerving disproportion between genius and talent.

To what extent was Stifter, the *déraciné* son of a smallholder from the Bohemian Forest, aware of the nature of his undertaking? In the famous preambles to some of his stories and in his letters he speaks mainly of his didactic intention, of the moral uplift he wishes to inculcate through his fiction. And there is certainly a good deal of highmindedness in most of what he writes. The moral suasion, like the Christian piety that often accompanies it, belongs to the style. But moral suasion is only one aspect of his art. Sometimes we notice that the moral tone becomes anxious, propitiatory, and that the propitiations fail to avert calamity, fail to reach the grounds of existence. The narrative movement characteristic of his stories begins with an elaborate description of natural setting. Wide-ranging, enumerative, and circumstantial, sometimes repetitious like a litany, the elements of the structure rise up and up, to the point where (so we feel) the very weight and size of the edifice will surely keep calamity out. And when all and more than all has been done towards that one end – what then? 'One must show everything, in all its detail, without in the least sparing oneself. . . . But when that too has been done, Mr Landsurveyor, then indeed, everything necessary has been accomplished, one must content oneself, and wait',* for now nemesis will strike.

Introducing one of the two main characters of *Der Waldgänger* (*The Forest Wanderer*, 1847), Stifter writes:

Far back in the region of memories stands an old man whom the author once knew, who spoke in a somewhat foreign manner, to whose sayings he [the author] often listened, and to whose fate he, absorbed in his own feelings which seemed to him the centre of the world, paid little attention. Because of their inconspicuousness this man's circumstances had not interested anybody, but after many years they became better known, and we wish to set them down for the sake of our recollection, *if indeed a thing so little articulated, which produces its effects through its simple existence rather than through being in a state of excitation, can be represented at all.*[5]

The meaning of this passage seems clear enough. The 'simple existence' together with its 'inconspicuous circumstances' amounts to 'the simple life'; this we readily (by way of a mental cliché) equate with 'the good life'; and to such a life, we agree, a 'state of excitation', the discord of passions and of human strife, is at best irrelevant. As a matter of fact, in the light of the story that follows, our reading

* Franz Kafka, *Das Schloss*, chapter 18; the official Bürgel is addressing the exhausted K.

in the course of which we equated 'simple existence' with 'good life', turns out to be quite wrong. The life which the story describes is tragic, flawed by a single wrong decision and its irredeemable consequences. ('Once you have answered the false alarm of the night bell', writes not Stifter but Kafka, '– all, all, is lost.') All, all the accoutrements of the good life have been accumulated and enumerated to no avail. But when nemesis strikes it is, even at the climax, not in the form of an excitation but of calm desolation. The tragedy lies at the very core of that 'simple existence' which is *not*, in this story at all events, 'the good life'. The solitary wanderer's fate is desolate (as it is in the Anglo-Saxon poem of that name), but as such it too belongs to the order of existence. 'Aber auch das ist im Recht': 'that too is the law', Rilke writes in the sonnet on the treacherous hunt of the doves[6] – another tragic image relieved (or deprived) of the tension of drama. Tragedy without the tension of drama is like interest without an object, like the evocation of 'pure beauty unadulterated by anything that is beautiful'.

If, then, the life recalled in that casually placed passage I quoted is less idyllic than it seemed, what is this 'articulation', 'etwas so wenig Gegliedertes', the absence of which is said to make the storyteller's task so difficult? It is contrasted with, and preceded by, 'simple existence'. For Schopenhauer, Stifter's contemporary, this 'articulation' is the process of individuation; a Christian theologian would see it as the fall of man. The detailed consequences of that fall are most appropriately described in narrative prose. Indeed, what else do the great European realists of Stifter's age do except retrace the discrete shapes of the worldly obstacles that God has put into the path of men? But 'the hardly individuated thing', *existence in and by itself* – how can narrative prose ever communicate that? A poet may try –

> The inner freedom from the practical desire,
> The release from action and suffering, release from the inner
> And the outer compulsion, yet surrounded
> By a grace of sense, a white light still and moving.
> *Erhebung* without motion, concentration
> Without elimination. . . .*

– mainly by enumerating what it is not. But a storyteller? How is he to begin? 'Once upon a time there was no man who had no house in

* T. S. Eliot, *Four Quartets*, 'Burnt Norton', ii.

which he *was*, all alone'? He can hardly tell us more than that saddest of all fairy-tales which a grandmother tells the children at the end of Georg Büchner's *Woyzeck* (1837):

> Come, you shrimps. Once upon a time there was a poor child that had no father and no mother, they were all dead, and there was no one left in the world. They were all dead, and so it set off and searched night and day. And as there was no one left on the earth it wanted to go up in the sky, and the moon seemed to have a friendly face. But when it came to the moon, it found it was a piece of rotten wood. So then it went to the sun, and when it came to the sun it was only a withered sunflower. And when it came to the stars they were little golden gnats, stuck on pins just as the shrike sticks them on the blackthorn. And when it wanted to go back to earth, the earth was just a pot that had been turned upside down. And it was all alone. So it sat down and cried, and it is still sitting there all alone.

For the Christian, the fall of man is preceded by a state of being he calls Paradise. This, something like this, is the setting of Stifter's greatest novel, *Der Nachsommer* (1857). But how to explain the sad isolation of Paradise? And what if that simple, undivided being which precedes individuation is itself not positive but negative? What if the Ancients were right who saw in Fate 'the terrible ultimate stark ground of events . . . the last ultimate unreason of existence'?[7]

Adalbert Stifter was born in 1805 in the village of Oberplan near the sources of the Vltava, Bohemia's main river, in a region that contains some of the last remaining virgin forest of Europe. He died in 1868 as a retired inspector of schools, little known among a wider public, in Linz on the Danube, the capital of Upper Austria. A distance of some forty miles separates the two places. A few episodic stills may help us to identify the man: the penniless student, employed as a tutor to the children of the upper bourgeoisie and aristocracy of Vienna (including the Metternichs), is standing in the courtyard of a patrician house, the wheels of a carriage spatter mud on his best suit; the lover, oppressed by feelings of his social inferiority, has resigned his hopes of marrying a merchant's daughter even before he has been rejected; the unsuccessful painter of melancholy yet luminous rural landscapes translates his passion for the order and symmetry of Nature from canvas to prose; briefly involved in the Viennese uprising of March 1848, the unsuccessful candidate for various educational posts moves hastily to Linz, settling there for the rest of his life; the prematurely ageing school-inspector is forever planning a journey to Italy, potters among cacti, keeps an exact record of the Havanas he smokes and the sweet wines he drinks; the elderly recluse writes letters of high moral seriousness and aesthetic import to a publisher who exploits him whenever he is in financial straits, writes letters of loving homage to an ignorant shrewish wife; the man who saw in his childless marriage a judgement of God adopts three girls and loses all of them through early death; the writer who hardly ever mentions so indelicate a matter as money yet speculates in dubious shares, totters from one financial crisis to the next, puts all his hopes in the state lottery (like a character from those Nestroy comedies he despised as immoral); and there is, finally, the invalid who, tormented for years by colics, abdominal spasms and cirrhosis of the liver, in a last moment of unbearable pain takes his own life. What deprivations, what narrowness of worldly experience, what need for solace and enrichment through Nature and Mind are manifest in this life, contemporary French and English writers would have been hard put to imagine.[8] Yet its tenor is not exceptional. In its narrowness and resignation as well as in its absence of dramatic turning-points, his life is fully representative of the lives of most nineteenth-century German poets. Paris, London, the Empire overseas . . .: the words have an exotic, adventurous sound to German ears. They speak of vice and splendour, of *worldliness*, of an established and richly varied social order as well as of a freedom beyond the German experience. A country-house party in Meredith – lords and ladies of dubious descent and rich genteel bankers, all stripped of their finery by the shrewd pen of a tailor's son – is a party held on another planet; but so is Stephen Blackpool's bitter conversation with Mr Gradgrind; so is the funeral of Poor Jo.

Most of Stifter's work runs counter to the tenor of his life. This is not to say that his living experience doesn't enter it. On the contrary, the work never moves far away from the cares his life inflicted on him, his creative imagination remains fettered to them. The facts of his life are not omitted but idealised and carefully veiled in his stories. In examining the fabric of his work it is relevant to know that its purpose to him was that of a beautiful veil. However, what that veil hides is the pettiness of his circumstances, not the tragic nature of his life. Simple existence, we have suggested, is not necessarily the same as the good life; the image that shines through the beautiful veil is something quite other than a harmless village idyll.

Stifter's first Novelle, *Condor*, was published in 1840; some eight volumes of his collected stories appeared in his lifetime. Most of his Novellen, first appearing in magazines, were heavily revised for their publication in book form. Recent reprints[9] of the original versions show that most of the revisions are designed to smooth out as many contours of individuation as possible, to add and superadd nature descriptions, to replace dramatic and even melodramatic effects by parasyntactic constructions and partial repetitions which have the effect of litanies and incantations. *Der beschriebene Tännling* (*The Inscribed Fir Tree*) was first published in 1845, and revised for the second volume of *Studien* in 1850; it is thus a representative Novelle of Stifter's mature phase.

The story and its overt message have the naïveté of a tale found in a village almanac. The bare retelling of it makes a modern reader blush with embarrassment (unless he puts on his Great Literature face, when he becomes impervious to anything). The tale, set in the early eighteenth century, concerns mainly a poor and beautiful girl, Hanna, who lives with her old mother in a solitary mountain cottage near a well consecrated to the Holy Virgin; and a hot-tempered lumberman, Hanns, who is in love with the girl and uses his hard-earned wages to buy her precious gifts. An elaborate deer hunt is arranged in the region for the entertainment of the feudal prince (who owns the lands in which the tale is set) and of his numerous entourage of lords and ladies, among them Guido, who falls in love with Hanna. Hanns is determined to take his revenge on Guido, but in a dream a vision of the Virgin Mary saves him from committing the murder he had planned. The two men never meet; Hanna leaves with Guido for the great city and marries him; and the story closes with Hanna's visit to her native region a great many years later:

Sie hatte eine dunkle, sammtne Überhülle um ihren Körper und war in den Wagen zurück gelehnt. Ihr Angesicht war fein und bleich, die Augen standen ruhig unter der Stirne, die Lippen waren ebenfalls schier bleich und der Leib war runder und voller geworden. Hanns, dessen Angesicht Furchen hatte, stand auf dem Wege.

She had a dark velvet cloak around her body and sat leaning back in the carriage. Her face was finely drawn and pale, her eyes lay calmly under her brow, her lips too were quite pale, and her body had become rounder and heavier. Hanns, whose face was full of wrinkles, stood by the wayside.

She doesn't recognise him. The final paragraph underlines the message of the tale. Both had prayed to the Virgin of the Well; Hanna (according to ancient custom) on the day of her first confession had asked for a fine silken dress embroidered with gold and silver; what Hanns prayed for while contemplating the murder of Guido we are not told. When, after hearing of Hanna's wedding in the distant city, the village girls recall that her wish was granted, an old smith replies: 'She received the Virgin's curse, not her grace – the Virgin's wisdom, grace and miracle were granted to quite another person.'

This tale could be told (and in a sense *is* told) in a very few pages. If we add up the passages in which the action is described, the very few lines of terse dialogue, the few paragraphs containing simple and unprobing character-descriptions, we shall find that most of the story's fifty-odd closely printed pages are devoted to its natural setting, to recitals of the various customs associated with the places of the action and other places nearby, and to a description of the hunt. Thus the girl, Hanna, is introduced only after more than six pages giving a detailed account of the mountainous landscape not far from the southwestern border of Bohemia and Upper Austria, an account which ranges widely over the whole area. The narrator begins as one who is finding his place on a detailed map of the region. He pinpoints the fir tree of the title, its trunk covered with mementoes carved once in the sapling, but now scarred and gnarled throughout many decades of the tree's vigorous growth. He moves to a hill – but it is not yet the one on which stands the bare little house where Hanna will live with her mother; he moves on, to another neighbouring forest and meadow; contemplates the effect of clouds and morning air on the colour of the distant Alps; pauses near two solitary houses; moves to the little church nearby, dedicated to the Virgin of the Blessed Well in which Hanns will bathe his eyes and face; moves on, to the village of Oberplan, to tell the story of the first miracle that happened at the well, and finally describes the house near the church in which Hanna is brought up.

Why does he linger so? We feel that he would much rather not tell the story at all, not disrupt the natural setting – which is no longer merely a 'setting' but the centre of his attention, the very substance and core of his tale. It is as if he were unwilling to turn to the tale of passion, betrayal and desolation. We notice that the story is divided into four sections, entitled 'The Grey Bush', 'The Clearing of Many Colours' (Hanns's place of work), 'The Green Forest' (containing the description of the hunt), and 'The Dark Tree' (in which Hanns, waiting for Guido, has the saving vision). But again, this division is more meaningful in terms of the changing landscapes than of the stages of the action to which it roughly corresponds. The greyish-green hill; the clearing in the forest gleaming with the brilliant scarlet of wild strawberries and the mauve of raspberries, with the golden brown of singed bracken and the heavy black of bare earth; the sharply bounded lethal area of the dark-green forest ('Jagdraum') into which the wild animals are driven for massacre; the skyscapes – pristine blue, watery grey, dappled with baroque Bohemian cloud, hidden behind whitish mists – are not all these more important than the figures in the landscape? Certainly it is they rather than the figures that are the bearers of existence; they *are*. And what (the bewildered reader will ask) does *that* mean, what could it possibly mean?

A good part of the story of Stifter's later prose could be told by examining the ways in which he uses such simple parts of speech as the verb 'to be'. As an exercise in 'stylistics' such an examination sounds dull enough. Yet we would readily find a great many passages where the verb is used not as an inconspicuous link between subject and predicate nor yet as an auxiliary. We would find that in some peculiar and quite idiosyncratic way it becomes 'ontic', it sets out to intimate bare existence. English renderings of such passages are not illuminating, they fail to convey an effect which in German is unique and strange. Here are some examples from the first three pages of our story. Such a sentence as

Aber nicht bloss wegen seiner Aussicht kommt der Kreuzberg in Betracht, sondern es sind auch mehrere Dinge auf ihm, die ihn den Oberplanern bedeutsam und merkwürdig machen.

However, it is not only because of its panoramic view that the Kreuzberg is to be considered – there are also many things on it which make it memorable to the villagers.

does not strike one as unusual. But when these bare constructions are repeated in sentence after sentence –

Die Säulen der Milchbäuerin *sind* durch feine aber deutlich unterscheidbare Spalten geschieden. Einige *sind* höher, andere niederer. Sie *sind* alle von oben so glatt und eben abgeschnitten, dass . . .

The pillars of rock [called the Milkmaid] are separated from each other by thin but distinct crevices. Some are higher, some lower. All are smoothly and evenly sliced off at the top, so that . . .

Ausser den drei Dingen, der Milchbäuerin, dem Brunnenhäuschen und dem Kirchlein, *ist* noch ein viertes, das die Aufmerksamkeit auf sich zieht. Es *ist* ein alter Weg, der ein wenig unterhalb des Kirchleins ein Stück durch den Raxn dahingeht und dann aufhört, ohne zu etwas zu führen. Er *ist* von alten gehauenen Steinen gebaut, und an seinen Seiten stehen alte Linden; aber die Steine *sind* schon eingesunken . . .
Die obenerwähnten Bäume *sind* die einzigen, die der Berg hat, sowie der Felsen der Milchbäuerin der einzige bedeutende *ist*.

Apart from the three things – the rock pillars, the little well house and the chapel, there is yet a fourth that attracts the attention. It is an old path, which for a while goes through the lawn that lies a little below the chapel, and then stops without leading anywhere. It is built of old hewn stone and lined on both sides with linden trees; but the stones are sunk in . . .
The trees mentioned above are the only ones the mountain has, likewise the rock is the only important one.

– we begin to wonder whether what shapes this prose are peasant simplicities or high ontological aims. The natural tendency of German syntax to separate the auxiliary from the main verb is so intensified that the auxiliary *almost* ceases to communicate with the main verb or predicate. Thus in our first quotation 'sind' is used three times in much the same way, so that in the first and third sentence it ceases to function as an 'auxiliary' and assumes an expressive gravity all its own; and this is done, not crudely, by multiplying intervening constructions, but through short, bare sentences. Some of these turns and phrases[10] derive, no doubt unconsciously, from the contemporary *Amtssprache* – the official diction Stifter used in his voluminous memoranda[11] to the local school boards and the ministry in Vienna. But this explanation does not contradict, it complements my understanding of Stifter's prose. To us all forms of 'officialese' seem inhuman because we feel (or at least we claim to feel) that all bureaucracy is inhuman. But this is surely absurd. The primary function of every 'Whereas . . .' is to secure justice and equity against partiality and misinterpretation, not to deny them; and something like this is Stifter's aim. His 'official' diction expresses a certain idealised and impersonal norm. Its intention is to impose a harmonious pattern and order on things and people, an order which is to be impervious to subjectivity; however, the danger is (as with 'officialese') that an intimation of this order ends up by being indifferent to the human lot. (Again we are reminded of Kafka, whose delicate lacework patterns of official procedure are equally indifferent to his heroes' welfare.)

At this point, when we have assembled a few of Stifter's apparently simple devices, we notice that the spell of boredom this prose weaves begins to yield to a curious fascination. We sense uneasily that the simplest of means – and language yields no simpler statement than 'the forest is green' or 'the child . . . was beautiful' or 'the trees which . . . the mountain has' – are employed in the service of an intention that is both complex and unrealisable. For of course what Stifter attempts cannot ultimately be done. No verb can stand without its predicate. Existence in and by itself, uncontaminated by anything existing, cannot be expressed. Individuation is inescapable. (When at the end of his life he moves towards ever more relentless attempts to escape the inescapable, his prose – in *Witiko* – ceases to be readable.) Yet if this 'ontological' style fails to achieve its ultimate object, what it does achieve is remarkable enough.

The things of Nature participate in an order of Being, this prose tells us, which men can do little more than disrupt. Some – a few villagers, barely mentioned – live close to that order. Hanna and Hanns too (their names distinguished by a single letter) initially belong to this order – she through her beauty, he through his vigour and energy. This order of natural being is presented as propitious and benign, but it is not the only order of being. Men – at least to the extent that they live in 'the world' – belong to another order. The prince and his courtiers bring havoc to the countryside, slaughtering the animals of the forest, throwing the villagers into a state of 'excitation and wild spirits' ('Erregung und Übermut'). At the climax of their bacchic abandon following the first part of the hunt, the crowd of villagers singles out Guido and Hanna and, with the repeated shout of 'This is the most beautiful couple!' seals their fate. But this other order too, in all its violence and destructiveness, has a strangely impersonal, 'ontic' quality about it.

The hunt, not the personal fate it changes, is the story's true climax. We recognise it as the symbol of Hanna's abrupt movement from the pastoral setting to the worldliness of the prince's court, from one order to the other. This movement has been prepared for – even as a girl Hanna was shown to be susceptible to the fine clothes and jewels that Guido's world promises. Yet when the change comes, it comes suddenly and silently; only a single brief, wholly impersonal comment from the author describes her feelings. As for Guido's feelings, they are conveyed by static images: a confusion, a deep blush, the picture, seen from afar, of him kneeling before Hanna – that is all. While two pages are given to the festive meal after the first meet, Hanna and Guido exchange not a single word. Hanns, we read, 'knew nothing of all this'; then 'he learned all'; and his night of agony, prayer and deliverance is conveyed, not through his emotions, but solely through the simple things he does, the places he goes to. These characterisations could not be more bare or more effective, nor could the contrast between them and their 'settings' be more marked. Just as the descriptions of the countryside were more than symbols of human peace, so the description of the hunt is more than a symbol of human fate. For the hunt, once it has been elaborately planned by the prince's servants and organised with the help of some of the villagers, doesn't give the impression of a human action at all. The extremely powerful passage in which it is described begins with a piece of music ('eine rauschende Waldmusik') played on wind instruments, which the forest echoes in 'notes of terror and sudden calls of fear, since the forest knew only the sounds of thunder and storm, not the terrible sounds of music'. There follows the call of a single hunting horn. Dogs are let loose into an area of the forest which has been roped off all round by impenetrable nets. A shot is heard. An anguished stag hurls himself against the canvas, a wild cat dashes up a tree. Guns discharge their loads, bullets hit, explosions flash, white smoke fills the lethal area. But there are no people. The narrative voice is mainly passive, once or twice the impersonal 'one saw . . . one heard . . .' is used, for the rest it is the objects and animals themselves that seem to perform this rite of death; only when the hunt is over do the servants move in, to gather the corpses.

There are no elaborate verbal simplicities in this passage; it is full of strife where the earlier scenes were full of peace. But once more we have the impression that something other than a human agency is at work, something other than the wills of individual men. It is again existence in and by itself, this time bearing death and destruction, that is invoked. It becomes clear that neither the fates of the main characters nor even these two images of a countryside at peace and 'the world' bearing terror and discord and desolation, fully contain the story's theme. What the story intimates is this, this almost unutterable muted juxtaposition of two modes of existence, one positive the other negative, in which men are involved but which extend beyond, behind them.

But surely, may not all this be taken as an example of the pathetic fallacy, an age-old device for bodying forth human emotions? Stifter himself, in an earlier story, tells us so:

> there lies a propriety, I might almost say an expression of virtue, in the countenance of Nature before it has ever been touched by the hand of man, to which the soul must bow as to something virginal, pure and divine, – *and yet* it is after all man's soul alone which carries all its own inward greatness into the image of Nature. [12]

It seems that, just as with his verbs of Being Stifter is attempting the impossible, so here he is merely stating the obvious. Or is there not a profound contradiction in that brief '– and yet . . .'? What kind of life is it that informs his characters? If, returning to our story, we look at the way 'man's soul' speaks to us we shall find that most of the human feelings and reactions too are rendered impersonally:

> Die Liebe, die Zuneigung und die Anhänglichkeit wuchs immer mehr und mehr . . .

> The love [between Hanna and Hanns], the sympathy and the attachment grew ever more . . .

And later, after the great hunt:

> Das zufällige Nebeneinanderstehen Hannas und des schönen jungen Herrn war nicht ohne weitere Folgen geblieben.
> Weil die andern Herren, welche zur Besichtigung mancher Werke der Gegend fortgeritten waren, viele Tage ausblieben, konnte die Sache in Gang kommen und Hanna von Empfindungen ergriffen werden.
> Endlich bemächtigte sich der Ruf dieser Sache und trug seine Gerüchte in der Gegendherum.

> The accidental encounter of Hanna and the handsome young nobleman did not remain without further consequences.
> Because the other lords had ridden away to inspect several work-places in the region, staying away a number of days, the affair could start on its course and Hanna be gripped by emotions.
> At last rumour took hold of the affair, and carried its gossip into the region.

Finally, there is the remarkable scene of the roll call (relentlessly repeated over and over again in *Witiko*). In preparation for the second meet the prince reads out the places of ambush, to make sure that each hunter knows where he has been posted. He begins: 'Herr Andreas bei der roten Lake.' ('Lord Andreas, by the Red Pool.') The reply is simple enough – 'Weiss sie nicht' – and quite untranslatable. For one thing, English has no means of conveying Stifter's majestic use of 'wissen' instead of the common 'kennen'. Moreover, if we heighten 'I do not know the place' or rather 'He does not know it' into the terse and impersonal 'not known', then the effect of the whole passage will be more like that of an Anglo-Saxon saga than a mid-nineteenth-century Novelle:

'Herr Andreas bei der roten Lake.'
'Weiss sie nicht.'
'Gidi wird dich hinführen'.
'Herr Gunibald bei der Kreixe.'
'Weiss sie.'
'Herr Friedrich vom Eschberg am gebrannten Steine.'
'Weiss ihn nicht.'
'Der Schmied Fierer wird Euch begleiten.'
'Herr Guido am beschriebenen Tännling.'
'Weiss ihn.'

'Lord Andreas by the Red Pool.'
'Not known.'
'Gideon will lead you.'
'Lord Gunibald near the old hut.'
'Known.'
'Lord Friedrich von Eschberg near the Burnt Rock.'
'Not known.'
'Fierer the blacksmith will accompany you.'
'Lord Guido near the Inscribed Fir Tree.'
'Known.'

Yet this archaic bareness* evokes no mock-heroic tableau; it is, we now see, only one more way in which Stifter attempts to go beyond the limits of individuation. More recent attempts of this kind – Ernst Jünger's coldly inhuman language of 'the storm of steel', Michel Butor's 'chosisme' – are not strictly relevant parallels. Stifter's characteristic mode is not inhuman. Existence, he implies, has a measure of *order* and personal meaning. Both Hanna's and Hanns's prayers are in some way answered by a just and merciful divinity. And yet, even this story leaves us with the impression that the search for existence is also a flight from the human world – or rather, not a flight but a gentle and relentless moving away.

This is all very well (a sceptical reader will exclaim, by now somewhat impatiently) – let us grant that you have made your point about Stifter's impersonal mode of writing, his relentless moving

* In the dialogues of *For Whom the Bell Tolls* Ernest Hemingway uses similar devices; his aim, presumably, is folkish authenticity.

away from the human world of everyday experience, etc. Granted that you have shown up some of the peculiarities and idiosyncrasies of Stifter's style – does *that* justify your talk of 'orders of Being' and other such occult matters? A critic who appears to be arguing at such a remove from the author's declared intentions (which amount to hardly more than a high-minded didacticism) – must not such a critic feel thoroughly uncomfortable about his undertaking? In brief, if what Stifter is 'really' concerned with is some kind of high ontological aim, why doesn't he say so? Not by way of 'stylistic intimations', but explicitly, 'in so many words'?

There is an answer to these objections, though it is unlikely to lead us out of the woods of speculation into the daylight of fact. Stifter received his education in the Benedictine abbey at Krems on the Danube, and remained a Catholic throughout his life; he believed in the sacrament of marriage and clung to it throughout the long years of a troubled and probably joyless union; and in his political writings[13] advocated the ideals of a Christian hierarchic conservatism. The poetic vision of Being, on the other hand, which I believe is embodied in the stories of his maturity, is ultimately incompatible with any Christian orthodoxy; it is much closer to the German *Naturphilosophie* of his age, a metaphysical substitutute for Christianity. No letter of his survives to tell us whether he was conscious of this incompatibility, all we have is the unresolved contradiction.

I chose *Der beschriebene Tännling* for my text because its story of Catholic piety brings this problem more nearly to the surface than the stories which don't explicitly refer to the Christian faith, and in which the world of Nature (and thus of Being) rules supreme. The problem I speak of is brought into the open in St Augustine's comments on Psalms 144 and 145:

Is not the Earth His work? Are not the trees His work? Cattle, beasts, fish, fowl, are not they His works? Plainly they too are. And how shall these too praise Him? . . . *But let none think that the dumb stone or the dumb animal has reason wherewith to comprehend God.* . . . Wherefore then does all praise God? Because *when you consider* the Earth and its beauty, *you* in it praise a voice of the dumb Earth. *You* attend to and see its beauty, *you* see its fruitfulness, its strength, how it receives the seed, how it often brings forth what is not sown; this you see, and *by your contemplation* of it you *as it were* question the Earth; your very enquiry is a questioning of it.[14]

This, this doctrine of 'as it were', determines the scope of any symbolism within the boundaries of Christian orthodoxy. Presented with St Augustine's text, Stifter would no doubt have assented to it. Perhaps he really believed that in his stories he was doing precisely what the Exposition advocates, that his 'and yet' is the same as St Augustine's 'as it were' (see my quotation from *Der Hochwald*, p. 113 above). He was no *esprit fort*. Literature was to him no battlefield of conflicting world views. The protracted anguish of his private life as well as his distaste for the contemporary world made him turn to literature as a solace, the private stronghold from which to send forth missives of pure beauty. If indeed there was a conflict within, it was smothered not faced – hence the painstaking, elaborate, defensive nature of his prose.

In Stifter's stories, and in his great novel too, a most delicate balance is struck between the barest of actions, the simplest psychology, and a high ontological aim. He doesn't suggest that man, the issue of individuation, is (as Roquentin puts it) *in the way* – not quite. Whenever he has occasion for an explicit statement, he affirms that man is able to participate in natural existence, and live in harmony with its order. *To be* in that region, however, to melt into its dark-green forests and bare grey rocks and bluish-white glaciers, is no longer to be quite recognisable in ours.

It may well be that my earlier comparison with Sartre's Roquentin seems adventitious, a mere fashionable anachronism. Certainly the difference in narrative tenors – in the means of the quest for Being – could hardly be greater. Yet the fundamental metaphysical intention, it seems to me, remains the same. At the end of his fruitless search for Being Roquentin is leaving Bouville. At the railway station he resolves to write a book. A novel? We don't know:

'I don't quite know what kind of a book – but you would have to guess, behind the printed words, behind the pages, at something which would not exist, which would be above existence. A story, for example, something that could never happen, an adventure.

It would have to be beautiful, and hard as steel, and make people ashamed of their existence.

Here Sartre's book closes and Stifter's *Der Nachsommer (Indian Summer,* 1857) begins. It must be one of the most single-minded fictions ever written. Beyond and behind its utopian construction, its didactic intention, its Goethean nature worship; beyond the moral and aesthetic lesson it teaches and behind the endless array of implements and things and *objets d'art, Der Nachsommer* is an attempt to evoke undivided, beautiful Being, that which 'could never happen', that which by implication and by its inherent perfection would 'make people ashamed of their existence' and exclude them from its sphere:

> In einem Tale an einem sehr klaren Wasser sah ich einmal einen toten Hirsch. Er war gejagt worden, eine Kugel hatte seine Seite getroffen, und er mochte das frische Wasser gesucht haben, um seinen Schmerz zu kühlen. Er war aber an dem Wasser gestorben. Jetzt lag er an demselben so, dass sein Haupt in den Sand gebettet war, und seine Vorderfüsse in die reine Flut ragten. Ringsum war kein lebendiges Wesen zu sehen. Das Tier gefiel mir so, dass ich seine Schönheit bewunderte, und mit ihm grosses Mitleid empfand. Sein Auge war noch kaum gebrochen, es glänzte noch in einem schmerzlichen Glanze, und dasselbe, so wie das Antlitz, das mir fast sprechend erschien, war gleichsam ein Vorwurf gegen seine Mörder. Ich griff den Hirsch an, er war noch nicht kalt. Als ich eine Weile bei dem toten Tier gestanden war, hörte ich Laute in den Wäldern des Gebirges, die wie Jauchzen und wie Heulen von Hunden klangen. . . .
>
> Der Hirsch, den ich gesehen hatte, schwebte mir immer vor den Augen. *Er war ein edler gefallner Held, und war ein reines Wesen.* Auch die Hunde seine Feinde erschienen mir berechtigt wie in ihrem Berufe. Die schlanken springenden und gleichsam geschnellten Gestalten blieben mir ebenfalls vor den Augen. Nur die Menschen, welche das Tier geschossen hatten, waren mir widerwärtig, da sie daraus gleichsam ein Fest gemacht hatten.[15]

Once in a valley beside a very clear stream I saw a dead stag. He had been hunted, a bullet had struck him in the side, and no doubt he had made for the fresh water to cool his hurt. But he had died beside the water. Now he lay by it with his head resting on the sand and his forelegs stretched out into the pure stream. Not a living creature was to be seen anywhere about. The animal appealed to me so much that I stood admiring his beauty and felt great pity for him. His eye had hardly glazed over, it still shone with a gleam full of pain, and it, and his head, which seemed to me almost expressive, were like a reproach to his murderers. I touched the stag, he was not yet cold. When I had stood beside the dead animal for a time, I heard sounds from the mountain forest, like joyful shouts and the baying of hounds.

The stag I had seen was constantly present to my eyes. He was a noble fallen hero, and was a pure being. The hounds too, his enemies, appeared to me justified, following their bent. Their slender forms, leaping as though propelled, also remained before my eyes. Only the men who had shot the animal were hateful to me, because they had seemed to make a festival of it.

To the nobility of that 'pure being' which fills the pages of *Der Nachsommer* Christian piety is irrelevant. Men are not excluded from it, but only a select few may share it. The ontological mode now extends from nature descriptions to the objects of men's daily use, their buildings and works of art, all of them arrayed in an unbroken continuity. The psychology remains rudimentary, unsearching and idealised. The novel addresses itself to the positive, propitious order of Being only; purposefully, relentlessly it excludes (as far as possible) the negative, destructive order. The drama we know to be inherent in human relations is smoothed out, the element of 'excitation' is conveyed through a cautionary tale hidden in the novel's distant past. Thus the impression of a nearly hermetic idyll is created.

In *Der beschriebene Tännling* Stifter took for his narrative structure a simple tale of love and betrayal; in *Der Nachsommer* he uses the device of the *Bildungsroman*. But whereas in all other such novels of initiation the central theme is not a state of being but a process of becoming (see below, pp. 125–6), in Stifter's hands the genre is radically transformed. He conveys no feeling of fleetingness, and even the movement of 'Werden', of becoming, is stilled. Certainly, the young hero *learns*, is engaged in a process of refinement and cultivation of mind. There is, too, a rudimentary sequence of experiences. But there is no restlessness of expectation, the provisional recedes behind an inexorable idyll. The journey is no longer more absorbing than its goal, simply because the journey *is* the goal: 'becoming' becomes being. The grand device that enables Stifter to square the circle is simple enough: the life *for* which Heinrich Drendorf, the hero, is being prepared is the life *in* which his preparation takes place. And 'the world' isn't a goal at all but merely one of the stations briefly passed on the way. The hero gets older but time stands still. A state of finality replaces the provisional and experimental mode of the *Bildungsroman*, but it isn't the finality of experience as we know it. The journey isn't a journey but a composition, a still life; that is, an assembling of the diverse elements of *Bildung* – moral, spiritual and emotional as well as scientific and aesthetic – into a unified whole.

In an unusually revealing letter to his publisher (21 December 1861) Stifter described his method of work. He begins (he tells us) by first pondering on his main theme and working out its details in his mind. But the first visible stage of composition is 'an outline of individual details, sentences, expressions, and *scenes*, in pencil, all on separate slips of paper (for this I use the best hours of my day)'.[16] It is a surprisingly synthetic, synchronic method, more reminiscent of Mallarmé or James Joyce than of Biedermeier literature. The 'separate slips of paper' will eventually be integrated into a consecutive order: a novel must tell a sequential story: prose is 'ein Nacheinander'; just so (to recall earlier parts of the argument), a verb must have a predicate, and individuation is inescapable. But Stifter's *Nachsommer* goes as far as it seems possible to go in challenge of these truisms. It gives us a measure of how far, before the onset of naturalism and the experimental prose in its wake, it is possible to go from story to image and yet remain within the orbit of narrative prose.

'Our dream pictures of the Happy Place where suffering and evil are unknown are of two kinds, the Edens and the Happy Jerusalems,' writes W. H. Auden. *Der Nachsommer* is, in the terms of this distinction, not a Utopia (as critics have claimed)* but a Garden of Eden:

> In their relation to the actual fallen world, the difference between Eden and New Jerusalem is a temporal one. Eden is a past world in which the contradictions of the present world have not yet arisen; New Jerusalem is a future world in which they have at last been resolved. . . .

---

* The present writer among them; see *Re-Interpretations* (London, 1964), 296.

Eden is a world of pure being and absolute uniqueness.

The self is satisfied whatever it demands; the ego is approved of whatever it chooses.

There is no distinction between the objective and the subjective. What a person appears to others to be is identical with what he is to himself. His name and his clothes are as much *his* as his body. . . . Space is both safe and free. There are walled gardens but no dungeons, open roads in all directions but no wandering in the wilderness.

Temporal novelty is without anxiety, temporal repetition without boredom.

Whatever the social pattern, each member of society is satisfied according to his conception of his needs. If it is a hierarchical society, all masters are kind and generous, all servants faithful old retainers.

Whatever people do, whether alone or in company, is some kind of play. The only motive for an action is the pleasure it gives the actor, and no deed has a goal or an effect beyond itself.*

The only kind of erotic life we find in Eden is that of 'courting couples whose relation is potential rather than actual', for the rest all is 'the chastity of natural celibates who are without desire'. Finally,

Though there can be no suffering or grief, there can be death. If a death occurs, it is not a cause for sorrow – the dead are not missed – but a social occasion for a lovely funeral.

(Were a funeral to occur in Stifter's novel, there is no doubt it would take the Austrian form of 'eine schöne Leich'.)

The felicity towards which Utopia aspires is social, whereas the felicity of Eden is private. *Der Nachsommer* cannot of course do entirely without a social structure. It is even possible to argue[17] that this

* See W. H. Auden's essay on 'Dingley Dell and the Fleet' in *The Dyer's Hand and other Essays* (London, 1962), 409 ff. So accurate is Mr Auden's description of the sort of novel that Stifter wrote that one is surprised at his surprise that 'the only creators of Edens during the last three centuries have all been English', namely Dickens, Oscar Wilde, Ronald Firbank and P. G. Wodehouse. Our surprise is compounded when we realise that one of Mr Auden's domiciles is less than fifty miles from the place where *Der Nachsommer* was written.

feudal structure represents certain aspirations – at once utopian and outdated – of the *haute bourgeoisie* of Stifter's Austria, the class towards which he himself aspired. In a very precise sense Stifter follows the practice, which Karl Marx had ascribed to the ruling class, of presenting a given set of social conditions as 'natural' ('naturwüchsig'); only ill-will and disobedience, he tells us, can alter them. The paradigm of this society is the family – the situation and the lives portrayed are thus as nearly private as we are likely to find in any novel short of the solipsistic *anti-romans* of our own day.

A country estate whose exquisite and prudent husbandry is rewarded by plentiful harvests and perfect harmony vouchsafes that 'inner freedom from the practical desire' of which the poet speaks. 'The release from action and suffering' is attained by placing all action and all suffering far back in the distant past. Instead of 'the inner and outer compulsion', the hero is guided by gentle precept and a free inward development. 'A grace of sense, a white light still and moving' illuminates every scene, every carefully wrought meeting and every gentle, undramatic parting. 'Concentration without elimination' is attained by means of enumerations of objects and a circumstantiality without parallel in German, perhaps European, fiction. The novel reaches towards a quietus beyond individuation, it seeks to attain the unattainable. If indeed there is such a thing as '*Erhebung* without motion', then *Der Nachsommer* is the work in which it is achieved.

SIX

Gottfried Keller:
Realism and Fairy-tale

> . . . *the embedding of random persons and events in the general course of
> contemporary history, the fluid historical background*. . . .
>
> (Erich Auerbach, *Mimesis*)

It may now be salutary to move from the ontological solitudes of
the Bohemian Forest to the less exacting region of Swiss democracy.
The works of German prose in the age of European realism fall into
place on a scale whose least realistic – that is, most characteristically
German – point is marked by the writings of Stifter; the work of
Theodor Fontane lies at the other end of that scale. The fiction of
Gottfried Keller (1819–1890) lies close to Fontane's, yet it does not
commit itself to the *données* of the contemporary social world with
Fontane's singlemindedness. *Der grüne Heinrich* (*Green Henry*) is the
last major work in German to stand under the direct impact of the
Goethean tradition; as a *Bildungsroman*, a novel of development and
initiation, it shares some of the Goethean values. Yet at the same
time it represents something of a compromise between the Goethean
notion of 'becoming', which is a display of the human potentialities
for growth and refinement, and the claims of realism, which insist
on subordinating those potentialities to the prosy responsibilities of
social life.

In its first version (1854) Keller's novel was such a flop that his
sister used the unsold copies as winter fuel. The second version
(1879) differs from the first in presenting the hero's life in the first
person, and it ends on a positive note (rather than with his somewhat
unconvincing death). 'The final version', it has been said,[1] 'asserts
the vitality of social life and makes the individual, even in his
eccentric course, a representative man.' It remains to be seen quite
how strong is this vitality of the social world as presented in the
novel.

It describes the boyhood, adolescence and early manhood of Heinrich Lee, known from his manner of dressing, and also from a certain callowness, as 'Green Henry'. Through pride, affection and fortuitous circumstances the boy comes to think of his minor talent for drawing and painting as a great artistic gift. He leaves his native Swiss town and the village in which he spent some of his boyhood to study art in Munich, from the 1840s onward the artistic centre of Germany. There he abysmally fails to make even a modest living from his art. And he finally returns, via some very romantic detours, to a modest post in the civil administration of his home town. Heinrich's widowed mother, his rustic relations, schoolfriends, several art teachers, two girlfriends, the companions of his bohemian life in Munich, and an aristocratic protector who turns out to have watched the young man's fortunes with a benevolent eye – these are the main background figures against which Heinrich's development is traced out.

The book is remarkable above all for its refreshing honesty and lack of pretension. Keller's narrative manner, for three-quarters of the way, is determined by a lively and clear-sighted impartiality. He consistently refuses to sentimentalise his hero's self-imposed predicament or to extenuate his failings. The accuracy of Keller's psychological insights, especially in the early chapters, is matched by forthright moral indictments which have hardly a trace of the didactic about them; soberly, and with some dry humour, they are presented in scenes in which the circumstances of Heinrich Lee's life are pared away, one by one, until the effects of his self-absorption or indulgence emerge with startling clarity. At these points the road on which he has been travelling becomes so narrow that he can no longer avert his eye from the havoc he has wrought.

We recognise the device of the *Bildungsroman*, from Wieland's *Agathon* (1766/1798) through K. P. Moritz's *Anton Reiser* (1785 f.), Goethe's *Wilhelm Meister* (1795 f.), and Mörike's *Maler Nolten* (1832) to Stifter's *Der Nachsommer* (1857) and Keller's novel as a distinct genre of German literature. Its central theme is not a state of being but a process of becoming. It is a description of a journey, from inexperience, egotism and emotional self-absorption into – 'life'. It is always a story of initiation and preparation – a story of provisional states of mind all pointing towards a goal. But this goal is either not quite reached or else only perfunctorily described. The journey is incomparably more absorbing than its end. If the hero's emotional entanglements and social encounters have something incomplete and provisional about them (in Stifter, see p. 119, the provisional is made permanent without gaining in finality), this is because all that happens to him is made meaningful not in its own terms but as part of a development, of a *Bildung* of character and heart. As for those who accompany him a little of the way, they are usually no more than means to his end. The matter is neatly, if somewhat polemically, summed up by Clavdia Chauchat, the enigmatic heroine of Thomas Mann's *Magic Mountain*; in a conversation with the hero, Hans Castorp, she remarks: 'To be passionate – that means to live for the sake of living. But one knows that you [Germans] all live for the sake of experience. Passion, that's forgetting yourself. But what you all want is self-enrichment – c'est ça.'

These are some of the narrative strands, the *données*, of the 'novel of initiation', which any practitioner of the genre is bound to take issue with. Keller places his hero in a fairly well-defined social context that is governed by a simple and unprobing 'bürgerlich' morality. His task is to adjust the pre-determining aspects of the genre to the claims of realism. More specifically, the question arises how he will set about accommodating the morality of means-to-an-end, a kind of 'moralité par provision', to a less flexible morality of good and evil. The episode of Heinrich's dealings with one of his art teachers, a man called Römer, is one of several instances which point up the novelist's task.

Römer is presented as that which Heinrich Lee is not, a genuine artist. He has come to Heinrich's native town (Zürich) after many failures, accompanied by sinister rumours concerning his past life. Heinrich lends him some of his mother's money. At a crucial point in Römer's haunted life, Heinrich, in a pique of vanity and self-righteousness, asks for the return of the money in a letter that is little short of blackmail. Römer instantly pays up and leaves, and is never seen again. In a subsequent venomous letter from Paris, addressed to 'my dear young friend', Römer makes it abundantly clear that Heinrich's action was the *coup-de-grâce* which has pushed him into abject poverty and moral disintegration. Some time later (volume iii, chapter 5) Heinrich confesses his perfidy to Judith, the more mature of the two girls to whom he is attached. He does so contritely, adding that 'the story will be a warning to me'; by his self-reproaches, he feels, he has as good as atoned for the misdeed. Judith indignantly repudiates the suggestion: atonement is not so easily come by (she tells him), Heinrich has done enough harm to reproach himself for the rest of his life, 'and this bread is good for you', she adds, 'and I'll certainly not spread the butter of forgiveness on it.' 'Then she stood still, looked at me, and said, "Why Heinrich, do you really know that you now have a life on your green conscience?"' In such forthright statements of the irretrievable nature of past experience, of the finality of wrong-doing, Keller's novel presents an advance on Goethe's *Wilhelm Meister*. For there the genre itself, with its underlying view of experience as a series of experiments, had run counter to the making of such clear-cut moral judgements. However, in the next few lines the solipsistic philosophy of the genre re-asserts itself. Heinrich doesn't reply to Judith's accusation. But in his own mind he finds it only too easy to assimilate the experience, 'because, after all, it belongs to my person, to my story, to my nature, otherwise it wouldn't have happened!' The objective aspect of the deed recedes behind its subjective meaning. In the moral indictment, the Goethean view of character-development is briefly widened, but in Heinrich's self-conscious rationalisation of the deed the genre catches up with the judgement and neutralises it.

Keller's engaging honesty consists quite simply in his refusal to do what almost every other author of a '*Künstlerroman*' has done – to make Heinrich into a great artist who is misunderstood. He is ready to show that what Heinrich is abandoning when he decides to give up his artistic ambitions is no more than a mediocre dilettantism, that at this point all is gain and nothing sacrifice. Keller exposes this dilettantism in detailed stages, unsparingly revealing the process at work in all inauthentic displays of talent, which he is old-fashioned enough to regard as a piece of self-indulgence. The dilemma he thus exposes is known to every man who has applied himself to a creative task for which he is inadequately equipped by nature, and which he has chosen for wrong reasons, mainly of vanity. All this is anti-romantic and honest, involving Heinrich in the kind of disillusionment that is germane to realistic fiction; but alas it is also somewhat undramatic. Bad art is equated with irre-sponsibility, which may come as something of a relief to readers saturated with literature about the 'a-moralism' or 'demonism' of art. But Keller seems unaware of slipping into the opposite (and equally egregious) attitude – I mean into the philistinism, writ large by the 'socialist realists' of our own time, which equates good art with social responsibility. A possible conflict between the social and the aesthetic is not explored (the Römer episode is, after all, only a means to Heinrich's end) – perhaps Keller felt the theme had been done too often before. Long novels, E. M. Forster once observed, are apt to need winding up. When no other major conflict intervenes the book begins to flag, and well before the end all but collapses: similarly Keller's 'bread-and-butter' style with its sensible, petit-bourgeois metaphors drops from agreeable sobriety to flatness. The message Heinrich discovers is simply 'This way is no way.' If the paean in praise of adult social responsibility on which the novel closes is unexciting, not to say insipid, then here again the genre asserts itself; the journey, in this kind of novel, is always so much more absorbing than its goal. Finally, as for the journey's relevance to the goal, the reader remains less than fully convinced. The prospect before him at the end is a lifetime's loyal service as a municipal pen-pusher.

What has gone wrong? Once more we find the philosophy of the Goethean *Bildungsroman* encroaching on Keller's realistic intention. More than any other kind of novel, the genre answers to the feeling we have for the fleetingness of experience, for the promise of fulfil-ment just round the next corner and always in the moment to come. It takes the sting of finality out of experience, and replaces it not only (as we have seen) by the notion of development but also by a *plan*. Wieland's, Goethe's and Stifter's heroes all discover that their progress has been benevolently watched over – not by a divine Providence but by a philosopher, a club of freemasons, a wise old man or (in Heinrich Lee's case) a rich count. It is a half-hearted solution, which pays lip service to realism by employing a human agency, and at the same time disrupts it by showing how innocuous and harmless were the hero's acrobatics in the world when all the while there was a safety-net spread out under him. (Thomas Mann in the *Joseph* tetralogy, 1933–1943, will go all the way, and show a hero who even *knows*, at the very moment when he is languishing at the bottom of that famous well, that he can come to no harm.) What is it that prevents Keller (as it prevented his predecessors) from launching his hero whole-heartedly, unprotected by anticipation, on the stormy seas of the real world? It isn't simply the idea of 'self-enrichment' with which Clavdia Chauchat had taunted her young friend.

No character in fiction is more bent on 'experiences', more determined to enrich his self, than Stendhal's Julien Sorel. Yet it is in a comparison with *Le Rouge et le Noir*, another variation on the theme of 'development', that the weakness of Keller's novel becomes clear. Moreover, what is revealed is characteristic of the whole tradition which Keller's realism challenges but which he cannot shake off.

The most obvious thing to insist on in such a comparison is the unabating vitality of almost every one of Stendhal's characters. By this I mean that the forces in conflict with each other in his novel are incomparably greater, incomparably more violent. The social inertia, the *resistance* which the world offers to Julien Sorel's ambitions, is magnificently powerful. The measure of these forces is not so much that they will lead to his violent end but that each, hero *and* world, gives as good as it gets. Leaving his father's sawmill, Julien enters a world depicted with such assurance, such single-mindedness of reference, such relevant circumstantiality, as is displayed in no German novel of the nineteenth century before Fontane. To compare the political cabbala in which Julien gets involved in Paris with the lengthy discussions on road planning and civic duties which teach Heinrich Lee how to become a responsible member of the Helvetic Confederation is like moving from a city jungle of predatory animals to the bovine economy of alpine pastures. It is to recall the narrowness of the Swiss – or, for that matter the German – social and literary scene and Keller's acquiescence in it. True, the novel contains a good many social observations and realistic details of the kind that delights the devotee of nineteenth-century fiction; for instance, on 'the false consciousness' of small-holders:

Weil jeder auf seinem Hofe solche uralte unablösliche Schuld-verpflichtungen hatte und sich selbst als den Bezahler aller der ewigen Zinsen betrachtete, so hielten sie die nehmende Hand der wechselnden Gläubiger für etwas ebenso Unsterbliches und legten dem betreffenden Instrumente einen geheimnisvoll höhern Wert bei, als ihm zukam.

Because each of them, on his own homestead, had similar time-honoured unredeemable debts and regarded himself as the disburser of all those eternal interest-payments, [the farmers] thought of the outstretched hand of the changing creditors [in the city] as something equally eternal, and attributed to the relevant document a mysteriously higher value than it really possessed.

With passages like these, the Marxists' appropriation of Keller,[2] one would have thought, could hardly go wrong. But alas, such observations remain isolated, nothing is made of them in the plot. Unlike the detailed reports of Julien Sorel's financial transactions, Keller's occasional excursions into social realism are transparently didactic.

The irony with which Stendhal reports on Julien's progress has none of Keller's gentleness and bemused detachment. Stendhal's almost Flaubertian wryness implies a supreme narrative confidence, a perfect rapport between author and public that is free from didacticism and high-mindedness alike – and again this confidence has no equivalent in the German literature of the age outside the pages of Heine. The *Bildungsroman* makes of the hero's entry into the world something of a problem – shall he, shan't he? – as though he could somehow avoid it. For Stendhal the idea that world and society are anything but the firm *données* of the hero's situation doesn't arise. The idea that society will in some mysterious way yield before the hero's *weaknesses* – which is what it does in Keller's novel – is quite alien to Stendhal's scheme of things; and, it may not be irrelevant to add, to life as we know it. (Little wonder that Nietzsche, surrounded as he was by such conflicts of troubled inwardness, fell in love with the Will to Power.) Whatever Sorel wants he must fight for. The passion displayed in the course of that fight gives Stendhal's novel a dimension that is lacking in Keller's. Hence the scheme of moral values challenged through Julien's actions is consistently more important and interesting. Heinrich is engaged in a protracted tussle with his art and his conscience; in a conflict with selfishness, heartlessness, irresponsibility. Yet all these are *his* qualities: once he has sorted them out, the world offers no challenge. Certainly, the problems Heinrich has to face intimate much more than a mere 'aesthetic' concern, for his 'art' symbolises a defective moral sensibility. Yet in this way too the circle of the self is merely widened, never breached. All *comes* at him, a means to his end; the world is hardly more than his world: not exactly unreal but malleable.

Once again it is the precept of Goethe's work which, taken out of the context he created for it, imports a doubtful logic into Keller's novel. The subtle balances that inform Goethe's work were unique, its conditions unrepeatable. We saw the results of Stifter's attempt to re-enact them. Goethe had made available to German, indeed to European literature the realm of Nature, yet his human wisdom and creative tact alike had preserved a fruitful equilibrium between the human and the natural spheres. In Stifter's work, where Nature becomes supreme, this subtle balance is upset: as he sees it, the self-determination of man is always wilful, froward and arbitrary, an irredeemable fall from his natural grace, opposed by an order of Being, not by other men. In Keller's *Bildungsroman* the precept leads to a different kind of imbalance. The novel's worst flaw is its humdrum ending, the way it offers no convincing answer to the question, Was Heinrich's journey really necessary? The teleology of Heinrich's experiences – that which gives them coherence and meaning – is still the Goethean teleology: every encounter, whatever its outcome for the other person, is intended to contribute to an enrichment and refinement of Heinrich's world of experience. In Goethe's writings, the teleology receives its sanction from the final goal achieved. Its product is the hero as 'der Kunstfreund', a personality informed by a richly developed aesthetic sensibility – where for Goethe the aesthetic is a full subsuming, not an aestheticist attenuating, of experience. The coherence of ends and means is firmly established, since the society Wilhelm Meister eventually enters is in its turn predominantly cultural and artistic. Whatever was valuable in an education (or rather *Bildung*) towards such a goal in Goethe's work becomes patently problematic in Keller's, for there the goal is precisely the opposite: renunciation of the artistic in favour of a modest bourgeois competence.

'. . . *whichever way you take it, we are dualistic fools.*'[3]

Keller's presentation of 'the world', then, lacks a last degree of seriousness. And this defect is paralleled – necessarily so – in his portrayal of the two women in Heinrich's life. Representatives of spirit and flesh respectively, they are mere literary clichés, they have been done over and over again throughout the nineteenth and early twentieth centuries, all the way down to Hermann Hesse. Anna has certain affinities with the Mignon figure of *Wilhelm Meister*, without any of Goethe's poetic overtones; a wraithlike creature who dies before she has ever quite lived. Judith, too obviously her Lawrentian opposite, makes her entries and exists to suit the convenience of the scheme of *Bildung*. The comparison with Stendhal is once more revealing. Unlike Mme de Rênal and Mathilde de La Mole, Anna and Judith don't exist outside the hero's emotional need of them (two souls, alas, live in his breast), and even on that doubtful premiss they don't come to life.

To have insisted on the firmness of the social fabric in Stendhal's novel is not to suggest that the hero's actions are fully determined by it. Underlying the novel is the intimation that, given a different setting, Julien's qualities of character might have led to different, positive ends. A less bigoted and class-conscious world might have accepted him without his having to turn his bright intelligence to cunning and deceit; and a less hypocritical world would have been less likely to excite his contempt; were not M. Valenod among the judges at his trial, Julien might not so readily put his head under the guillotine. These might-have-beens are not idle speculation any more than human freedom itself is. They are conveyed by means of a most delicate balance between self and world. This balance belongs among the finest achievements of European realism: the self respond-ing to the world but neither its mere victim nor its absolute usurper, the world real and powerful yet not wholly overwhelming. A freedom of choice is there, but it is a real, not an absolute freedom, offering a choice of actual possibilities: *that* Julien chooses is more his business than the world's, *what* he chooses is more the world's business than his. And Stendhal's business is to show world and self as ultimately inseparable, for it is the interaction of the two that determines the course of events and thus the shape of the novel.

Underlying several arguments of these studies has been the distinction between the private and the public spheres, personal idylls and social realities, between self and society. On this distinc-tion, basic to the ideology of European individualism, the German literature of the age is founded, from it that literature draws its most characteristic conflicts, its creative insights into the human condition. Yet even in the heyday of individualism a sense was alive that this might not be more than a working distinction, that there is a point – in theoretical thinking as well as in living experience – where self and world cannot be meaningfully separated. A situation arose in which theoretical thinkers were seeking to re-establish a unity which the realistic artists had never ceased to take for granted; just as they – the artists – had never questioned the verities of a naïve philosophical realism, whatever doubts idealistic philosophers professed about the existence of the external world. Early sociologists – among them Marx and Durckheim, but also Max Weber[4] – came to insist that *the self*, in any living sense, *even as a self*, is already inextricably involved in a social whole, that Robinson Crusoe is an Englishman and a native of the City of York.[5] A reader of realistic prose is likely to greet the sociologists' discovery (as he is likely to greet many of the discoveries of the psychologists) with a wry 'Better late than never'. For the sociologists merely provide theoretical structures for that complex interdependence which to the realistic novelists has always been the best part of their intuitive knowledge of the world – has always been a truth about life no less fundamental for being obvious.

On this intuitive recognition Stendhal bases a character at once unscrupulous and attractive, intelligent and vain, calculating and reckless, and passionate in all things. It is these qualities that make for life *and* for the intimation of values in the novel. Moral values are concentrations of human experience at a certain high degree of intensity. In realistic fiction they are usually shown forth negatively, that is, as being challenged and violated. The passions engaged in worldly conflict – negative and occasionally positive embodiments of moral values – go to the roots of the human condition: not 'the human condition as such' but always in a given time and space. This is Stendhal's major theme, but it is not quite Keller's in *Der grüne Heinrich*. The taint of a chimerical freedom – as though somehow it were possible *not* to enter the river of experience that flows all one way: as though a man could ever *choose* whether he will enter the social world or not – is indelibly imprinted on the novel.

Some of Keller's difficulties in the writing and rewriting of *Der grüne Heinrich* were no doubt due to his misgivings about telling his story through a first-person narrator. But that was not the only problem he encountered. Seeing that several chapters of the novel in its final version are apt to stand away from the main story as self-contained Novellen, we may wonder whether he had the narrative gift to 'go through to the end' with an extended novel – whether he had that energy which is the hallmark of the great novelist. Introducing a collection of his own short stories, Mr Mailer puts the matter with disarming simplicity: 'Anyone can be good for a week, but who can be good for a year, or two, or three?' Nietzsche, Keller's own contemporary, is less deprecating about the *petits genres*. Attacking Wagner's grandiose conception of the *Gesamtkunstwerk* (the 'total work of art'), he writes: 'Nowadays it is only the small thing that can be truly well made. Only in that is integrity still possible.'[6] And when Nietzsche goes on to praise the excellence of Keller's prose,[7] he has in mind not his novels but several collections of Novellen whose very form turns to good account one of the compositional weaknesses of *Der grüne Heinrich*.

Georg Lukács in his book on Keller enlarges on Nietzsche's historicism. Keller is fully alive to the contradictions inherent in bourgeois capitalism (Lukács argues), and it is his troubled social and political consciousness which doesn't allow him to achieve the 'epic totality' of the novel. In this, Lukács assumes a much more developed feeling of social responsibility and a much more acute political consciousness than he can show in Keller. Like all Marxist critics he takes it for granted that any social or political consciousness worth the name must be a Marxist – or at least a proto-Marxist – consciousness:* a consciousness that is bound to unearth the 'contradictions' inherent in every society except, presumably, that of the Marxist millennium; and hence to devise, or at least imply, a 'solution' of those contradictions. In other words, Lukács takes it for granted that political interest is the same as political advocacy, and that interest sufficiently 'developed' can only lead to one kind of advocacy.

And yet, freed from its notorious tautology, Lukács's argument does point in the direction of Keller's creative predicament, and that of many of his most gifted contemporaries. The realistic novel in the grand manner certainly doesn't depend on a 'positive' or

* As the Church Fathers had justified their admiration for the Greek philosophers by ascribing to them an *anima naturaliter christiana*, so Marxist critics argue that writers like Büchner and Keller lived and thought in a pre-Marxist limbo.

'mature' political consciousness in Lukács's sense; nor indeed upon a 'solution' of the contradiction of a given society. (Marx's admiration for the novels of Balzac, or Lukács's own two essays on Solzhenitsyn [1970] are proofs of that.) But the realistic novel does depend on a creative imagination at work in relative freedom on an abundant social fabric: contentious, contradictory that fabric may be, but it must also be rich and abundant and resistant to the imagination. What the realistic novel depends on is not advocacy but an acute interest in the social and political realities of an age: an interest, above all, of that non-ideological, pragmatic kind which the Marxists despise as 'mere praxis' and 'pseudo-concreteness'.

'Had we but world enough and time' is the motto from Andrew Marvell which Auerbach puts on the title-page of his *Mimesis*. That there is, for Keller and his contemporaries, not 'world enough' – that their social and political circumstances are too petty, too static to sustain their creative interest, is the view underlying all the studies of this book. However, the dogma that the manifold deprivations under which these writers lived can only be understood and cured by a Marxist consciousness is a symptom of those deprivations, not their cure.

All that Keller had available to him by way of an 'historical background' (see the quotation from Auerbach, p. 123 above) was the parish-pump politics of the Zürich municipal council whom he served as a clerk. He could neither enlarge it to the size of an 'epic totality' nor yet bypass it in the consistent way Stifter had done. He was neither willing to abandon the novelist's ambition nor impervious to the charms of the idyll. And so he shrinks the historical background to fit the pattern of the smaller genre: *Die Leute von Seldwyla* is the outcome of this compromise.

The ten Novellen assembled in the two volumes of that collection (i, 1856; ii, 1874) seem at first sight to be only loosely connected. They are all set in Seldwyla, an imaginary little Swiss town which, in its slothful and foolish ways, owes something to the Abdera of Aristophanes and Wieland. Yet for all their apparent variety of mood, narrative manner and sophistication, these Novellen have a unity reinforced by their common setting. Each of them is built round a mania, a single *idée fixe*, the staple of satirical comedy. The first tells of a drastic cure for sulking. The second, tragic in tone, is on the Romeo-and-Juliet theme in a village setting. The third is the story of a wastrel's ruin made good by a prudent wife and son. The fourth uses harsh satire to drive home the absurdity of maniacal thrift. Even in the fifth, a humorous fairy-tale with satirical undertones, a Faustian cat cheats a Mephistophelean magician by appealing to his greed for money. The next, which resembles the first story in style, ridicules the inhabitants of a neighbouring town for being taken in by fine clothes and an elegant coach and horses. The seventh satirises the love of titles and noble ancestry, while the eighth mocks the '*précieuses*' affectations of a housewife who has fallen in love with literature. The ninth is a historical tale less directly related to the rest (though its atmosphere of violence is reminiscent of the fourth, and the heroine's possessiveness, which she eventually abandons, is again typical of the main theme). And the tenth, which returns to the more or less contemporary setting, takes for its subject the destruction of family life by religious bigotry.

The narrative manner of each story is designed to bring out the kind of *idée fixe* of which it treats. Thus the cautionary tale of sulkiness is told in the tone of a child's story – not quite a fairy-tale but a curious anecdote about the real world as it might be told to a child. Then again the characters move jerkily, like marionettes; the charm of such stories lies in their lifelike artifice. Keller's stylistic range includes wit, light-hearted irony, farce, burlesque and caricature, through oblique and direct social criticism, all the way to the tragic manner, to harsh satire and the grotesque; among these, caricature is the most frequent device, because it is the most direct expression of that 'terrible constriction of life in one-sidedness' (the phrase is Hebbel's), of those life-denying manias which are Keller's unifying theme.

All this is crowded into Seldwyla, an imaginary yet realistic nineteenth-century small-town setting and its environs. And now, because Keller takes issue with the petit-bourgeois constriction – because he no longer acquiesces in it – the taint of provincialism is gone. Nowhere is this more patent than in 'Romeo und Julia auf dem Dorfe', in the way he reduces the grand Shakespearian theme to fit a different social situation. We witness the deterioration of two fathers from proud, patriarchal figures to litigious maniacs; their quarrel over a stony piece of land makes the two families abandon their farmsteads and move into the squalid quarters of the Seldwyler 'Lumpenproletariat'; and the two children-lovers, for all their innocent tenderness and all the love they bear each other, are held and at last crushed by the world of their parents which is the only world they know, the absolute horizon beyond which their imagination cannot reach. Theirs is the petit-bourgeois dispensation under which Gretchen had lived: 'Es ist so elend, betteln zu müssen,/und noch dazu mit schlechtem Gewissen.' ('It is so wretched to beg one's bread/And with a heavy conscience too.')[8] The Seldwyla setting, we can now see, is no fortuitous or fanciful framework but the precise and fitting condition of their lives: what is enacted in the Swiss backwater is a European theme.

At the same time we remain aware that the term 'social realism', which we readily apply to Balzac or Dickens, doesn't quite fit. Keller remains, as Fontane observed, '*au fond* a teller of fairy-tales'.[9] The structure of a cautionary tale, complete with a moral message, informs each of these stories. Underlying the various styles I have mentioned is a narrative manner that gently mocks at the reality of it all, and simplifies the psychology in the way a fairy-tale does. There is a great charm in this, but it is not the charm of a consistently realistic narrative.

The polarity of good and evil is not rigid – education, good will and good humour lead some of the Seldwylers to mend their ways – but the processes of moral improvement or deterioration are based on the simplest motives and issue in the simplest ends. And when, for once, Keller makes explicit that sense of civic responsibility for which Lukács had praised him, the positive values that emerge are somewhat banal (as were the values that emerged in the course of Heinrich Lee's education). The story 'Frau Regel Amrain und ihr Jüngster', is one of the few in which the realistic manner is sustained but, paradoxically, it is also the least interesting one in the collection. Yet the reason for this is patent. For is it not the paradox of realistic literature – one thinks of Dickens's Esther Summerson – that it is least successful where its narrative line is least exacting, where the values of the world it portrays are least challenged?

A spendthrift father has returned after years of fortune-hunting in America, to find that his wife and son have saved the family business he left on the verge of bankruptcy, and are unwilling to let him take over its management:

Er zog einige Wechselbriefe hervor, so wie einen mit Gold angefüllten Gurt, was er alles auf den Tisch warf, und es waren allerdings einige tausend Gulden oder Thaler. Allein er hatte sie nicht nach und nach erworben und verschwieg weislich, daß er diese Habe auf einmal durch irgend einen Glücksfall erwischt, nachdem er sich lange genug ärmlich herumgetrieben in allen nordamerikanischen Staaten. . . . So ging er in die Stube, die man ihm eingeräumt; dort warf deralternde Mann seine Barschaft unmutig in einen Winkel, setzte sich rittlings auf einen Stuhl, senkte den großen betrübten Kopf auf die Lehne und fing ganz bitterlich an zu weinen. Da trat seine Frau herein, sah, daß er sich elend fühlte, und mußte sein Elend achten. So wie sie aber wieder etwas an ihm achten konnte, kehrte ihre Liebe augenblicklich zurück.

He [the old man] brought out a few bills of exchange and a belt full of gold, threw it all on the table – and indeed, it came to several thousand florins or dollars. However, he had not amassed this fortune gradually, and he wisely omitted to mention that he had got hold of it at one swoop through some stroke of luck, having tramped around all the North American States for a long time in poverty. . . . He went into the room they had given him. There the ageing man threw all his money into a corner, sat down astraddle on a chair, placed his sad large head on its back, and began to weep bitterly. His wife came in, saw that he felt miserable, and she had to respect his misery. Now, as soon as she could respect something in him, her love instantly returned.[10]

We note the telling image of the childlike old man, the beautifully rendered detail of the chair. But we also note the curiously unprobing account of the husband's and wife's reactions, the absence of any comment on, or narrative dissociation from, the petit-bourgeois scheme of values that is implicit in these reactions. The love of two adolescents[11] could move no mountains. The love of two elderly people must go through the valley of shame. There is here nothing, no freedom of feeling, outside the social covenant. Does the covenant determine all? Perhaps the gentle humour and occasional irony that inform this story derive from a different dispensation. If so, we don't know what it is. Clearly, to these people money isn't everything; or rather, there seem to be two kinds of money, and only one – that acquired by thrift and hard work – has any value in their eyes. And in Keller's too? Beyond moderate thrift and prudent husbandry, decency and good humour and tolerance – is there no other value? He doesn't tell us.

Keller is at his best where he shows that trivial baseness is not really trivial, that the mood of *Gemütlichkeit* may on occasion stand in a terrifying alliance with depravity and cruelty (see below, p. 148); where he understands how close and powerful the alliance is, and how closely it is bound up with the stifling setting of the petit bourgeoisie; in fine, where he critically explores the social facts of the world he knew. What gives his work a European quality and relevance is the fact that this provincial milieu and its inbred morality are a European phenomenon. In the stories of Gogol, Dostoevsky, and Jan Neruda the satirical vein of Keller's Seldwyla is continued and intensified, the petit-bourgeois mentality dissected, the *idée fixe* which informs it shown up in all its harshness and, ultimately, its dæmonic obsessiveness. Keller's Novellen explore not the radical conclusions of one of the major themes of European realism but its less strenuous approaches. Occasionally his stories open towards tragedy or purposeful satire; more often their temper is that of an idyll or fairy-tale.

SEVEN

Wilhelm Raabe: Home and Abroad

Wilhelm Raabe's literary career is a prolonged and somewhat unhappy tussle with the public and critics of Wilhelminian Germany. His first novel, *Die Chronik der Sperlingsgasse*, 1857, achieved a popular success he never quite equalled in the half-century of novel-writing which followed it; and the masterpieces of his last decade were only written when he at last reconciled himself to the insecure position of a literary outsider. Yet throughout his long career the concerns of the German middle-class public remained intimately the concerns of his fiction. Raabe's novels, like those of Theodor Fontane, his senior by twelve years but his exact contemporary as a practising novelist, are created from a fruitful compromise between European realism and the German literary tradition. But whereas in Fontane the compromise is achieved on the European side, as a local variant of European realism, the work of Raabe's maturity lies well to the German side of the continuum of nineteenth-century literary conventions. Is Raabe's then another case of self-impalement through otherworldliness and provincialism? The suspicion is unjustified wherever he takes issue with it, by turning the conflict between the worldly world and German inwardness into a major theme of his fiction. Nor is there anything provincial about the fairly complex narrative techniques of those of his novels where a characteristic self-indulgence and prolixity of style is turned to parodistic and critical account. But the narrative manner is far from consistently critical, and to impose an overall pattern of conscious social criticism would be as misleading as in the case of Dickens. The fact is that neither early popular success nor later academic (and popular) neglect appears to have helped Raabe to cultivate a consistent understanding of his finest literary gifts. His lasting achievement springs neither from conformity nor open conflict with the society of his day and its professed ideals; nor could he create in such radical and occasionally indignant isolation as did Adalbert Stifter. His achievement is to be found where he writes as his society's sympathetic domestic chronicler and critic. This is Raabe's characteristic way of fulfilling one of the conditions, perhaps the most paradoxical, of nineteenth-century realistic prose, whose universal and permanent appeal springs from its creators' utmost immersion in the palpable circumstances of a very specific and particular time and place. The specificity of vision: the immersion in the domestic particular: the rendering of the familiar detail – these are the objects of the realist's Eros, and one of the main sources of his relevance beyond his time and place.

The narrator of *The Chronicle of Sparrow Lane* is that paragon of the cultural aspirations of the German middle class, 'ein Privatgelehrter',* taking time off from his labours on an obscure *magnum opus* of great erudition and Schopenhauerian dimensions, to be entitled *De vanitate hominum*. In the garrulously anecdotal and associative style of old age (and, incidentally, of *The Pickwick Papers*), Dr Johannes Wacholder recounts episodes from his life and the lives of a few of his friends and neighbours, all living cheek by jowl in an inconspicuous narrow side-street of old lodging houses and garrets; the locale is one of the poorer districts of Berlin. The artless way in which these reminiscences fill the pages of Dr Wacholder's chronicle is deceptive, for what at first looks like an ill-assorted huddle of tales turns out to be a carefully wrought sequence of contrasting moods. Lyrical evocations of childhood and early sorrow; pictures of the Hessian countryside and of Berlin in all seasons; the hurly-burly of liberal journalism under the Prussian censorship; the plight of proletarian emigrants on their way to America; old age and its moods of happy and melancholy recollection – all this would hardly make one suspect that the author of this *tour de force* was twenty-four years old, a hapless

---

* The fullest fictional account of the ethos of '*Wissenschaftlichkeit*' is given in Gustav Freytag's influential novel, *Die verlorene Handschrift* (1864); its theme is the heroic aspect of scholarly devotion and academic integrity.

bookseller's assistant lately turned student, who had never written a line of fiction.

The mastery Raabe achieved in the *Chronicle* seems all but lost in the writings that followed it. *Der Hungerpastor* (1864), which became almost as popular as the *Chronicle* though for worse reasons, takes up the structure of the traditional *Bildungsroman* and sentimentalises it into a self-consciously 'German' scheme of values. As to the Novellen and long historical novels of Raabe's middle period, there seems little point in attempting to rescue them from the limbo of literary history. Even *Abu Telfan* (1868), by which Raabe himself set great store, is disfigured by long-windedness and the author's uncertainty – reflected in its lopsided structure – as to what kind of novel he is writing and how seriously he wants us to take the social criticism it contains. Some of the most chauvinistic purple patches of these novels have been singled out for praise by the ideologists of the 1930s, among them the astonishing Alfred Rosenberg, and academic trimmers like Hermann Pongs. From this kind of advocacy, Raabe's reputation in Germany has not fully recovered to the present day.

It is more rewarding to concentrate on the masterpieces of Raabe's last decade, in which some of the contrasting moods and ideas of the early *Chronicle* reappear – moods and ideas, moreover, kindred to those which have occupied us throughout these studies. And this task is made all the easier through the work of Barker Fairley, in whom Raabe has found an undogmatic and happily perceptive critic. Fairley particularly excels at retracing the complex yet unemphatic narrative structures of Raabe's best novels. What these structures embody is an outlook which is consistent and yet has nothing of a raw *Weltanschauung* about it: 'It is [Raabe's] sense of life that makes his novels so cherishable, not his ideas about it.'[1] And, having quoted Raabe's praise of 'Treuherzigkeit' – 'Und ist nicht Treuherzigkeit das erste und letzte Zeichen eines wahren Kunstwerks?'[2] – that truthfulness and simplicity of the heart which, in German, is inseparable from a certain cosiness and, in Raabe's German, a certain good-humoured philistinism – Fairley concludes:

His outlook on life . . . was that of the plain man or of common humanity or whatever we like to call it when an author does not claim to have anything of his own that we could not reach without

him, or so he would say. . . . What [Raabe] succeeded in doing
was to carry his simple outlook, his 'Treuherzigkeit', to the summit
of life, of creative life, and vindicate it there, without abating a
jot of it or finessing with it in any slightest degree.

Author and critic, we can see, are bound by a special bond of
sympathy.

An old man, articulate to the point of loquacity yet self-effacing
at the same time, ponders on the events of his past life, and on the
fate of his childhood companions – such was the framework of the
early *Chronicle of Sparrow Lane*. The narrators of Raabe's last novels
are hardly more than middle-aged, and yet with them too we
feel that the emotionally rich days of their lives are over, and that
what is left is the routine existence of a settled job and family life.
Emphasising their own withdrawal, they often unwittingly betray
some good reason for not wishing to stress the part, considerable or
otherwise, which they played in the events they are unfolding. Now,
by the second half of the nineteenth century, this 'framework
narration' has become a fashionable device of German prose, used as
a means of securing greater credence or fictional authenticity for
inherently improbable events. If proof is needed that for Raabe the
framework technique is a good deal more than that, it is to be found
in the three great novels of his last phase – *Alte Nester* (1879)
Stopfkuchen (1890) and *Akten des Vogelsangs* (1895). Here the quiet of a
scholar's study, or the cabin of a ship on its voyage to the Cape of
Good Hope, provide a natural contrast to the turbulent world in
which the recollected stories were enacted (and incidentally the book-
lined garret offers an excuse for all those overt or playfully hidden
quotations – bookish and a little sententious but never falsely
'literary' – with which Raabe's novels abound). Moreover, Raabe
allows the framework to merge with the picture. By making the
narrator in his partial withdrawal an integral part of each plot and
story, he turns the formal device into a major part of the theme. The
contrast between the brown study and 'the world' (or '*Sæculum*', to
use a favourite expression of Raabe's) comes to be seen as one
example of a contrast and conflict which has many different forms.
The security of childhood, counterpointing the turmoil of adult life;
village life, or the old house on the edge of the forest, or again the
modest little castle above the village, contrasted with the uncertain

life of the city; family, friendship and love, contrasted with the ups and downs of professional life; the narrow life of the German provinces, made narrower still in the grand perspective of voyagers returning from Africa or America: these are some of the variations on the theme, which in Raabe's novels becomes a major German theme. Of course, there is nothing original in his choosing such contrasts for his novels; the numerous though questionable company he appears in seems to place him in the blighted region of sentimental patriotic clichés on the borderline of the nationalist ideology.

Is Raabe then a 'Heimatsdichter', a 'Poet of the Homeland' after all? No term in German literary criticism has suffered a worse fate at the hands of the nationalist mythmongers and literary chauvinists. Raabe himself, Stifter and the 'Nordic' Theodor Storm, Gustav Freytag and Mörike, the 'dæmonic' Annette von Droste-Hülshoff and even the sober-minded Fontane – they have all been subjected to the 'chthonic' or 'völkisch' treatment. Even Heine was included, by the simple device of calling the author of his most popular poems 'Anon'. They all emerge from this treatment as spokesmen for the 'Germanic' – later 'Aryan' – values of authenticity and honesty, depth of feeling and inwardness and starry-eyed innocence, determinedly facing French worldliness and (later) decadence, English commercialism, Semitic craftiness etc. These rhapsodies of the critics of yesteryear are not, alas, entirely unjustified. In Freytag's *Soll und Haben* (1855), for instance, the German business probity of a Silesian firm of merchant bankers is contrasted with Jewish sharp practice on the one hand and Polish lawlessness and 'Unkultur' on the other; and the difference between the (German) rate of interest up to 7 per cent and the (Jewish) rate of 10 per cent and over is raised to a metaphysical principle. Later German developments make it difficult to read this kind of fiction, to which Richard Wagner too contributed (*Ein Ende in Paris*, 1841), with the necessary scholarly detachment; and the effort to do so fails to be repaid by any literary interest. In *Der Hungerpastor*, it must be confessed, Raabe too exploits these familiar prejudices.*

* Barker Fairley is no longer likely to be right when he writes that *Der Hungerpastor* is 'among the half-dozen books most widely read in German'. However, of the central contrast 'of Semite v. anti-Semite' he says, justly and moderately, that it 'reduces the humanity of the book where it was at its

The scheme on which 'Heimatsdichtung' (in this chauvinistic sense) relies is simple enough. It has at all events this much in common with twentieth-century fascist literature, that it is essentially undialectical. It supports a black-and-white evaluation of the conflict and contrast between 'the world' (which is always wicked) and 'the German soul' (which is always pure, often a victim of 'the world's' sinister machinations). The 'conflict' has a foregone conclusion and the author's value judgements are always predictable – that is, clichés – simply because they follow a premeditated (or prefabricated) ideology, which the fiction illustrates and on occasions helps to propagate. 'What shall it profit a man if he shall gain the whole world, and lose his own fatherland' – this, roughly, is the theme; like the bulk of the nationalist ideology, it is derived from secularised and misappropriated Christian ideas. And if we ask why, in the heyday of European realism and after, this ideology hasn't produced a single work of lasting *literary* value (leaving aside the complex question of Wagner's libretti), the answer lies in its undialectical, predictable narratives, in its presumption that nothing of any value is to be discerned on the other side. Where realism refuses to commit itself to anything narrower than a perceptive concern for and an intelligent interest in the contingencies of social life (see above, p. 131), offering as its questionable 'social message' not advocacy but (if anything) disillusionment with advocacy, the literature of nationalism is unrealistic precisely because it advocates a scheme of values which is said to transcend all realistic considerations. The association of literary realism with a broadly democratic outlook, we can see, is not accidental.

The framework technique fashionable in German fiction has several uses. One of them is to accentuate the nationalistic bias by creating a perspective in which the movement of individual lives, and of the society they compose, is recorded from a point at rest. No more is needed than to make the point at rest safe and cosy, the movement precipitate and dangerous – and a whole set of contrasting loyalties, displaying always the same black-and-white pattern of values, falls into place.

best and most generous' – that is, in its depiction of the artisan milieu – 'and ensures that [the novel] will never be read abroad without distaste, whatever its popularity at home' (*Wilhelm Raabe: an Introduction to his Novels*, Oxford 1961, 172–3).

The novels of Raabe's maturity too use the technique and exploit the perspective, but they do so critically. It is their distinction that, while they too are founded in this commonplace contrast, there is nothing black-and-white about the way they present it. Here nothing is prefabricated. The value-judgements his later novels contain are unsentimental, subtle, and implicit: the way judgements are made and apportioned is integral to the development of each narrative. Provincial back-water, countryside or scholar's study are not necessarily a haven of authenticity, the great world is not necessarily Sodom and Gomorrha; the cosiness *can* be stifling, the world a liberation.

Somewhere near the core of each of these novels, hidden in the rural cosiness, there occurs a moment of violence and destruction. This moment has the appearance and suddenness of an unpremeditated revolt, yet a good deal of the narrative is devoted to motivating it, and yet again the final impression it leaves is of an *acte gratuit*. In an earlier novel, *Der Schüdderump* (1870), the act is primitive and direct. The setting is a manor house in the Harz mountains, ruled over by the squire's widow. With the help of two old gentlefolk (pensioners on the Lauenhof) and a few villagers she is doing her best, in sadly reduced circumstances, to bring up the son and heir of the rundown estate. (Georg Weerth, a footloose friend of Marx and Engels, had used the same milieu in a haphazardly constructed narrative published in 1849.[3]) Set against this well-meaning gentility teetering on the verge of bankruptcy, there is the luxurious and corrupt establishment of a speculator – originally the village barber – in Vienna, a city notorious in the Protestant north for its frenchified airs and lack of solid bürgerlich virtues. (On the other hand, Friedrich Engels in a letter to Minna Kautsky from London, 26 November 1885, calls Vienna 'the only German town which has a *society* [where] Berlin has only "certain circles"'.) The two milieux are connected through Tonie, an orphaned girl brought up in the manor house as little better than a menial, and taken away by the rich speculator who turns out to be her grandfather. The action is governed by a 'morality of inertia', of the undeveloped heart. As in E. M. Forster's early novels, the emotional issues are undramatic and mildly muddled and at the same time decisive. By the time young Hennig von Lauen wakes up to the girl's beauty and charm, both milieux – the Lauenhof and Vienna – have done their work. He attempts to rescue Tonie from her gilded cage, but once he is in Vienna, Hennig fails to find the strength of mind and heart to convince her of his love. He has to return to the native village without her, and Tonie (in accordance with that regrettable nineteenth-century convention) pines away and dies.

The curious title of the novel, a local name for a pest-cart, is misleading. Discovered by the narrator in a little folk-museum, 'der Schüdderump' is meant (not very subtly) to stand for a symbol of death and ineluctable fatality. But Raabe is too good a novelist to confide the novel's motivation to blind fate, its interest lies in the social and psychological motivation of Hennig's velleity. The boy's defective upbringing is in the hands of his forthright mother and his two indigent mentors, a kindly knight of the sad countenance called Herr von Glaubigern and a redoubtable and less kindly spinster called Adelaide de Saint-Trouin etc., etc., who traces her origin in a direct line to the Emperors of Byzantium. The two gentlefolk are kept on at the Lauenhof because there is nowhere else for them to go; and they 'educate' Hennig, and later Tonie, because there is nothing else for them to do. In their different ways they try to fill Hennig with their own unreal and outdated notions of life. The boy rejects the spinster's snobbery and can make little of the knight's otherworldly wisdom, yet apart from these doubtful precepts he has nothing to fall back on. His mother doesn't discourage Hennig's interest in Tonie (anyway, she is too busy looking after the house and the harvest), but neither does she regard Tonie as a person in her own right; when it comes to fighting for Tonie, Hennig will get no help from her. Adelaide – known to Hennig as 'das Frölen', to the rest as 'das Gnädige' – is disappointed to find in him a rough farmer's boy rather than a scholar, and looks on Tonie, as she had done on Tonie's mother, as a mere plaything. And the gentle von Glaubigern, he too, for all his chivalrous ideas and good intentions, is capable of no more than an ineffectual gesture. The crucial mis-timings which lead to the melancholy ending are the result not of fate but of hesitation; and they are indicative of an all-pervasive atmos-phere of indecisiveness and uncertainty of purpose, which in its turn is shown – or almost shown – to reflect the material strains and outdated social status of the Lauenhof. This is the atmosphere the boy couldn't escape at home; and this, too, the young man cannot shake off on his ineffectual and faintly ridiculous expedition to rescue Tonie from the snares of Vienna.

But what of Hennig himself? He had his chance, but when it came it was too early, and when he takes it it is too late. Of the two, the earlier occasion (chapter 10) is the more interesting. One cold grey day in late autumn Hennig and his two mentors are taking a walk in the Harz foothills beyond the Lauenhof. They ascend a steep meadow, and not far from the top of it are hit by a violent gust of wind:

Mit einemmal schien dem Jungen ein Licht darüber aufzugehen, wieviel vom Leben er infolge seiner trefflichen Erziehung bereits verloren habe. In einem langanhaltenden, dummen Geschrei machte er plötzlich seiner Entrüstung darüber Luft, tat einen Sprung über den Graben, lief den Abhang hinauf dem Walde zu und war verschwunden, ehe der Ritter und das Fräulein im geringsten fähig wurden, den Dämon, welcher ihren Zögling ergriffen hatte, zu begreifen und zu würdigen.

All at once the boy seemed aware of how much life he had already lost through his excellent education. He aired his indignation in a long-drawn stupid cry, took a leap over the nearest ditch, raced up the slope towards the forest, and was gone before knight and ancient damsel could so much as recognise and account for the demon that had seized their nursling.

And again:

Der im Wohlleben aufgewachsene Hennig besaß jenes animalische Gefühl für die Behaglichkeit des Lebens, welches man auch Gemütlichkeit zu nennen pflegt, im hohen Grade. Den Genuß, faul und fett am Fenster oder am warmen Ofen zu sitzen, wenn die Nebel von den Bergen niederstiegen, wenn die Blätter und der Wind und Regen rauschten, kannte er sehr wohl; und nun riß ihn an diesem dunklen Nachmittag ein anderer Geist zum erstenmal über diese bequemen Stimmungen hinaus.

Hennig, who had grown up in easy circumstances, had a well-developed feeling – known as *Gemütlichkeit* – for the creature comforts of life. He was quite familiar with the delight of sitting lazy and well-fed at the window or beside the warm stove when the mist is coming down from the hills, or when the leaves toss in the wind and rain; and now on this gloomy afternoon a different spirit seized on him, and for the first time whirled him out of this comfortable mood.

For the first time, and the last. On his heedless rush through the woods in a moment of adolescent *Sturm-und-Drang* Hennig meets Tonie and becomes aware of her as a person and a friend. But the awareness doesn't last. The *acte gratuit* results in nothing more decisive than a scolding and short commons for the night.

In the course of translating this passage, one is bound to run out of synonyms for that *Gemütlichkeit* which the adolescent Hennig is attempting to breach – and no wonder: it is, for Raabe, the quintessence of a German sense of life. Like the circumstantiality of Stifter's prose, like the 'ponderousness' which Schopenhauer satirises, like the stifling cosiness of Spitzweg's canvases, German *Gemütlichkeit* is a curious and unique configuration of time-honoured habits, rich meals, ancient or at least old-fashioned furniture, solid broadcloth and solid moral maxims, weighty and sententious, inward-looking and apprehensive of, often downright hostile to, the social world outside. A good deal less relaxed than the Austrian (or rather Viennese) manner of life that goes under the same name, less cheerful than Dickens's 'merry old England', but also a good deal less formal than the Victorian ethos, it is there in Mörike's *Maler Nolten*, in the inns of Keller's Seldwyla, in Fontane's middle-class interiors as well as in Carl Spitteler's Swiss farms; in the very air of Marx's house in Hampstead, in the early novels of Hermann Hesse, in Thomas Mann's first major novel, *Buddenbrooks* as well as in *Doktor Faustus*, his last, all the way to Günter Grass's Danzig and Heinrich Böll's Cologne before the bombs. So important, so characteristic is this notion of *Gemütlichkeit* for German fiction that we are bound to ask what storms rend the German seas that the ship of life should require so much ballast, such elaborate sheet-anchors.

There is a sense in which Raabe's evocations of this *Gemütlichkeit* are only too successful, where that 'coincidence of subject-matter and form' beloved by the critics leads to altogether unfortunate results. Little will here be said about the texture of Raabe's prose. The verbal elements which make up the pages of his novels aim at cumulative effects, making more than fair allowance for the forgetful reader. His prose is neither highly organised nor are its effects particularly original. Memorable metaphors are as rare as is intimation through aphorism; mannerisms of characterisation and speech are relentlessly repeated, and the case for regarding them as 'leitmotifs' is a good deal less convincing than it is in Thomas Mann's prose (how convincing *that* case is had better be left for another occasion). The wise saws of sententiousness are not always guyed; the archnesses of direct speech spill over into the authorial narrative; and a philistine smugness of life is sometimes conveyed all too closely by a regrettable stylistic *Gemütlichkeit*. All this of course impairs his novels, most seriously in the case of *Der Stopfkuchen* (which I shall thus omit), and it cannot be said in extenuation that Raabe's *longueurs* are compensated for by that sudden energy and breathtaking verbal inventiveness which flash through Dickens's dross. If nevertheless these faults don't consistently diminish the value and interest of his work, this is because (in spite of the ancient New Critics' claim to the contrary) the achievements of the realists are not necessarily tied to a high degree of verbal discrimination, so that, unless one's criteria are positively Nabokovian, Balzac and Dostoevsky are allowed to share Parnassus with St Flaubert.

Each of the three major novels of Raabe's maturity – *Alte Nester* (*The Old Nests*, 1879), *Stopfkuchen* (*Stuffguts*, 1890), and *Die Akten des Vogelsangs* (*Documents of the Birdsong District*, 1895) – is written in the 'framework' form I have described, and in each the narrator's withdrawal or uneasy reticence and its reasons are part of the story. A detailed evocation of a neighbourhood milieu ('the nest') – done with great affection but also with a fine critical perceptiveness – enables Raabe in each novel to dwell on the childhood of the main characters; enables him to show the decisive importance for the rest of their lives of the roles which the children assume, and to dwell on the lasting importance of the alliances and exclusions of childhood – and childhood ends with the moment of dispersal, the great voyage to far-off lands, the act of violence. There are similarities of narrative pattern here, embodying not a raw and ready-made scheme, but a broad and lyrical sense of life.

A group of children swinging high up in the branches of an Italian hazelnut tree; another group, fighting in the dusty bushes by the roadside; two boys and a girl, sitting on a bench at the edge of a wood, looking down on the town in the valley below . . .: what will become of them, where will their 'fate' – that which guides them from within, as well as that which prods or pushes or drives them from without – where will the spirit lead them? However small and intimate the company, one of them will always be the odd man out: the one who will travel to foreign lands and return, a self-made man, to bury his ambitions and at long last rediscover the life that was there, ready for the taking, before he ever set out, a second who will stay behind (being fat and somewhat unsteady on his pins), and do his good deed and live his good life a stone's throw from his birthplace; and a third who will travel round the world, return and despair. These are the central characters and indeed (they are not lacking in the proper attributes) heroes of Raabe's later fiction. What distinguishes them from their playmates and less than loyal friends seems to be a mere quirk: a fatal inability to 'take life as it is' and howl with the wolves, to acquiesce in the expediency and callousness which all around them acknowledge as 'the realities of life'. They will not accept accommodation – metaphorically, and often literally; what distinguishes them, in short, is the vulnerable heart. Will it lead them into disaster or serene contentment? Childhood here is the seedbox of life: a time not of idyll only but also of decisions made and resolutions taken, when the tasks of a life-time are chosen. The novels open when the childhood friends meet again, 'many years later', interrupting each other's tale with many a wistful 'Do you remember . . .?', yet the occasion is for the drawing up of accounts rather than for sentimentality; and in the course of the tale unexpectedly sharp moral judgements push through the gently ironical texture of the narrative.

Die Akten des Vogelsangs opens in a wholly conventional way. The narrator, an affectionate paterfamilias and distinguished senior official in the legal branch of the civil service ('Oberregierungsrat Dr jur. Karl Krumhardt'), receives a letter from a childhood friend, 'Helene Trotzendorff, widow Mungo', containing news of the death of Valentin Andres, known to Krumhardt and all his other friends of the Birdsong District as Velten; the story of his life will be retraced in the '*acta*' that follow. (Raabe, like Dickens, chooses his names for their meaningful associations: the woman's for defiance, the hero's for 'otherness', the narrator's for his stalwart 'bürgerlich' respectability.) Krumhardt's elaborate and often curiously formal recollection of their common past centres on the story of Velten's love for Helene (or Ellen, as she is known in her American incarnation). It is the passion of a life-time; yet Velten's relationship with Krumhardt (and all that he so explicitly stands for) is hardly less important.

Both Velten and Helene were fatherless and poor, which is the first and most obvious reason why Velten protected the fiery little girl who, with her mother, arrived one day from America to disturb the philistine peace of the Birdsong District. Velten's mother is the widow of an impecunious doctor, Ellen's mother is waiting for the day when her husband, who sent her 'back home to Germany' penniless, will come 'with his million' to take her 'back home to New York'. Of Mr Charley Trotzendorff and the great world in which he has his ups and downs we see very little, but clearly it is the exciting world of the 'fast buck', the very opposite of the sleepy and conventional German provincial capital. The fierce pride, independence of mind and defiance of conventions which bring the two children together are also the qualities that keep them apart. Velten follows Krumhardt to Berlin where he fails to get a degree, follows Ellen to New York where he fails to prevent her marrying one of her father's rich business associates, and finally returns to Germany: first to the Birdsong District to bury his mother, then to his old Berlin lodgings to die. Failure, begotten of a self-destructive humour, accompanies his every move and isolates him from all his friends, even in the last resort from Karl Krumhardt, who says of him, 'There was nothing in his life that I was in the dark about – except himself.' And the reader may feel that Raabe too doesn't fully understand his Velten, and is obliged to leave the outline of his character opaque; that there is in his presentation of this estranged hero an element of unclarity or mystification.

Raabe's compositional problem is given with his choice of Karl Krumhardt as the narrator, and with his decision to confine the story to Krumhardt's point of view. Velten has much of the Outsider of modern existentialist literature; Raabe himself, through his narrator, acknowledges in him something of Faust's demonic restlessness and barely concealed contempt for the certainties and values of bourgeois life. Yet he is presented through the eyes and the judicious and juridical pen of one who shares, indeed embodies, the values of the society from which Velten is excluded. Karl Krumhardt (one thinks of him as Wagner to Velten's Faust) is a sympathetic and affectionate narrator and friend, yet he cannot express

the full grounds of Velten's exclusion, the full reason for his alienation, if only because in writing about his life-long friend he is at
the same time defending himself against the lure, the fascination of
Velten's existence: 'My reason for having dragged him into the
world', Krumhardt quotes from Lessing, 'is that I didn't want to
live with him under one roof any longer.' It is not that Velten makes
demands upon his friends who then fail him – he is too shy and too
proud for that. Like Hamlet, or for that matter Faust, he has many
talents yet no clearly identifiable creative gifts, and yet again, he has
the aloofness and strange charm of genius. The reason why Krumhardt doesn't in the last resort know 'what to make of him' is the
same as the reason why Raabe cannot round him out to the last
secret of his lost soul. Velten lives, or rather *is*, the negation of the
'bürgerlich' life around him, and of almost everything it stands for.

Almost everything, for Velten fits no preconceived 'nihilistic'
pattern, his is not a radical (let alone a doctrinaire) negation. If he
is a nihilist, he is a gentle, good-humoured one. He believes in
loyalty and friendship; he is a devoted son and, once he has failed
to win Helene (or, as he puts it, 'to rescue her from Yggdrasil, the
tree of life'), he gives his love to his mother, making at least her death
less lonely than her life had been; and with Helene too, we gather,
he shared a few weeks – or was it only days? – of intimacy and
passionate love. But none of these ties endures, none of these feelings
thaws the solitude that freezes his soul. How does one embody a
negation? Hölderlin had invoked a man's property – 'mein Eigentum' (see below p. 210): *quae mihi propria sunt* – as the essential
condition of man's accommodation and rooting on this earth and in
this world. Kafka will sadly comment on the pun on '*sein*', which
divides its meaning between the ontological verb and the possessive
pronoun, between being and having. And Raabe portrays a man
who wilfully rids himself of all that the world (his world and ours)
regards as the necessary condition of worldliness and humanity alike
– a man, at the last, without property.

Raabe's novels are studded with quotations,[4] overt and concealed,
from the poets and philosophers and the Bible, from Shakespeare,
Montaigne, and a host of German writers. In *Die Akten* the beginning
of the young Goethe's third ode to Behrisch, 'Sei gefühllos!/Ein
leichtbewegtes Herz/Ist ein elend Gut/Auf der wankenden Erde'

('Be unfeeling!/A heart easily moved/Is but a wretched thing to own/On this inconstant earth'), is repeatedly quoted (Raabe is not one for subtle effects) to describe that condition between worldly wisdom, invulnerability and callousness which Velten aspires to in vain. But among the countless quotations of Raabe's last novels his favourite is one that we too have often relied on in these pages, St Matthew's 'Consider the lilies of the field . . .', with its serene refutation of all care and worldly foresight. However, the faith which the Gospel recommends as an alternative to the troubled *cura rerum* ('for your heavenly father knows that ye have need . . .') is transformed in Raabe's fiction – not, indeed, into the mercantile ethos of the Buddenbrooks with its perfunctory *'Dominus providebit'* – but into a wholly private and subjective belief founded in authentic feeling, in 'Treuherzigkeit'. In *Der Stopfkuchen* this inexpedient faith leads to happiness and contentment, with worldly goods and animal comforts thrown in as an unsought-for reward. But even when – as in *Die Akten* – it leads to disaster, the value of this faith, of the vulnerable heart from which it springs, is left unimpaired.

For Velten (as for Heinrich Schaumann, hero of *Der Stopfkuchen*) the exercise of this virtue is not a matter of choice. The self-destructive compulsion that has taken Velten round the world and, his purpose in life unaccomplished, to his death, is a foolish thing in the eyes of 'bürgerlich' society, obscure even, in the last resort, to Karl Krumhardt, that society's most sympathetic spokesman. Only the women – creatures of instinct rather than foresight, albeit of a life-preserving instinct – understand Velten: his mother and his remarkable Berlin landlady, Helene and Léonie (sister of his university friend Léon des Beaux), and Anna, Karl Krumhardt's wife – in their imaginative understanding these women are all on his, Velten's, side. (And these are the moments in the narrative when it touches, almost unawares it would seem, on the story of Christ.) Yet while the women have a very special sympathy for his vulnerability and strange unworldliness, they don't, for their own part, acquiesce in it. They sense the danger, the threat even, to any kind of settled life, above all to family life, which Velten represents. Here again a thread of the Faustian experience is woven into the fabric of Velten's existence. Two aspects of Eros govern it: woman in her sexual rôle drives him out into the world; woman in her motherly rôle offers him the comfort of an intuitive understanding, and a last place of rest.

But do *we* understand? The nature of Velten's genius, like the nature of the negation that is his life, is intimated rather than fully explored. Raabe ignores what in our own day would be the two most obvious means of illuminating his singularity: the social milieu which Velten rejects is not satirised, nor is he presented as a pathological case* – there is a homeliness about Raabe's style which excludes such radical solutions. The suggestion that Velten is 'too good for this wicked world' is made, but only faintly, for the world depicted is at worst obtuse rather than wicked, while Anna Krumhardt's anxiety lest 'her' Karl's admiration of Velten should estrange him from his family, is presented with only a few ironical undertones. What then is there to explain Velten's alienation?

The problem Raabe's narrative poses is related to the 'problem of Hamlet' as T. S. Eliot outlined it, though it receives a different answer. It may well be that Raabe wasn't fully aware of the difficulty his readers would have in trying to tie causes to effects, in accepting his motivation as convincing. The figure of Velten belongs to a kind of German fiction – one may almost speak of a literary convention – which, from the seventeenth century to Thomas Mann's *Doktor Faustus* (1947) and beyond, has given a special place to the Stranger, the 'unaccommodated man'.[5] It is a fiction which has never accepted the truism that man is a political or at all events a social animal, and whose major contribution to world literature has been the exploration of solitude,[6] itself a condition in which the causal ties of social life are strained or broken. In their portrayals of the Outsider, German writers have been fascinated by experiments with causality, finding it easy to dispense with what the convention of European realism has taught its readers to regard as adequate grounds for character motivation. In the wake of the Enlightenment, and often as a protest against its 'cause-mongering', they turned to Laurence Sterne for a literary inspiration which no English writer ever found in him. The literary convention in defiance of the social convention which now arose includes K. P. Moritz, Jung Stilling, Jean Paul, E. T. A. Hoffmann, Büchner and the early Stifter among Raabe's predecessors. Their characteristic writings testify with some explicitness to the disconcerting fact that conceptions of

* A mixture of these two strands of motivation is used in Thomas Mann's *Doktor Faustus*, whose remarkable affinities with Raabe's *Akten* are discussed below, p. 161.

causality change, that adequacy in the motivation of literary characters is after all a matter of historical and cultural determination. However, the literary convention defies the social convention by implication only: 'the Strangers' of German literature are not identical with 'the Underground Man' of realistic fiction⁷ – Dostoevsky's admiration for E. T. A. Hoffmann (which would suggest a close literary kinship) is a fruitful misunderstanding. The figure of the mysterious 'Underground Man' speaks to us as a comment – often a revolutionary comment – on the tragic condition of a section of nineteenth-century society; both the material and the spiritual grounds of his alienation are presented with equal seriousness. The Stranger of German fiction on the other hand, embodied in the eerie half-fiction of Kaspar Hauser, is wholly unrevolutionary. He is intended as a comment on the human condition irrespective of its specific circumstances, the ultimate grounds of his alienation remain as mysterious as human existence itself. Yet – here again is the riddle Stifter attempted to solve – how can fiction present 'the human condition irrespective of its specific circumstances'?

Raabe has no taste for Stifter's ontological simplicities (see above, p. 111). He is enough of a realist to want to present *some* grounds for his hero's estrangement from the world, implying at the same time that they aren't the full grounds, that there is a mystery which he, secure behind the persona of Karl Krumhardt, his narrator, does not propose to probe. In any event, what are the *full* grounds – when is motivation adequate? Does it come as readily to us as it did to his readers to measure adequacy in accordance with the nineteenth-century realistic convention? Can we disregard the fact that conceptions of causality change; that to live in another age means, among other things, to measure differently; that realism itself is not a static but a perennial, and therefore perennially changing, mode of writing? (What would Raabe have made of Vladimir and Estragon? And yet, are they not kith and kin to Velten Andres?)

Yet it isn't simply a matter of concluding that Raabe's feeling for what is or is not adequate motivation is different from ours. To say this and no more than this would be to disregard the major creative effort – a matter of straightforward realism – that he lavishes on his 'bürgerlich' interiors and reassuring landscapes, on the material and spiritual comfort of his settings; it would also make our own notions of motivation more stable and Victorian than they really are. The truth is more complex on both sides. Raabe *is* aware of the conflict between Biedermeier and alienation and the compositional problems it sets him, even if he doesn't fully solve them (hence Krumhardt's frequent avowals of his own narrative incompetence); while we for our part have recently had to learn to use new and more unsettling standards of motivation than those which the realists of Raabe's age have bequeathed to us. *Die Akten*, more than any other of Raabe's novels, is a work in which a strange new existential attitude is encompassed, albeit uneasily, by an old setting: a novel which is peculiarly behind its own times, and peculiarly relevant to ours. The situation is similar to that in which we dovetailed and contrasted Stifter's quest with Roquentin's. Velten anticipates the modern Outsider, yet the world in which he asserts his singularity has nothing of the cold indifference and implacable hostility which engulf the Outsider in the writings of Kafka, Sartre or Camus. What Velten possesses – or rather, is possessed by – is a new existential freedom: a bleak freedom which, even in *that* social situation, must manifest itself in negation, in the *acte gratuit*. If there is a last opaqueness, it is at one with the strange charm of the modern tragic hero in his self-imposed yet inescapable isolation.

The placid surfaces of Raabe's last novels, I suggested earlier (see above, p. 145), are disturbed by a moment of violence or destruction, which acts as a catalyst for the 'bürgerlich' emotions and values. In *Der Schüdderump* (1870), it was the adolescent hero's heedless rush into the woods, giving a brief taste of freedom and no more. In *Alte Nester* (*Old Nests*, 1880) another Velten goes out into the world to earn the big money that will enable him to reinstate his childhood companion in her old family mansion, only to find the house they treasured in their common memories in rack and ruin; and on their walk through its horrifying, hideous desolation they discover the full truth of their feeling for each other. In *Unruhige Gäste* (*Unquiet Guests*, 1880) it is the typhoid-stricken paupers' hut that brings two people together in a common care for its inhabitants, only to let them go their separate ways once the shared moment of danger and death has passed. *Der Stopfkuchen* (like *Horacker*, 1876) is built round a murder, or rather the false suspicion of murder, that affects the lives of the novel's main characters. A detective story, a nostalgic recollection of a common childhood past and of many other aeons of time, and a tale in praise of the vulnerable heart, are all tied together by a set of narrative devices which I find too elaborate and too mannered[8] – and again it is the violent act that throws into relief the values at stake and the characters' tenacity in asserting them. However, it is in *Die Akten* that the catalyst works most effectively (and most strangely), for it is here that the violent act challenges all that the age itself holds most dear.

The Vogelsang district, now rebuilt beyond recognition, does little to welcome Velten Andres when he returns to it from America, to bury his mother. True, he has achieved the kind of success that 'the District' and its worthies, now scattered all over the town, expect of one whom, somewhat grudgingly, they regard as their own. We gather that he has made a good deal of money – enough for an independent existence, at all events – and 'the Town' expects him to put it to some use: to engage in some commercial enterprise that would at last *involve* him, involve him in other men's affairs and concerns. Needless to say, Velten disappoints them. The money – which turns out to be quite literally the proverbial walletful of dollars – means nothing to him, changes nothing, counts for nothing in his life. He re-establishes contact with Karl, there are a few walks and a few discussions in Velten's house – but again, this link of friendship means little, next to nothing. Like a man afflicted by some contagion, or as in some strange ceremony of self-immolation, Velten is isolated – or isolates himself – from the rest of the world by a void, a circle of solitude which not even Karl can effectively penetrate. Indeed, Karl tries; dutifully, he expresses concern for Velten's future:

'Beruhige dich und alle, die Interesse daran nehmen, in dieser Hinsicht völlig. Grade nicht hier am Ort, doch habe ich grade am Ort hier die schönste Gelegenheit, sie noch sicherer zu stellen, ich erwarte nur noch das erste Ofenfeuer dazu.'

'Das erste Ofenfeuer?'

'Mir ist niemals ein Winter zu meinem Fortkommen im Leben mehr zupaß gekommen, als wie der diesjährige. Jawohl, demnächst heizen wir, Krumhardt.' –

Ja, und er ist so gut wie sein Wort gewesen. Als das Wetterglas seines Vaters nach Réaumur unter zwölf Grad in der Wohnstube seiner Eltern sank, fing er an zu heizen, und zwar mit seinem Erbteil am und vom Vogelsang. Er heizte mit seinem Hausrat.

'You and all who take an interest in it [Velten replies] can set
your minds at rest about it. I'm not planning to settle in this place,
but the place gives me the best opportunity to lay my plans
securely. I'm only waiting for the first day when I can light the
stove.'

'Light the stove?'

'There's never been a winter more auspicious for my future
progress in life than this year's. Indeed, Krumhardt, we'll soon
be stoking up.'

Well, and he was as good as his word. When his father's
barometer in his parents' front parlour sank below twelve degrees
Réaumur, he began to make up the fire in his stove – with his
Vogelsang patrimony. And with his household goods he kept the
stove going.

'. . . mit seinem Hausrat': the word had, even for Faust, a solemnity, the connotations of a *pietas*, and it is through the ruins of his
worldly goods that Velten will make his exit. The familiar furniture,
encrusted with the marks of a lifetime's daily use; the trinkets and
mementoes of a lost past; the very doors and doorposts, gates and
fences and window-frames of the family house – amidst the chorus of
scandalised neighbours, Velten feeds the bric-à-brac of generations
to the flames, 'day after day during that hard winter', until only the
odd beam and architrave are left for the paupers to drag away. Then
the last house of the old Vogelsang district is gone.

What meaning are we to give to this holocaust? Velten's self-
dispossession is the penultimate act in defence of the vulnerable
heart. (And his death, that has no other cause than 'tiredness, a
boundless tiredness', that is, a defective will to live, follows soon
after.) Furthermore, the act is also (not indeed the Gospel's but) the
gentle nihilist's way of showing up the vanity of King Solomon and
his raiment in all its glory. But finally, the fact that Velten, at other
times a generous man, can't bear to give away, even to the poor,
anything that has the marks of his living existence on it, also
throws annihilating doubt on the value of the comforts of people who
are a good deal humbler, and a good deal more needy, than the
famed Hebrew king. And this is the meaning of the act on which,
after some hesitation, the novel will close. Again, one might expect
Raabe to sharpen the meaning of the act by underscoring its Biblical

parallel. Are we to see Velten as 'the young man . . . who had great possessions' and who, on being told to 'go and sell all that thou hast', obeyed? But who, in that interpretation, is there that said, 'come and follow me'?

Even now, during his last days in 'the District', Velten's solitude is not absolute, there is always Karl Krumhardt. 'During the day I really couldn't spare the time from the office', Karl tells us, for he has to attend to all the quarrels over property and goods and chattels which are a lawyer's daily work. Only in the evening does he call on his friend:

> Ich konnte ihm bei meinem Eintritt weiter nichts sagen als:
> 'Es ist unheimlich warm bei dir, Velten!'

> On entering his house, all that I could say was, 'It's uncannily warm in here, Velten!'

But Velten corrects him:

> 'Gemütlich! . . . Deutsch-gemütlich, was? Ihr habt ja den Ausdruck, macht Anspruch drauf, ihn in der Welt allein zu haben, also bleib auch du ganz ruhig bei ihm, Krumhardt.'

> 'Gemütlich! . . . Deutsch-gemütlich, isn't it? Why, it's *your* expression, isn't it? It's *you* [Germans] who claim it as yours and yours alone in the whole wide world – so you may as well stick to the word, Krumhardt. . . .'

This is the nearest we get to an explicit awareness of what the conflagration means (which is little enough for a novelist who at other times is not exactly taciturn); the rest we must puzzle out for ourselves.

Like the thick red line that Hanno Buddenbrook rules under his name in the family bible, Velten's act and fate sets an end to a mode of life, and casts up the final account for a set of values; Velten confides his feeling through another quotation from Goethe:

> Hier ist der Abschluß! Alles ist getan,
> Und nichts kann mehr geschehn! Das Land, das Meer,
> Das Reich, die Kirche, das Gericht, das Heer,
> Sie sind verschwunden, alles ist nicht mehr.

> Here is conclusion. All is now done,
> And nothing more can happen. Land and sea,
> Empire, Church, the Law, and might of arms
> Are now no more. All, all are gone.[9]

Do we understand what has led to this end? Not, certainly, in terms of nineteenth-century realistic fiction. In *those* terms, in that literary and living practice, what Velten is doing is an outrageous piece of wilfulness, sheer madness. 'Du hast sie zerstört, die schöne Welt', the spirits call in anguish to Faust: the metaphysical assurance founded in material possessions, the ethical tie-up between property and propriety, retraced in the realists' practice of shoring up things (realism comes from *res*) against the flux of time and against their destruction through oblivion – these are the household gods of the age, these Velten has destroyed. (And Raabe is probably innocent of the kind of literary selfconsciousness that would make of the holocaust a symbol of the realist's predicament in an alienated world.) But in the supremely exacting and at times self-destructive mode of literature of the subsequent age, whose values will be created from the débris of bourgeois culture, whose affirmations will be as distant and as improbable of attainment as the creative ingenuity of its authors can make them,[10] and whose only freedom will be the bleak freedom of the gratuitous deed (since every other deed is tainted with the false comforts of expediency and worthless purpose) – in *that* mode and in *that* age it will make for a sense we understand and are familiar with.

Yet this is not Raabe's last word (nor would it be right to place *Die Akten* too near the centre of Raabe's work).* His evaluation of Velten's act and life places them on the margins of the social world to which he commits his narratives. Velten is more than a mere oddity, and yet he doesn't carry the whole meaning of the novel. His act is shown as an act of personal, existential freedom, a value inside a negation that leaves the rest of the world unharmed. Karl Krumhardt's respectability is not ridiculous, nor are we allowed to identify his wife Anna's anxious concern for the family with that hen-like consciousness which goes under the cliché of 'Kinder, Kirche, Küche', the three holy Ks of Wilhelminian domesticity.

---

* I take Barker Fairley's hint (op. cit., 251) without fully accepting his view that the book is an exception in Raabe's œuvre.

True enough, life goes on. And to that life – Anna and Karl Krumhardt's and their children's life – the singularity asserted in Velten's existence (the value inside the negation) must remain an alien threat, a mode of experience intuitively understood and pitied, and rejected. But the strength of the family ethos that rejects it is not an insensitive strength – not yet, we are tempted to say, with half an eye on Thomas Mann's Buddenbrooks.

A comparison with *Doktor Faustus* may help to show more clearly what divides us from the world of Raabe's masterpieces. Thomas Mann too entrusts his story to a scholarly, slightly pedantic paterfamilias: owing to this device (the centre at rest in a perilous world) the two novels have a similarity of structure that is one of the puzzles of literary history,[11] Serenus Zeitblom, like Raabe's Karl Krumhardt, is tied to his hero by bonds of a less than fully perceptive friendship. Zeitblom too understands only imperfectly the demon that drives his friend into isolation, and he too intimates a fuller understanding through occasional obtuseness alternating with deep wonder. Adrian Leverkühn, like Raabe's Velten Andres, derives a temporary peace of mind from the intuitive sympathy of women. Where the precise nature of Velten's gifts could be left unspecified, there Leverkühn's musical genius provides the novelist with a new dimension of meaning. Leverkühn too breaks out of the confines of humble middle-class existence by an *acte gratuit* – the pact with the devil; and what he purchases, over and above Velten's bleak freedom, is a renewal of his musical inspiration. The world from which Leverkühn isolates himself by his self-destructive act is not the placid scene of Wilhelminian materialism but the radical evil of National Socialist Germany (to which Zeitblom is prepared to accommodate for worse reasons than those Krumhardt lists to excuse *his* compromise). Yet Leverkühn's icy solitude has more than a private meaning. It is the condition in which alone his musical gifts can flourish, yet by means of these gifts he is able to re-enact 'the life of the Will in the language of music' (as Schopenhauer would put it): born of his solitude, Leverkühn's music pierces it and creates a commentary on the horrors and depravities of contemporary Germany. Both the negation (that is Leverkühn's life) and the value inside the negation (that is his art) belong to another age.

It is the work of Fontane, his own contemporary, that provides a

L

less glaring contrast with Raabe's undertaking. Both draw on the conflict between the values of the heart and the virtues of privacy on the one hand, and the public values of decorum and service on the other. The charm of institutions and the conflicts of public office, on which Fontane lavishes his finest stylistic gifts, have little meaning for Raabe. Since the social and worldly dimension of his work has little of the intricacy and complex richness of Fontane's milieux, he is apt to slant such contrasts toward the private sphere of experience, and it is in that sphere alone that the values are tested. With Raabe's domestic interiors goes a greater emphasis on *Stimmung* (achieved at some expense of plot and action, above all of control over the stylistic detail): Velten is both a character and the embodiment of a mood, a stranger who yet lives on the margins of the homely and familiar. There is here an incompleteness of motivation and hence of narrative structure as the realists understood the terms, which we don't find in Fontane. But then, he never attempted that glimpse of the Absurd which we get from the tranquil setting of *Die Akten des Vogelsangs*.

EIGHT

Theodor Fontane:
The Realism of Assessment

With Theodor Fontane (1819–1898) nineteenth-century German literature fully enters the tradition of European realism, not a moment too soon. His major novels are written at a time when that tradition is about to be superseded by the experimental schools of French and German naturalism, in whose prose works the focus shifts from integrated scenes of social life to blow-ups of discrete, often discontinuous details.

The son of a Gascon Huguenot father and a Cévenoise mother, Fontane was born and bred on the North Sea coast of Prussia. No writer ever took the grades to Parnassus more circumspectly and with more deliberation. In 1850, aged thirty, Fontane gave up both a reasonably good job as pharmaceutical dispenser and his liberal opinions, and accepted a post in the press office of the Prussian government, taking over its shortlived London correspondence in 1855, and resigning his agency in 1858. There now followed a chequered career of journalistic, literary and educational ventures. As correspondent of various mainly reactionary Berlin papers, including the notorious *Kreuzzeitung*, Fontane made a name for himself with reports from the War of Schleswig-Holstein of 1864, the Austrian Campaign of 1866, and the Franco-Prussian War (in the course of which he was arrested as a spy and spent a short time as prisoner of war on the Ile d'Oléron). Throughout the '50s and '60s he had received various government grants for work on historical studies in Mark Brandenburg, and in 1876 he accepted the secretary-ship of the Prussian Royal Academy of Arts. The promised sinecure turned out to be an imposition and, against strong protests from

wife and family, he again resigned. By this time he had published
two war books, four volumes of travels in Mark Brandenburg full of
picturesque local history, a slim volume of ballads inspired by Sir
Walter Scott, a volume of impressions of London (the outcome of
three long visits as a correspondent). There is a good deal of charm
and wry humour in these descriptive books but, like Dickens's
American Notes and Henry James's *A Little Tour of France*, they are
approaches to literature rather than the thing itself.

At the age of fifty-six – the lateness is without parallel among great
writers – he took the last step towards his art. The bits and pieces of
a lifetime – the realist's *bricolage* – fell into place. Commercial
experience, service in the army and the Prussian bureaucracy,
landed *Junkers* and ironical generals, small shopkeepers, Protestant
parsons and Catholic *dévots*, conservative *von und zu*'s and progressive
schoolmasters; a few dogs and elegant Englishmen and picturesque
Austrians in the margin; marriages and divorces, bankruptcies and
get-rich-quick schemes, duels and illnesses and the gentle sloping of
life towards death. . . . He 'knew it all inside out', it was all merely
waiting for him to set it down. At his death, twenty-two years later,
he could look back on a harvest of seventeen novels and Novellen
(and a number of short stories) at least half of them major achievements, and confess that he had 'accomplished what I had been
destined for from the beginning'. And when a friend wrote that
'perhaps you could have done better if you hadn't been kept
back by perpetual "hard struggling"', Fontane replied, 'All that
business about "struggling" is superficially true. But even if I'd had
to struggle less [*wenn ich weniger gestruggelt hätte*], I wouldn't have
achieved more. The little that was in me came out in that way too.
I've no complaint against my fate.' The understatement is characteristic of Fontane; one can't think of many German writers, past or
present, who would have made it as unaffectedly.

For of course Fontane *is* a German novelist. Intellectual bad
manners, especially nationalistic ones, have a tenacious life. Among
some German academic critics of the older generation Fontane is
still regarded as something of an alien intruder (see his family background). His favourite genre, the *Gesellschaftsroman*, the novel of
good society, is in their eyes too frivolous and worldly, too 'French',
to deserve serious scholarly attention; and his achievement is seen as

the end-product of a spent tradition. These disparagements throw more light into the oubliettes of the arbiters of yesterday than they do on a writer whose achievement is only now being made available to the English-speaking public by a faithful and sympathetic translator.[1] Fontane may be a late-comer in European terms, in German literature he is above all an innovator. His narrative work contains strands of a specifically German literary tradition, but these are integrated into an overall conception of the historical and social novel which is cosmopolitan in its outlook and in its very structure indifferent to national jealousies. He has learned a great deal from Sir Walter Scott, Thackeray, and Dickens; from Balzac, and probably also from Flaubert; he is fully alive to his contemporaries Ibsen and Zola – he is, in other words, a European novelist. And as such he creates a locale as specific and unmistakable as Dickens's London, Flaubert's Paris, Tolstoy's Moscow, Jan Neruda's Prague or Eça de Queiros's Lisbon: he is *the* novelist of the Berlin, Prussia and Germany of the Second Reich 'as it really happened'. The notion that these twin aspects of Fontane's art – its international connection and its stable local setting – are somehow incompatible could occur only to those who believed that the Wilhelminians lived on the moon or in Never-Neverland (as some of his and our contemporaries appear to do). The whole scale of milieux from the lower middle class to the *Junkers* and the courtly entourage of Berlin – the working classes are on the whole outside Fontane's range – has such a fascination for him that occasionally he contents himself with presenting milieux almost as the substance of a story, as a five-finger exercise on an instrument which he plays with an unparalleled virtuosity and assurance. One such story[2] offers him an occasion for summing up the complicated relationship between Germany and 'the West' to which, twenty-odd years later, his heir Thomas Mann devoted a long and far from exhilarating book.[3] There are many such detachable passages in Fontane, yet his fiction is unselfconscious, and the context in which they are placed tends to dissolve them, once stated, in the medium of extended conversations – and the wealth and variety of his kinds of conversation has only recently been fully appreciated.[4] The tolerantly-ironical yet incisive tone of such passages is characteristic of his art.

The observation (it will be remembered, see p. 13 above) states the contrast between the man who 'can take life as it really is, . . .

what nowadays they call a realist' and the illusionist who 'simply can't exist without a fata morgana with palms and odalisques and all that sort of thing'. But is the statement really relevant to the Germany of Fontane's day? Are we not quoting out of context, which (in this story) is the impoverishment and decline of a minor aristocratic family? After all, what Fontane depicts is the Germany of the heirs of Bismarck, of the *Junkertum* and 'Kaiser Willem der Zwote', of the 'Pickelhaube' and 'Reichsadler' and the Prussian civil service; lobster-and-Vouvray at Kempinski's; the Krupps and Ballins . . . Who is there, in this rich and assertive society, who 'hasn't anything, and who has to live in a Sahara desert'?

It is Thomas Mann's *Buddenbrooks* (1901) that explicitly takes issue with the contradiction characteristic of the German *fin de siècle*, the contradiction between a growing material enrichment and a growing spiritual discontent and alienation from the materialistic civilisation of the age. Mann resolves it, with narrative means of a radically ironic kind, by placing the contradiction firmly in the centre of his stage. Fontane's irony is much gentler, more tolerant, his novels are structured less antithetically. He senses and intimates the velleities of his contemporary world, but he is too deeply involved in that world, he cares for it too much and too directly, to become a 'good' prophet of the bad. In their métier, at all events, the great realistic novelists are on the whole indifferent prophets. The prophecies of doom they must leave to the philosophers. For prophecy implies the possibility of an alternative interpretation of experience, and thus a detachment from the encompassing reality of the world; whereas realism is founded in a creative acknowledgement of social reality, an assent (however critical) to the world, not as an interpretation at all but as the one and only bedrock certainty there is. The philosopher, interested as he is in the interpretability of the world, offers alternative points of view, moral or metaphysical. No sooner does Nietzsche praise 'our present delight in the Real' (the basis of Fontane's work), welcoming it as a reaction against 'our old delight in the Unreal, which we have indulged in for so long and to excess', than he proceeds to question 'our problematic lack of discrimination and finesse in respect of that Real'.[5] What Nietzsche criticises is not an inadequate moral (let alone ethical) discrimination but a crudely self-assured – that is a philistine – epistemological and existential attitude. Moving further and further away from proposals for a reform of existing contemporary reality, or rather, caring less and less for the 'realism' of such proposals, Nietzsche is increasingly committed to another, a new kind of reality altogether, the realm of the Superman: a realm (passionately invoked but speculative and spectral for all that) which the realistic *romanciers* may not enter.

Fontane too is critical of contemporary vulgarities, material and spiritual alike. But the alternative values he intimates are as firmly embedded in the encompassing 'Real' as are the vulgarities of fanaticism, intolerance and bad taste. He has an innate sympathy for those who 'cannot exist without a fata morgana'; on the bio-graphical level, his uneasy and restless search for the right job, the right environment, bears this out. Those of his characters who experience this need – they are varied and come from all the walks of life he presents – tend to live on the ineffectual margins of society. But they are not Veltens, nor the 'alienated outsiders' of existentialist literature. Their morality is in several ways different from the morality of the people nearer the centre of society, their lives are above all more private. But after all, that inner circle too, with its notoriously cold and often inhuman ethos of the Prussian imperative, is upheld by living people – that is, by people full of private doubts and mental reservations under their self-imposed discipline. The centre itself, the centre of power where 'historic' decisions are made, Fontane doesn't depict (nor does he construct a theory that offers an alternative account of the course of history, as Tolstoy did in the last chapters of *War and Peace*). But the people *near* the centre of power as Fontane presents them are not without a secret sympathy with those whom it is their rôle to govern and quite generally keep on a short rein – the fata-morganists of all kinds.

Fontane has been accused of snobbery in the choice of his milieux; of siding with the aristocracy against the common people; and of depicting the latter only in their comic or sentimental aspect. It is certainly true that he has no eye for the economic plight of the proletariat, for what the naturalists called 'the Social Problem'. As to the lower middle classes, their representatives tend to become comic when they move out of their proper sphere, into the ambience of political radicals and rabble-rousing reforms. Yet the heroine of *Irrungen, Wirrungen* (*Trials and Tribulations*, 1888), a working girl living in the most modest circumstances, possesses an honesty and intensity of emotion which are not matched by her aristocratic lover. The strength and beauty of her character lie in her capacity not to allow the inevitable parting to impair the quality of the love that precedes it. Lene's renunciation of Botho involves suffering but no disillusionment, because it has been anticipated and accepted throughout the affair. Her acknowledgement of the ways of the world implies no conformism on Fontane's part. His judgement on Botho, the dashing young officer who dutifully leaves Lene and marries into 'family' and money, is as subtle and unemphatic as is the rest of the story. The wife Botho eventually marries is pretty and charming, and . . . :

Und nun umspannte er ihre Taille und hob sie hoch in die Höh'. 'Käthe, Puppe, liebe Puppe.'
'Puppe, liebe Puppe', das sollt' ich eigentlich übelnehmen, Botho. Denn mit Puppen spielt man. Aber ich nehm' es nicht übel, im Gegenteil. Puppen werden am meisten geliebt und am besten behandelt. Und darauf kommt es mir an.'

And he clasped his hands round her waist and lifted her high into the air: 'Kate, my doll, my dear doll,' he said. 'My dear doll . . . [she replies] I should really resent being called that, Botho. Dolls are for playing with. But I don't resent it. On the contrary. Dolls get most love, and the best treatment. And that's what matters to me.'

whereas Lene marries one Gideon Francke, a somewhat solemn foreman in a metal-factory (visiting in top-hat, black gloves and all) and a lay preacher of the Pietist persuasion. A figure of fun? Not quite. In an interview with Botho, whom he has come to question about Lene's past, Francke turns out to be a man of the utmost tolerance, honesty, seriousness, and loving concern. The comic aspect of the man is not hidden: 'Ja, Herr Baron, auf die Proppertät kommt es an und auf die Honnetität kommt es an, und auf die Reelität' ('You see, sir, what really matters is decency and honesty, sir, and reliability!'), nor is the fact that he has gone a long way for his convictions: 'I was over in the States for a good while. And even though not everything over there is pure gold, no more than here, *one* thing *is* true: you learn to look at things differently, not always through the same spectacles.' It is not Gideon Francke who is the fool at this interview.

Fontane knows that the 'good society' from which his novels are drawn is, if not doomed, yet certainly ill-equipped for survival. He knows that its notion of a man's 'proper place in life' is upheld by an outdated ethos, and that social changes, involving the demise of the old families, are in the air: 'I'm becoming more and more democratic [he writes in a letter, 29 January 1894], and the real nobility is just about the only clan left that I can still value and appreciate. All that lies between and betwixt – *Spiessbürger*, *bourgeois*, officials, the so-called 'cultured' classes – gives me little joy.' His fastidious dislike of ostentation, pretentiousness, and of great fortunes new or old, goes hand in hand with a very special affection for the paternal benevolence, frugality and quixotic innocence of the *Junkers* of the old, that is the Frederician, school. They are to him quite the most picturesque and absorbing figures on the social scene, and thus the proper objects of his creative attention. Twenty years before he set out on his literary career, Fontane confessed to a friend (in a letter from London, 25 April 1856) that 'my occupation with politics is, after all, only literary', yet in the same breath he criticised 'our habit of over-estimating *art* at the expense of *life*'. Scornful of the self-importance of the politicking *littérateur*, he at the same time questions the ethos of *l'art pour l'art*: the remark is characteristic of his freedom from every fanaticism, political or aesthetic. I have quoted it to offer reassurance to our democratic sensibilities: more important than Fontane's partisanship of the landed gentry is his informed and critical interest in their reactions to the process of social change.

Fontane depicts the reality that is, and its antecedents in the recent past, not the utopia that might or should be. His love of anecdote, in the service of that past, makes him occasionally err on the side of prolixity. His narrative mode is social, which means that in his treatment of intimate situations he preserves an unprobing decorum. An adulterous affair is in progress, but the author has left the pine forest by the sand dunes where it began.[6] Or again: an elderly man, Count and Privy Councillor, has entered a village church, to view the body of his only son, killed in a futile sortie.[7] Only an old sexton is his guide in the darkening church:

Anfangs schien es, daß sie wieder verlöschen wollten, aber zuletzt brannten sie, und der Alte, während er jetzt die Bahrdecke fortnahm und auf die Altarstufen niederlegte, sagte ruhig: 'Nu, mit Gott, gnäd'ger Herr.'

Ladalinski hatte sich erhoben und stellte sich an die eine Schmalseite des Sarges.

'Steh' ich zu Häupten oder zu Füßen?' fragte er.

'Zu Häupten.'

'Ich will doch lieber zu Füßen stehen.'

Danach wechselten sie die Plätze und hoben nun den Deckel ab, der alte Geheimrat mit krampfhaft geschlossenem Auge.

Und nun erst sah er auf den Sohn, fest und lange, und fand zu seiner eigenen Überraschung, daß sein Herz immer ruhiger schlug.

At first it seemed as if the candles would go out, but then they started to burn properly. Taking up the cloth that covered the bier and placing it on the altar steps, the old man said quietly: 'Well, the Lord be with you, my dear sir.' Count Ladalinski had risen and stood at the narrow end of the bier. 'Am I at his head or at his feet?' he asked. 'At his head.' 'I think I'd rather stand at his feet.' After this they changed places and lifted the lid, the old Privy Councillor keeping his eyes firmly shut. Only then did he look at his son, steadily and for a long time, and to his own surprise he found that his heart was beating more and more calmly.

What informs Fontane's realism is a spirit of sympathetic but far from undiscriminating tolerance, and a decorum which encompasses but doesn't intrude on men's deepest feelings. It is this twin quality of his style which, at a time such as ours, when the literary shocks of sex and violence are ten a penny, makes for the value and interest of his work.

Fontane's *Vor dem Sturm* (*Before the Storm*, 1878), his first work of fiction, is his and German literature's masterpiece in the genre of the historical novel. It derives many of its settings from Fontane's early volumes of travels in the Prussian province of Brandenburg (1862–82), through which he first became known to a wider public. Like *War and Peace* (1869), it is a panorama of life in the Napoleonic era, presenting the intertwining fortunes of a number of families and private persons in the shadow of the warlike action, though it is cast on an altogether smaller scale. Its events and complex plot span the time between Christmas Eve 1812 and early Spring 1813; the locale is delimited by the triangle Berlin–Küstrin–Frankfurt an der Oder, and the countryside between. This concentration in time and space is abandoned only where Fontane's episodic vein takes us into the histories of the families depicted, or where the Spanish War of Succession, Borodino, or Napoleon's Russian campaign are discussed by the leading characters of the novel. If, in this account, I don't dwell on the several love-affairs, elopements, and the like; if, furthermore, I omit the activities of several literary circles (one very French, two others very German in their tastes) in which some of the leading characters are involved, this is because the uniqueness and distinction of *Vor dem Sturm* seems to me to lie in the political conflict into which both the sentimental attachments and the literary activities are subtly laced. This conflict involves a variety of nationalistic attitudes; it demands moral decisions, and raises questions fundamental to the whole social edifice of the Prussian state. The conflict is argued out step by step, and it is acted out in life and death. In taking up this major political theme and bringing it to its conclusion undistracted by promptings from a 'higher sphere',* the novel achieves a distinction unique in German fiction.

The remnants of Napoleon's army, victors of the Battle of Jena (1806), are retreating through the Prussian countryside. Should Prussia follow the example of Spain and conduct guerrilla campaigns against an enemy army in disarray? This is the central political issue of the novel, and with it are connected the personal fates of all its major characters. The King, Frederick William III, ineffectual grand-nephew of Frederick the Great, is undecided and will not give the order for a popular uprising. In the calculation of the Berlin court the existing social order, which such an uprising might destroy, is more important than the threatened political order. For while an alliance with the French Emperor is likely to enable the Prussian state to weather the storm and in the long run to emerge unscathed, the unleashing of 'the popular will' is incalculable in its consequences:

'Ich kenne das Volk; ich habe mit ihm gelebt. In meinen
hohen Jahren, wo sich der Sinn für vieles schließt, öffnet er sich

---

* The only other major German novel dealing with nationalism, Franz Werfel's *Die vierzig Tage des Musa Dagh* (*The Forty Days of Musa Dagh*, 1933), is impaired in just this way.

für anderes, und so sage ich, weil ich es weiß, es ist ein gutes Volk. Ich sehe es so klar, als ob es vor meinem leiblichen Auge stünde. Aber der König ist eingeschüchtert; er hat viel Schmerzliches erlebt und nicht das Große, das meine jungen Tage gesehen haben. Ich kenne ihn genau. Er schließt lieber ein Bündnis mit seinem Feinde, vorausgesetzt, daß ihm dieser Feind in Gestalt eines Machthabers oder einer geordneten Regierung entgegentritt, als mit seinem eigenen, in hundert Willen geteilten, aus dem Geleise des Gehorsams herausgekommenen Volke.'

'I know the people; I have lived among them. In my old age, when the mind is closed to many things, it opens up to others. I know that they are a good people. I see them as clearly as if they stood before my very eyes. But the King is intimidated. He has seen much that was painful, and none of the great things that I saw in my own early days. I know him well. He will rather conclude an alliance with the enemy, assuming that the enemy is represented by a ruler or a properly appointed government, than with his own people, where that people is divided into a hundred factions and has left the path of obedience.'

The speaker (chapter 37) is the aged Prince Ferdinand, sole surviving brother of Prussia's greatest king. His protagonist in this remarkable conversation is Berndt von Vitzewitz, a Prussian *Junker* and father of Lewin, the novel's nominal hero;[8] the date is 1 January 1813.

Old Berndt Vitzewitz has come to Berlin (somewhat as Kleist's Colonel Kottwitz came to Potsdam) to find his worst suspicion confirmed: the Prussian government is in the hands of the trimmers. He returns to his country seat determined to organise his peasants into a 'self-help' action against the French, invoking not only their patriotism but also their fealty to the feudal lord – a threat, ultimately, to the royal authority. Moved by harsh chauvinism and a hatred of everything French, Berndt will have his will and lead his band of partisans into a disastrous skirmish. Yet it is characteristic of the living ironies with which the novel abounds that, hidden in the depths of Berndt's rigid character, there lies a sorrow, mixed with guilt, for the early death of his French wife; and that he sums up his audience of the Prince with the remark, 'I am not afraid of the people, I am not afraid to go *with* them. It is foolish to count on the mistakes or weaknesses of your enemy if you have the power to make him obey your orders. To remain inactive is as often to doubt the ways of God as it is to trust in Him. *Aide toi-même et le ciel t'aidera.*'

Politics, in a warlike situation especially, makes for strange bedfellows. The conception of *étatisme* which Prince Ferdinand upholds is part of the conservatism of the ruling class of courtiers and ministers, but their opposition to an attack on the French is shared by men in Berndt's own camp. Kniehase, Berndt's village magistrate, argues (chapter 30) against independent military action on grounds of loyalty to the King; Konrektor Othegraven, a young parson of strong liberal views, repudiates such action on Christian grounds; and Lewin, Berndt's own son, condemns the proposed attack against a beaten and retreating enemy as unchivalrous and barbaric. And yet, all three, and a host of other men, each with a more or less clear view of the rights and wrongs of the military coup, will be behind Berndt and the retired Major-General Bamme, who is in command of the partisan battalions, when the attack is launched: in political action association prevails; but each will have made his decision on personal and moral grounds. And in his awareness of this double aspect of his chosen theme – the inalienable connection between the public and the private – Fontane achieves some of his finest triumphs.

These, much foreshortened, are the ideological fronts 'before the storm'. And in the no-man's-land between them is the German intellectual. His position is outlined with the seriousness of a heartfelt conviction in a statement full of sound and fury, signifying nothing. His position is of course anti-French; but beyond that? With the young Lewin von Vitzewitz we attend (chapter 42) a university lecture by the renowned Professor Johann Gottlieb Fichte,[9] who recently addressed the same audience with his notorious *Speeches to the German Nation* (Winter Semester 1807–8). The news of General Yorck's capitulation to the Russians at Tauroggen (30 December 1812) has just reached Berlin. Has Yorck decided on this step in order to gather his forces for an attack, or is he preparing to join them? Has he acted on orders from the King or against his orders? Nobody in Berlin knows, least of all Professor Fichte. But this doesn't prevent the philosopher from fanning his student audience into a high enthusiasm:

'Meine Herren', begann er, nachdem er nicht ohne ein Lächeln der Befriedigung seinen Blick über das Auditorium hatte hingleiten lassen, 'meine Herren, wir sind alle unter dem Eindruck einer großen Nachricht, die nicht kennen zu wollen mir in diesem Augenblick als eine Affektation oder eine Feigheit, das eine so schlimm wie das andere, erscheinen würde. Sie wissen, worauf ich hinziele: General Yorck hat kapituliert. Das Wort hat sonst einen schlimmen Klang, aber da ist nichts, das gut oder böse wäre an sich; wir kennen den General und wissen deshalb, in welchem Geiste wir sein Tun zu deuten haben.'

'Gentlemen', he began, as he allowed his glance to pass over the auditorium with a smile that was not without complacency, 'Gentlemen, we are all under the impression of great news. To pretend not to know this news would seem to me at this moment either an affection or a piece of cowardice – one as bad as t'other. You know to what I allude. General Yorck has capitulated. At other times than these the word has an ugly sound, but there is nothing that is evil in itself. We know the General, and therefore we know in what spirit to interpret his action.'

In fact, nobody has any idea; Fichte continues:

Ich meinesteils bin sicher, daß dies der erste Schritt ist, der, während er uns zu erniedrigen scheint, uns aus der Erniedrigung in die Erhöhung führt.

I for my part am certain that this is the first step which, while it appears to humiliate us, will lead us out of our humiliation and will raise us up.

Nobody even remotely knows how this is to be accomplished. High-sounding phrases and grand metaphors – 'An eagle's eyrie is not a crow's nest' – roll from the rostrum, all informed by the same intolerable earnestness of commitment to nothing at all save the gesture itself:

Es kann nicht sein, daß die große Tat kleinmütig gemißbilligt worden sei, und wär' es doch, nun so kräftige sich in uns der Glaube: es ist nicht, auch wenn es ist.

It cannot be that the deed was met by timid disapproval [of the king]. And even *if* it were, why then let it only strengthen the faith that is in us: *I mean our faith that it is not even if it is.*

What is that 'it' that also is not? The dark words (shades of Professor Heidegger's rectoral address in 1933) are not explained; instead, Professor Fichte concludes:

Seien wir voll der Hoffnung, die Mut, und voll des Mutes, der Hoffnung gibt. Vor allem tun wir, was der tapfere General tat, d.h. entscheiden wir uns.

Let us be full of the hope that gives courage, full of the courage that gives hope. Above all, let us do what the brave general did, let us *decide*.

Decide to do what? But there is no need for an answer. Instead, 'the auditorium responded enthusiastically' – as on such occasions it usually does. Fontane leaves the scene uncommented. Was he aware of its full import? Was he something of a prophet after all? However that may be, there is no need to dwell on the startling relevance of the Fichtean gobbledygook to similar declarations in the century Fontane did not live to see. When Max Weber (in an essay of 1919) criticised the 'idolatry of "sensation" and "personality"' as substitutes for responsible social and political thinking, he might well have turned to this tirade as a splendid example of the intellectual vices he castigated. To students of recent German intellectual history its ring is depressingly familiar.

The patriotic action for which Berndt von Vitzewitz has striven, a carefully prepared attack on the French who are occupying Frankfurt an der Oder, fails abysmally. The partisans suffer some losses, are repulsed, and beat a hasty but orderly retreat. Among the killed is the poet and critic Hansen-Grell (perhaps something of an authorial self-portrait), one of those mildly eccentric figures whose nonconformism and poetic enthusiasm turns out to be accompanied by a surprising amount of 'Zivilcourage'. Lewin Vitzewitz is taken prisoner and Pastor Othegraven, who had organised a counterthrust from inside the city, is tried by a French court martial and shot. Berndt is shaken from his fanaticism and left a prey to dire self-doubts. Lewin's closest friend, Tubal Ladalinski, son of a Polish count in German ministerial service, is killed (see above, p. 170) in the course of rescuing Lewin from the Küstrin prison to which he was taken. The fiasco is complete – one of the last and finest scenes of the novel (chapter 81) is given over to a conversation between Berndt and Bamme, the retired General who led the action. What went wrong, they ask. The Russians had promised support and failed to give it (one thinks of Warsaw in 1944), the morale and ingenuity of the French forces had been badly underestimated, but it is no longer the tactical shortcomings of the affair that occupy the minds of the two elderly men as they ride out to visit a neighbour.

Berndt opens the conversation by announcing Lewin's betrothal. He does so with misgivings, for his son's bride Marie, Kniehase's foster-child, is a girl of dubious background and no 'family' at all. How will his caustic friend General Bamme take it? For Bamme the news is the occasion for a long discourse on the gentry's need for new blood –

> 'Ich perhorresziere dies ganze Vettern- und Muhmenprinzip, und am meisten, wenn es ans Heiraten und Fortpflanzen geht. . . . Ein Zieten eine Bamme, ein Bamme eine Zieten. Und was kam schließlich dabei heraus? Das hier!' Und dabei schlug er mit dem Fischbeinstock an seine hohen Stiefelschäfte. 'Ja, das hier, und ich bin nicht dumm genug, Vitzewitz, mich für ein Prachtexemplar der Menschheit zu halten.'

> 'I loathe this whole network system of cousins and more cousins . . . a Zieten marrying a Bamme, a Bamme a Zieten, and what is the end of it all? *This!*' And he switched his whalebone riding-crop against the leg of his riding-boot. 'Yes, *this*. I am not so stupid, Vitzewitz, as to regard myself as humanity's masterpiece.'

And now, as with a magic wand (but it is the great realist's pen), Fontane turns the argument from a private deliberation into a clear-sighted analysis of the national and political predicament. With Bamme's concluding speech (still part of the same dialogue) the last irony of the novel is turned, its theme is resolved, and the travail of the next hundred years of German conservatism begins:

> '. . . Eines wenigstens glaubten wir gepachtet zu haben: den Mut, und nun kommt dieser Kakerlaken-Grell und stirbt wie ein Held

mit dem Säbel in der Hand. Von dem Konrektor sprech' ich gar
nicht erst; ein solcher Tod kann einen alten Soldaten beschämen.
Und woher das alles? Sie wissen es. Von drüben: Westwind. Ich
mache mir nichts aus diesen Windbeuteln von Franzosen, aber in
all ihrem dummen Zeug steckt immer eine Prise Wahrheit. Mit
ihrer Brüderlichkeit wird es nicht viel werden, und mit der
Freiheit auch nicht; aber mit dem, was sie dazwischengestellt
haben, hat es was auf sich. Denn was heißt es am Ende anders als:
Mensch ist Mensch. Ich darf so sprechen, Vitzewitz, denn die
Bammes sterben mit mir aus, ein Ereignis, um das der Vorhang
des Tempels nicht zerreißen wird, und nicht einmal ein Namens-
vetter ist da, den ich in seinem Standesbewußtsein kränken
oder schädigen könnte. Denn, im Vertrauen gesagt, das Kränken
fängt bei uns immer erst mit der Schädigung an.'

'The one thing we thought nobody else had was courage. And
now a nobody with a funny name like Hansen-Grell comes along
and dies like a hero, with a sword in his hand. I won't even
mention the parson, Othegraven. *There's* a death can put an old
soldier to shame. And where does it all come from? You know it as
well as I do. From the other side. West wind. I don't care twopence
for those Froggies, but in all their silly ideas there's always a grain
of truth. As for their fraternity, there's not much future in that,
nor in their liberty. But what they've put in between, *that's* valid
enough. Why, what else does it mean, when all is said and done,
than that one man is as good as another man. I may speak freely,
Vitzewitz, because when I die the Bammes will have died out, an
event which is unlikely to cause the veil of the temple to be rent in
twain, and I don't even have a namesake whom I could insult or
injure in his social pride. Confidentially, you know, it's only *after*
we've been injured that we ever feel insulted. . . .'

Fidelity to what happens in the real world – to what could be said
by a disillusioned old general to his friend, who remains a little
naïve in spite of all that has happened – governs this passage. The
apparent discursiveness is deceptive, verbal precision of a high order
(an accurate retracing of the scene before the inner eye, the eye of
fiction) guides Fontane's hand. It is the general's moment of insight.
First he drily explores the revolutionary tag, then plays caustically on

M

the New Testament image, finally concentrates the argument into the aphoristic antithesis (worthy of a Montaigne) between insult and injury: nothing could be more steeped in that social world which once securely enveloped the two old men and now is collapsing around them; and when all this is couched in an unstrenuous, relaxed, colloquial mode of speech, all conditions of genre and kind are fulfilled – this is 'realism of assessment'[10] at its most memorable.

NINE

Fiction and the Immutable Self

From Goethe's *Werther* (1774) and *The Elective Affinities* (1809) through Rilke's *Notebooks of Malte Laurids Brigge* (1910) to Thomas Mann's *Doktor Faustus* (1947) the twin themes of solitude and isolation have formed a major aspect of German narrative prose; hence my earlier claim that in the exploration of solitary experience lies its major contribution to world literature. Some of the formal problems to which these explorations gave rise in the age of European realism have been mentioned. The characteristic solution, as we find it in the stories of Adalbert Stifter, combines a parochial setting with existential depth.

Rilke's artist as a young man is absolutely alone, the hostile city that surrounds Malte is a world not of people but of things, his only company are his childhood memories. Where solitude falls short of such radical alienation, as it does in most nineteenth-century stories, there the simplest and least extended social organisations will serve best to embody it. Thus the society that Stifter presents is insistently paternalistic. He confines his stories to the master-servant, father-son, old man-youth, husband-wife relationships; and even in *Witiko*, his last novel, the attempt to present the wider canvases of a warlike situation recedes behind pedagogic intentions realised within a feudal nexus, where fealty to the lord and king is still based on a pattern of familial values.

In the stories of Theodor Storm (1817–1888) the themes of solitude and isolation form a dominant dialectic of guilt and punishment.[1] Solitude as a 'natural', that is initially given, disposition of mind is no longer the ground of personal value (as it was with Stifter), but the isolation and inconsolable loneliness to which it leads are experienced as a punishment. The guilt of the solitary man, in Storm's early stories, is not a moral failing but a predicament of his individual fate. Sometimes (as in *Immensee*, 1832) it is manifest in an inability to divulge and conquer the deprivation; at other times (*Viola Tricolor*, 1874) love and sympathy in the face of mortal danger succeed in bridging the gulf; then again (*Aquis Submersus*, 1877) moral guilt is added to the fated predicament. In *Carsten Curator* (1878) and several other stories the brief happiness by which an elderly man's marriage is attended leaves him on his bereavement overwhelmed with responsibilities and an unabating sense of loss. In his last and perhaps greatest Novelle, *Der Schimmelreiter* (*The White Horseman*, 1888), Storm embodies the deprivation in a charismatic figure. Hauke Haien's life's work, the building of a dyke in his Frisian village, is achieved at the price of his increasing isolation from the community whose safety and survival his work was intended to safeguard; but it is this same heroic alienation that leads to his doom. We have here a faint glimpse of that glorification of sacrifice on behalf of the community which was to be cheapened and exploited by the ideologists of the Third Reich.

The development of Storm's prose fiction from the lyrical and yielding solitude of *Immensee* to the heroic and self-assertive isolation of *Der Schimmelreiter*, which coincides in time with the political career of Bismarck, Germany's 'Iron Chancellor', is symptomatic of an important change in her writers' view of human character and destiny; a change, moreover, which is so consistent and general that we may see in it literature's response to Germany's new rôle in the European balance of power. The Swiss C. F. Meyer's decision, after the foundation of the Second Reich, to write in German rather than French is as symptomatic of this nexus between politics and literature as is, on the other side of the coin, Nietzsche's famous dictum on the first page of his *Unzeitgemässe Betrachtungen* (*Thoughts Out of Season*, vol. i, 1873), where he castigates the nascent nationalism (the attitude that is presumably behind Meyer's decision) as liable to 'turn our victory [of 1871] into utter defeat – into the defeat, nay extirpation, of the German spirit in favour of the "German Reich".' The final quotation marks, it should be added, are Nietzsche's.

In 1825 the political scientist Adam Müller had coined the term 'geschlossene Persönlichkeit'; translated into fiction, this enclosed or rather embattled personality now emerges as a character whose contacts with the outside world are narrowed down to the assertion of his purposeful and uncompromising will to power. In a century at whose beginning stands the figure of Napoleon, this conception of human character becomes dominant throughout Western literature (but not, see Moscow 1812, in Russia). It is embodied in Stendhal's Count Mosca and Balzac's Vautrin, in Melville's Captain Ahab and Dickens's Mr Dombey, in the father-figure of Otto Ludwig's *Zwischen Himmel und Erde* (*Between Heaven and Earth*, 1856), in the tyrants that dominate Hebbel's dramas, as well as in Storm's Hauke Haien. These men are, in a metaphorical sense, the creators of the worlds they command; at the moment when his immovable will collapses, 'Mr Dombey's World' (this is Dickens's own chapter heading) dissolves also. Arthur Schopenhauer, the philosopher of 'the embattled personality', whose works Hitler claimed to have read in the trenches, builds his system by taking the metaphor seriously; and it is significant that this system, first conceived in 1818, has to wait some thirty years before it makes its impact on a wider public.

The charismatic leader-figure in his essential isolation is central to the prose work of the Swiss Conrad Ferdinand Meyer (1825–1898), whose historical novels and Novellen have worn less well than his poetry. Highly charged contrasts of moods and colours, which in the stories make for melodrama, are perfectly contained and balanced in short lyrical poems intimating the enticement of tranquillity and death. Dark surfaces and landscapes are briefly illuminated by sharp streaks of colour, moods of sultry repose or melancholy issue in moments of clarity and insight. A sonnet-like impression of a nocturnal journey on the lake of Zürich hides in its core a moment of mystery, and again the poem ends on a note at once melancholy and enticing: 'Schmerz und Lust erleiden sanften Tod' ('Pain and joy endure a gentle death'). Meyer's poems point the way from *fin de siècle* decadence to the near-identity of thing, word and experience of the 'Dinggedichte' ('object poems') of Rilke's *Neue Gedichte* (i, 1907) and to the Paris of Malte Laurids Brigge. In Meyer's poem 'Schwarzschattende Kastanie' the firmly evoked sense-impression of a chestnut tree on the lake shore is briefly contrasted with a merry group of bathing children; but the group is not wholly dominated by the shadow of the central image, it has a life of its own. Such poems as 'Zwei Segel' ('Two Sails') and 'Der römische Brunnen' ('Roman Fountain') on the other hand, are wholly confined to the evocation of objects of the outer world; their contours are made meaningful both as parts of reality *and* as discrete symbols of a vision in which explicitly human elements are no longer mentioned; twentieth-century imagism has its ancestry in these poems.

In Meyer's stories, on the other hand, elements of 'poison, passion, putrefaction' are handled all too freely. His great 'renaissance' personalities may be fantasy compensations for his own psychological inadequacies; as to their 'amoral' greatness, it often seems more like a pose than a convincing mode of life. The novel *Jürg Jenatsch, eine Bündnergeschichte* (1874) tells of the high adventures and gory death of a Lutheran buccaneering parson of the early seventeenth century, whose heroic life is divided between Swiss patriotism, anti-Hapsburg guerrilla warfare, and amorous intrigues. In a scene before the altar of a Venetian church (book II, chapter 3) are assembled all the most perishable ingredients of historical romance: a group of youthful warriors under a picture by 'Maestro Titiano', a pack of elegant greyhounds, searing amorous glances behind veils of black lace. Actually, what Meyer's tableaux recall is not Titian but Hitler's favourite painter, Hans Makart (1840–1884), whose luxuriant costume canvases and stage décors were all the rage in the Second German Empire. The prose is not free from theatricalities – a riot of verbs of violent motion and emotion gives it an effect of breathlessness, though occasionally (especially in *Der Schuss von der Kanzel, A Shot from the Pulpit*, 1883) it is relieved by touches of humour and ironical characterisation. Meyer's attempts at exploring a spiritual conflict in his charismatic heroes leave one worse than disappointed. Of all the interpretations the life of St Thomas à Becket has received, *Der Heilige* (*The Saint*, 1879) is surely the least commensurate with its subject, the conflict between King and Archbishop being motivated by the former's seduction of the latter's daughter.

With Annette von Droste-Hülshoff's Novelle *Die Judenbuche* (*Jew's Beech*, 1845) we return to the localised setting (Westphalia); here a strong fate-element, superstitions, and peasant avarice combine into a detective story whose mystery is solved by the workings of retributive justice. Similar ingredients go into the Novelle *Die*

Schwarze Spinne (*The Black Spider*, 1842–1846) by the Swiss parson Jeremias Gotthelf (1797–1834). In his patriarchal ethos, his simple psychology, as well as in his distrust of urban life, Gotthelf shows affinities with Stifter; however, the interest of his novel sequences is confined to readers who are willing to equate highmindedness and didacticism with literary values.

The terminology of 'inner-directed' and 'outer-directed' man (coined by David Riesmann) makes available to modern social studies a dichotomy in which nineteenth-century writers saw the central enigma of individual human characters; indeed, the hostile brothers of Otto Ludwig's *Between Heaven and Earth* might have been written in illustration of Riesmann's thesis. The German Naturalists, in an effort to emulate the new biological and social sciences, present a similar dichotomy in terms of genetic inheritance *versus* 'environment' and 'milieu'. But while in their theoretical writings they emphasise the difference between these two sources of human behaviour, and in their political articles concentrate on the need for social and eugenic remedies of the ills of contemporary society, in their plays and Novellen they make little or no attempt at working out the distinction ('Corrupted in our disposition, corrupted in our upbringing', is the summary judgement of one of Gerhart Hauptmann's characters.) Moreover, the Naturalists' commitment to a 'scientific' view of life has been exaggerated, by them as well as by their critics. For while they show a genuine concern with presenting the effects of biological and social determination on the stage, dramatists like Sudermann, Anzengruber and Hauptmann still insist that the roots of human behaviour lie deeper, beyond the reach of remediable determinants or rational investigation. The blanket notion of an impersonal and supernatural fate dies hard. Ever more tenuously connected with the idea of a Christian Providence but hallowed by popular and literary tradition alike, this notion remains a powerful if ultimately obscure motivating agent in their writings. The view of human character it entails harks back to the most influential philosophy of this period, Arthur Schopenhauer's *Die Welt als Wille und Vorstellung* (*The World as Will and Idea*, [1]1818, [2]1844, complete [3]1859).

Even though Schopenhauer's philosophy is essentially monistic, his view of human character anticipates the dichotomies I have mentioned. A man's fundamental and fundamentally unalterable personality, ancestor to the congenitally inherited character of the Naturalists and to Riesmann's 'inner-directed man', Schopenhauer calls his 'intelligible self' and sees as coincident with a man's 'moment of individuation', his birth. Society is to Schopenhauer almost as inauthentic a thing as is Martin Heidegger's sphere of '*man*' (where attitudes are determined not by 'what I do' but 'what *one* does'). Social life imposes on a man's 'intelligible self' certain character traits which are determined mainly by his fear of other men. Chief among these traits are his practical ambitions, his skills in satisfying them, his ability to get by and to get on with others. And this acquired character Schopenhauer calls 'the empirical self', leaving us in no doubt as to its derivative nature. When, in our lives, we are faced with important decisions, we go through the motions of rational deliberation, seemingly consulting our empirical self in the process. A mere delusion, the caustic philosopher assures us – we have made up our minds long before, the *intelligible* self has done it for us. *Its* origin is shrouded in the mystery of individuation, he tells us, an event out of time and space because it itself is the ground of time and space. (The logical conundrum inherent in this method of arguing he bequeathed to Nietzsche.)

Now, since the vast majority of men live out their lives in delusion, the philosopher's discovery of the truth of the human condition is unlikely to make any great difference to them. They will go on regardless, as long as life – that is, their will – serves them: wanting all that is not worth having; trying to satisfy desires which grow on the satisfactions with which they are fed; failing to avoid even those sufferings which a little more self-knowledge would enable them to avoid; valuing the valueless and the ephemeral; taunting and injuring each other in the vain hope of impunity, and in the act of procreation dragging at the cosmic bait of momentary lust and thus perpetuating the tragi-comedy yet once more. And the great wheel of human history is no more than the sum total of all of these vanities projected in the continuum of time, while time itself is merely another product of the delusive will of the unregenerated self. On the other hand there are the few who see the human situation for what, according to Schopenhauer, it really is. They cannot but choose to opt out of it – not by suicide (like all acts of violence, suicide would only be another gesture of delusion), but by cultivating the detachment, désinvolture, of an observer, a philosopher, an artist, a saint; this is Schopenhauer's hierarchy of the truly virtuous. A man may – indeed he should – do all he can to get an ever better insight into his 'intelligible self', by clearing away as much as he can of the worthless rubble that his ambitions, assertiveness and involvement in the world have produced. But how much *can* he do? Again it is his fixed, unalterable self which will ultimately determine with what success his disinterested search for the truth of the human condition, that is of his own condition, will be attended. The stronger a man's 'intelligible self', the more ready he will be for the knowledge of the vanity of all earthly things; the more ready to sacrifice the ambition of his worldly will for the sake of a union (which we call death) with that all-encompassing, cosmic Will that precedes all individuation, all phenomena in the world. The darkness from which we come and into which we go is for Schopenhauer the eerie light of Nirvana. (It may not be irrelevant to add that the resemblance of this philosophy to the Christian doctrine of redemption and grace is somewhat disingenuous.) In the moment of union, or rather reunion, all that exists in the world will be taken back by the cosmic Will into its Nirvana, which is beyond time and space, beyond history and world.

It is impossible to decide with any degree of certainty how much of Schopenhauer's philosophy Fontane knew and how strong an influence it exercised on him.[2] He certainly has little of the philosopher's cavalier attitude to the social world; he is incurious about Schopenhauer's aesthetics and his metaphysics of the cosmic Will (as he is about any metaphysics). On the other hand Schopenhauer's doctrine of the immutable 'intelligible self' corresponds by and large to the view of the human character that informs Fontane's novels. For this, however, no 'influence' need be postulated, for both novelist and philosopher articulate the beliefs of their age; they voice, and thus to some extent determine, the Hegelian *Zeitgeist* itself.[3] Fontane's Huguenot background too, it might be argued, made him familiar with the Calvinistic doctrine of predestination,[4] whose affinities with Schopenhauer's characterology on the one hand and the contemporary cult of 'die geschlossene Persönlichkeit' on the other are not far to seek. But again it is the ethos of contemporary society, as reflected in its institutions *and* in Fontane's realism, which provides the likelier source.

With Schopenhauer too, then, we are back at the notion of supernatural fate. The notorious lack of fluidity in the Prussian and German caste system; the notion of mother-tongue and (later) race as the true criteria of nationality; the contemporary attitude to Slav minorities and neighbours; the considered, that is 'scientific' nature of German anti-Semitism; the conformism and political fatalism of the middle classes; the insistence, even among the Naturalists, on the element of ineluctable fate as the deepest motive of human actions – all these aspects of the radically anti-democratic temper of the Second Reich have their political and social explanations. All of these social attitudes spring from a conscious preference for a 'natural' and 'instinctive' as against a rational and conscious set of values. And all of them are social, literary and moral variations on the contemporary belief in the (divinely or otherwise) *given* and fixed nature of the self. The reaction against the Romantic notions of 'Eternal Becoming' and of the unlimited development of the human personality sets in as soon as 'Realpolitik' (a term coined in the 1820s) becomes dominant. The industrialisation and economic growth of Germany, her European and colonial expansion, are not at odds with the doctrine of the immutable 'intelligible self'. On the contrary, Germany's imperial ambitions are underpinned by a belief in her 'mission for all the nations of the world',[5] in an ordinance divinely decreed. There may be various views as to who exactly is responsible for the decree, whether it is the Christian God, 'the logic' and 'inevitability' of history, or some cosmic or biological process. However that may be, the task of each individual is to work out what has been implanted in him from the beginning, to aspire to no higher station in life and to no greater power than that which is his lot, lest in the ensuing confusion the nation itself should be incapacitated for *its* preordained task. Although Fontane is critical of the temper of his age (and his private letters show that he had no illusions about its morality and some doubts about its future), his realism does not allow him to look far beyond it.

On the question of 'who or what moves the wheel of human history' the (relatively) early *Vor dem Sturm* confines itself to the individual reactions of the people near the *ad hoc* centre of power. Men like Prince Ferdinand (spokesman of the King), Berndt von Vitzewitz or Konrektor Othegraven do not directly determine the fate of the German nation any more than any single person can, yet they certainly contribute to the gathering storm. But Fontane's later work will never again steer so close to the centre of power. In the novels that follow – they are the bulk of his writings – he moves away from that centre, to points where the ethos of contemporary society, finely established through characterisation, plot and story, is not so much fashioned as enacted. The importance of his superb characterisations lies in his recognition that he who enacts an order or ethical code also to some extent fashions it, but at the same time disclaims responsibility for it; and, by and large, Fontane accepts, even if he doesn't approve of, the disclaimer. Thus *Effi Briest* (1895) culminates in a profoundly illuminating discussion (chapter 27) in which the harsh dictates of the Prussian code of honour are defended – on grounds which are no less effective, as far as the subsequent plot of that novel is concerned, for being shown up and acknowledged by the partners in that conversation as hollow, inhuman and hypocritical. (The way Fontane here exposes the peculiar delusion that all effective action must be based on 'genuine' belief has never, as far as I know, been equalled.) Again, it is a case of injury before insult. But once the exposure of 'our service to an idol' has been accomplished, the only alternative scheme of values Fontane suggests is a purely private one; it is the wisdom of 'forget and forgive'.

Fontane the novelist is not interested in the typical. 'This is what happened', he is saying, not, 'Here is an example of what happens in our society'. It is his reader who recognises the protagonists of that famous conversation as typical, *after* the novelist has retraced them for him in their living, individual reactions to the dictates of the code. In his last novel, *Der Stechlin* (1899) he once more returns to the questions which concerned him in *Vor dem Sturm*: 'Who is in charge? Who *is* the régime? Is it the machine itself, whose old-fashioned works just keep on clattering away, or is it the fellow in charge of the machine?' (chapter 29). He asks the question, but stays not for an answer. Of course, *pace* Tolstoy, the realistic novelist cannot offer an overall answer, an answer apart from or beyond the detailed, piecemeal answers given in the doings and deliberations of his characters. But having said this, we must add that here for once Fontane doesn't avail himself of the full possibilities of his craft. Standing at the beginning of an alas relatively brief period of German realistic fiction (brief as far as distinguished works are concerned), the novelist is, after all, too ready to accept at their face value the encompassing forces of society; the realistic novelist *can* give fuller answers than Fontane is able to give here. His greatest virtue is also the source of our occasional disappointment. He is not much given to passionate 'struggling' (see above, p. 164), certainly not where a conflict of the individual with society is concerned. There are non-conformists in his novels, but they are always 'originals', men and women who preserve a colourful and attractive personal integrity on the margins of society, but never engage with the leviathan.

In *Unwiederbringlich* (*Beyond Recall*, 1891), among his crowning achievements, Fontane unites the European tradition of social realism with a characteristically German theme. The novel has been compared with *Madame Bovary*, but the parallel will not take us further than the fact that the act of adultery (central to both) is partly founded in the contrast between the boredom of provincial life and the exciting social whirl of the city; the two characters chafing under the matrimonial yoke – Emma Bovary and Count Holk – are made of different stuff, and their conflicts are of a very different order.

The chosen settings of the action – Schloss Holkenäs on the North Sea coast of Schleswig-Holstein; the Danish capital with its rococo residence, Tivoli Gardens and the minuscule royal court; and Schloss Friedrichsburg, the Danish Princess Royal's favourite castle – are described with that eye for architectural detail which is one of the delights of Fontane's prose. The narrative manner is again unemphatic and unstrenuous. Buildings, interiors, and the niceties of social intercourse are all firmly related to the story, as yet there is little of that emphasis on the symbolising function of the objects that make up the milieu which we shall find in the early work of Thomas Mann, Fontane's only great disciple. The story is the unfolding of a marital incompatibility between Count Helmuth von Holk and his wife Christine. It begins with the abandoning of the old castle of Holkenäs; the building of a new one, indicative of Holk's restlessness, fills Christine with forebodings. (One is reminded of a similar episode in *Buddenbrooks*, where it marks the first step of the Firm's decline; but also of Goethe's *Elective Affinities*, where the planning of new architectural and landscape designs is similarly indicative of the hero's restlessness and boredom.) Step by step, hint by hint, the two central characters are portrayed. Holk, an attractive and not unintelligent 'nobleman in the prime of life' (to quote the beginning of Goethe's novel) has the virtues and weaknesses of his comfortable character. He is easy-going yet with a sense of decorum and even self-importance; neither thoughtless of his family nor consistently frivolous; pleasure-seeking yet with occasional qualms of conscience. There is about him a certain suggestibility which waits for the occasion but does not determine it, and his self-knowledge too is at best limited to the occasion at hand. He has many of the qualities of Eduard, the hero of Goethe's novel, short of Eduard's generous impetuosity; in terms of Schopenhauer's characterology Holk is nearly all 'empirical self', and has only mutability for his immutable substance. His wife Christine, on the other hand, is all that Holk is not: brought up on the strict religious principles of pietist Herrnhut, she is by nature at once melancholy, severe, and inclined to censoriousness. She is not without a streak of superstitiousness, which she disapproves of in herself as in others. She is determined to guide their children in the path of righteousness, and has the strength of convictions firmly held and uncompromisingly practised. Yet she is sufficiently self-critical, in the earlier parts of the story at all events, to be wary of her own moments of religiosity and fanaticism, and in adversity it is her injured pride, not her faith, that comes uppermost. In her rigidness she approaches the condition of that 'intelligible self' which is increasingly scornful of all that the 'empirical' world has to offer. Unlike Ottilie, the young heroine of *Elective Affinities*, Christine undergoes no dramatic development. But she resembles the Ottilie of the last part of Goethe's novel in the severity of her withdrawal and in the impenetrable solitude of her end.

Fontane's novel of course contains no such abridged summary of the two characters as I have presented. The story opens on a fairly harmonious and happy relationship. Each conversation between Holk and Christine, and with other members of the family and household and neighbourhood of Holkenäs, serves to underline the contrast and growing conflict, each ensuing event widens the gulf. In his letters Fontane voices his conviction that marriage based on 'the principle of complementaries', on a union of opposite characters, doesn't work: Holk and Christine bring out the worst in each other.

It is Holk 'from whom scandal cometh'. Called to do his stint as the Princess's gentleman-in-waiting in Copenhagen, he finds himself amused, distracted, stimulated by life in the capital: he flirts with the married daughter of his landlady; falls in love with Ebba von Rosenfeld, a lady-in-waiting of whom he sees more than is good for him in the course of his not very onerous duties at court; saves Ebba from a conflagration at Schloss Friedrichsburg, which dramatically ends their only night of love; and insists on a separation from Christine, only to find himself rejected by Ebba. Yet in all this Holk is moved by no passion, no clear intention even, but by each occasion as it presents itself to his yielding character. Christine too is not without blame in all this. In her distaste for the frivolous court-life she encourages Holk to go alone to Copenhagen, in her severity and pride she taunts him with his weaknesses and impairs the chance of a reconciliation even before the adultery has occurred, and before he has taken his unfortunate (and, in the event, ridiculous) decision to propose to Ebba. It is her severity and pride that offers the occasions which he is only too glad to convert into causes. Fontane apportions no guilt and pronounces no judgement; the story is the working out of an incompatibility which no good intention on either side can alter, since all intentions are worsted by the fixed character of one and the wayward character of the other.

The social realism of the novel is built from the dominant contrast between the somewhat sombre and simple North German life at Holkenäs and the 'Parisian' life round an aged princess (shade of Dickens's 'Cleopatra'[6]) whose social graces are not free from cynicism and whose love of intrigue is not without a touch of evil. Unlike Dickens, Fontane never speaks of evil; all he does is to let the Princess arrange Ebba's and Holk's lodgings in the same outlying tower of Schloss Friedrichsburg (chapter 19). A subtler intimation of her delight in seeing the intrigue grow occurs during the sledging expedition that ends chapter 25. Ebba and Holk have left the company and are skating down a frozen waterway that issues into Lake Arre and beyond it into the open sea. As they speed towards the narrow belt of ice, the disposition of three wills (Ebba's and Holk's but also the absent Princess's) in the strategy of the affair is firmly established:

... Ihre Blicke suchten einander und schienen zu fragen: 'Soll es so sein?' Und die Antwort war zum mindesten keine Verneinung. Aber im selben Augenblicke, wo sie die durch eine Reihe kleiner

Kiefern als letzte Sicherheitsgrenze bezeichnete Linie passieren wollten, bog Holk mit rascher Wendung rechts und riß auch Ebba mit sich herum.

'Hier ist die Grenze, Ebba. Wollen wir drüber hinaus?' Ebba stieß den Schlittschuh ins Eis und sagte: 'Wer an zurück denkt, der will zurück. Und ich bin's zufrieden. Erichsen und die Schimmelmann werden uns ohnehin erwarten, – die Prinzessin vielleicht nicht.'

Their eyes met and seemed to be asking: 'Shall we?' And the answer was, at least, not a refusal; but just as they were about to pass a line of small firs marking the final limit of safety, Holk suddenly swung towards the right, pulling Ebba with him. 'We've reached the limit, Ebba. Shall we go beyond it?' Ebba drove the points of her skates into the ice and said: 'If you are thinking of going back, that means that you want to, and that's good enough for me. In any case, Erichsen and the Schimmelmann woman [two further members of the party] will be expecting us, though perhaps not the Princess.'[7]

Some of the contrast between Holkenäs and Copenhagen rubs off on Holk. To his wife he is bound to appear at his most frivolous and worldly, whereas at court he is apt to cut the somewhat awkward figure of a country nobleman; in fact he is not quite at home in either. An example of what Ebba von Rosenberg will ridicule as Holk's 'misplaced solemnity' recalls to us the strong sense, in this novel of emotional conflict too, of Fontane's tolerant yet purposeful realism. During one of his first meetings with her (chapter 13) Holk airs his somewhat pompous knowledge of genealogy by informing Ebba that his own great-uncle's second wife was a Rosenberg, that 'all the Rosenbergs descended from the brother of the Archbishop of Prague', and other sundry matters of consuming interest of which Ebba confesses herself ignorant:

'Woraus mir nur hervorgehen würde, daß Sie, statt dem Gruszczynskischen, wahrscheinlich dem Lipinskischen Zweige der Familie zugehören.'
'Zu meinem Bedauern auch das nicht. Freilich, wenn ich Lipinski mit Lipesohn übersetzen darf, ein Unterfangen, das mir die berühmte Familie verzeihen wolle, so würde sich, von dem in

dieser Form auftretenden Namen aus, vielleicht eine Brücke zu
mir und meiner Familie herüber schlagen lassen. Ich bin nämlich
eine Rosenberg-Meyer oder richtiger eine Meyer-Rosenberg,
Enkelstochter des in der Schwedischen Geschichte wohlbekannten
Meyer-Rosenberg, Lieblings- und Leibjuden König Gustavs III.'

'From which I should deduce [Holk continues] that you
probably belong to the Lipinsky and not to the Gruszczynski
branch of the family.'

'To my great regret, not even that. True, if I'm allowed to
put Lipeson instead of Lipinsky, a boldness which that illustrious
family will, I trust, forgive, then perhaps I might claim a link
between me and that family by using that form of the name. You
see, I'm a Rosenberg-Meyer or more correctly a Meyer-
Rosenberg, granddaughter of the Meyer-Rosenberg who was well
known in Swedish history as King Gustav III's personal pet Jew.'[8]

Well may the relentless genealogist wince.

After this we are hardly surprised that it is Ebba who, first in the
course of a conversation with the Princess (chapter 18), then in her
scathing rejection of Holk's suit, gives us the fullest explicit insight
into his character. Seeing her for the first time after the Friedrichsburg escapade, Holk has come to press his claim on her, but he does
not get beyond telling her that he has left his wife. Instantly and
without the slightest compunction she rebuts his advances:

'Freund, Sie sind unverbesserlich. Ich entsinne mich, Ihnen
gleich am Anfang unserer Bekanntschaft und dann auch später
noch, jedenfalls mehr als einmal gesagt zu haben, Sie stünden
nicht am richtigen Fleck. Und davon kann ich nichts zurück-
nehmen; im Gegenteil. Alles, was ich damals in übermütiger
Laune nur so hinsprach, bloß um Sie zu necken und ein wenig zu
reizen, das muß ich Ihnen in vollem Ernst und in mindestens
halber Anklage wiederholen. Sie wollen Hofmann und Lebe-
mann sein und sind weder das eine noch das andere. Sie sind ein
Halber und versündigen sich nach beiden Seiten hin gegen das
Einmaleins, das nun mal jede Sache hat und nun gar die Sache,
die uns hier beschäftigt. Wie kann man sich einer Dame gegen-
über auf Worte berufen, die die Dame töricht oder vielleicht auch
liebenswürdig genug war, in einer unbewachten Stunde zu

sprechen? Es fehlt nur noch, daß Sie sich auch auf Geschehnisse berufen, und der Kavalier ist fertig. Unterbrechen Sie mich nicht, Sie müssen noch Schlimmeres hören. Allmutter Natur hat Ihnen, wenn man von der Beständigkeit absieht, das Material zu einem guten Ehemanne gegeben, und dabei mußten Sie bleiben. Auf dem Nachbargebiete sind Sie fremd und verfallen aus Fehler in Fehler.

My dear friend, you're quite incorrigible. I remember telling you at the very beginning of our acquaintance and later on as well, in any case, more than once, that you were on the wrong track. Nor will I take anything back, on the contrary. All those things that I used to mention merely to tease you and irritate you a little when I was feeling impertinent, I shall now repeat in deadly earnest and even as an accusation. You try to be a courtier and a man of the world, and you are neither one nor the other. You're half-hearted in both and you're always sinning against the most elementary rules of the game – particularly at the present moment. How can anyone, where a lady is concerned, refer to words that she was foolish enough – or perhaps kind enough – to utter in an unguarded moment? All that remains now is for you to mention certain *happenings* and you'll be the perfect gentleman. Don't interrupt, I've worse things to say to you yet. Except for the small matter of constancy, Mother Nature has endowed you with everything needed to make a good husband and you should have been content with that. In any neighbouring territory, you're completely at a loss and you only go from one blunder to another.[9]

It is entirely characteristic of the tolerant realist that the truth about his hero should come not from Christine who takes a pride in her righteousness, but from Ebba who is certainly no better than she should be; truth, for Fontane, is not the prerogative of the truthful.

After Holk's slightly ridiculous suit ('ein Korb . . . einer der rundesten . . .') has been rejected, he spends eighteen months aimlessly travelling about and kicking his heels (in a somewhat similar situation Eduard, the hero of Goethe's novel, departs for a convenient war). At the end of this time we find Holk looking down on a fashionable square near Hyde Park and poring over the announcement of Ebba's marriage in the society columns of *The Times*.

Negotiations between husband and wife are taken up by Christine's brother Arne and Schwarzkoppen the family parson, and at last a reconciliation is effected. As in *Effi Briest* so here too there is something of a hiatus; between climax and final disaster the novelist is playing for time. For two brief chapters he accompanies Holk on his futile travels, has him kept informed of events at home, but leaves Christine's solitude unexplored. The reconciliation is strengthened by a solemn re-consecration of their marriage vows; chapter 33 begins, 'However, the feeling of sadness that had dominated the moving ceremony appeared to be unjustified', and 'the happiness of Holkenäs seemed really to be returning.' But while Holk resumes the relationship as if nothing had happened, Christine is unable to forget the betrayal. There are no more reproaches; on the contrary, Holk is conscious of Christine's 'desire to forget', but her 'empirical self' is fighting an unequal battle. One by one Christine sheds her ties. The children have no more need of her, her feeling towards Holk is dominated by resignation, even her old confidante, Fräulein Julie Dobschütz, is excluded from her intimacy, until at last her solitude becomes absolute. This is Fontane's return to the old German theme, to that condition of isolation, at once implanted by fate and self-imposed by the will, in which Goethe's Ottilie too ends her life. One is reminded of Raabe's Velten, but Fontane interposes no fictitious narrator and thus faces a different problem of motivation. In abandoning Christine after the climax, he had allowed himself little room to show at all fully how her last ties with the world break under the weight of her melancholy and severity. Once again Fontane's decorum prevails. The novelist does not, after all, care for too much intimacy; preferring to suggest causes through their effects, he does not accompany her on her last journey but turns away from the solitary soul's desolation and final despair.

A simple little ballad about the happiness of days beyond recall is sung by one of the children; it ends with the lines, 'Doch die mir die liebsten gewesen sind,/Ich wünsche sie nicht zurück.' 'But those days that were dearest to me,/I do not wish them back.' This is the last word on Christine's life, under this motto she sets out on her last journey. Through her suicide no moral retribution is exacted, as it is through Anna Karenina's; nor is she driven to it by a round of trivial contingencies, as is Emma Bovary. We hear of a brief moment of hesitation but of no last anguished confusion; however, we have only 'dear Dobschütz's' letter to go by. For Schopenhauer, we recall, suicide was not a redemption but a last act of the unredeemed, self-assertive will. And so it is here: it is still her immutable, uncommunicating will that moves her as she walks out into the sea at Holkenäs. Once wounded, 'the intelligible self' can never heal again.

Christine's spirituality as Fontane portrays it – the spirituality of 'geschlossene Persönlichkeit' – is hostile to the one value to which, in his novels, all others are related. This value is not happiness – to set up happiness as essential to human life would have seemed unrealistic to a man who had not too much of it in his own life. Nor is it justice or truthfulness or integrity – all of which splendid virtues he is apt to depict at precisely the points at which they cease to be virtues and become excuses for fanaticism or self-assertion. The central value that emerges from his novels is involved, though none too securely, in all these. It is tolerance – a value, it may be relevant to add, with which neither his world nor ours is over-endowed.

TEN

Friedrich Nietzsche: The Birth of a Myth?

Tolerance? Away with it and with all the other mildew virtues that grow in the dank ruins of the temple of the Judaeo-Christian God. Pity and charity, denial of the unregenerated will and love of your neighbour? Subterfuges, all of them, hide-outs of the weak and 'underprivileged' ('die Schlechtweggekommenen') in body and soul. The brazen Nietzschean message heralds a new age, the age of modern wars, racism and genocide, that seems wholly disconnected from the age to which these studies have been devoted. And the German student-soldiers of the First World War, who are reported to have carried Goethe's and Mörike's poems in one pocket of their knapsacks and Nietzsche's *Zarathustra* in the other, belong to a generation that never recovered from the conflict of divided allegiances.

Yet Nietzsche was anything but a Nietzschean, the connection between his writings and its ideological 'message' is hardly more than adventitious. He is the first and remains the greatest anti-systematic philosopher of modern Europe. The true posthumous history of his ideas is simple enough; it is summed up by Vauvenargues's reflection, 'Great men, while teaching little men to think, have set them on the path of error.' His thinking and writing at its best displays a vital, passionate commitment to an uncompromising truthfulness, of which his lack of discursiveness and his aphoristic style are the hallmarks; whereas, as F. H. Bradley observed, 'Our live experiences, fixed in aphorisms, stiffen into cold epigram' or, in the case of the Nietzscheans, into lifeless and life-destroying ideology. His finest insights have been turned into a rag-bag of -isms: vitalism, racialism, social Darwinism and anti-Semitism, and they became a main part of the superstructure of fascism. His writings, and especially the notebooks published posthumously by his sister under the title *Der Wille zur Macht* (*The Will to Power*, 1902 f.), contain elements of all these doctrines; they also contain thoughts scathingly critical of their contemporary uses. It is the advantage as it is the curse of those least restrictive forms he increasingly chose – aphorism, question-and-answer paragraph, brief or extended reflection – that they are able to accommodate and give expression to an unnerving speculative freedom, that in these forms *almost anything can be said*. This is the formal, stylistic correlative of his critique of traditional morality, of which he says that it is about to be superseded by a new licence whose motto is 'Everything is permitted' (meaning the heroic and noble deed as well as the dastardly one). What saves the greater part of his work from chaotic or sterile contradictoriness (and we shall see that not all his contradictions lead to chaos), what the 'Nietz-scheans' were bound to ignore, is the style and temper of his thinking. And if an excuse is needed for including a sketch of at least one of Nietzsche's books in a study of German literature, it lies in the fact that an original style of thinking and writing is deployed in the service not of an ideology, not of a novel system of values even, but of a new style of life.

Whatever other intellectual vices Nietzsche may display, he never allows himself the comfort of an easy way out. He is the most energetic and strenuous of thinkers, who comes to see a major value in the personal and 'existential' (the term is Kierkegaard's, not his) commitment of a man to his thinking, and who judges ideas primarily by a man's existential right to them. It was Nietzsche (not Sartre) who first saw man as the creator of his own values, and who demanded that 'our thinking and hypothesising shall reach no further than [our] creative will'.[1] This demand for a harmony between a man's vital powers on one hand and his reflective and cognitive capacities on the other Nietzsche does not always restrict to high philosophical matters: 'Worthy did this man seem to me, and ripe for the meaning of the earth. But when I beheld his wife, the earth seemed to me like a dwelling-place of the senseless.'[2] Again and again, in Nietzsche's observations on the thinkers and men of action of the past, it is not their detached opinions or achievements that matter to him but the quantity of personal being involved in their opinions or beliefs together with the quality of that being: 'God is an hypothesis. But who is there that could drink all the bitter torment of that hypothesis without dying.' Moreover, this unity of a man's thinking and doing, enjoined by Nietzsche from his earliest books to his last jottings, is not a matter of exhortation only. The aspiration towards it forms a major aspect of his manner of philosophising, of his several literary styles, and imposes at least some measure of coherence on the seemingly absolute speculative licence.

It is only in terms of this unity of living and thinking that Nietzsche's work as a critic of the culture of his age makes sense. The burden of his attack on contemporary Christianity, on academic scholarship and the 'disinterested' pursuit of knowledge as well as on the preoccupations with 'monumental' history and comparative religion have as their common source his concern for a balance between 'what we are' and 'what we should know': there is an innate balance between our vital resources and our capacity for belief or knowledge (he asserts), which must not be upset. He never tires of exposing the disharmony, the disproportion he sees at the root of modern life. 'God is dead'[3] because, even if he were alive, he wouldn't make the least difference to the life of modern man; the Socratic or scientific disposition of mind is harmful to 'the hygiene of life',[4] because scientific curiosity in its boundlessness may lead a man anywhere, even to the destruction of life; and a healthy forgetting and ignorance may on occasion serve the vital forces of life and man's true culture better than the dwarfing knowledge of an unmanageable past.

On occasion: in the face of the German idealist tradition that had addressed itself to 'man as such', to the *semper et ubique* of 'the human condition', Nietzsche's existentialism (somewhat like Marx's materialism) makes an issue of man's historicity by relating all insights explicitly and aggressively to his present condition, to 'the knowledge of his circumstances'.[5] And these 'circumstances' are still by and large our own. To take the conflict of 'knowledge' versus 'life': we are certain to have the gravest doubts about the solutions Nietzsche offers to the many problems that arise from it. We may even suspect that *some* of these problems arise through his habit of hypostatising concepts like 'life' and 'knowledge' in order to dramatise the conflict. But the burden of his attack remains unanswered, the problems have become more urgent than they ever were in his time.

It is no doubt true that Nietzsche himself failed to attain to that unity in which he came to see the only source of personal and philosophical authenticity – but not for want of trying. Indeed, the story of his conscious life, with its painful rejection of old friends and old ideas, and its several self-refutations, is hardly more than a series of strenuous attempts to live what he thought. Whereas the Nietzschean ideologists, it need hardly be added, meek fellow-travellers of tyranny, sought merely to justify their wretched conformism before their wretched 'philosophical' conscience in order to curry favour with their illiterate masters. The care and characteristic mode of his thinking, the fact that every 'solution' he offers is relative to the quality of a man's being and falsified outside that relation, they were bound to ignore. But the Fascist and National Socialist intellectuals are not alone when it comes to flattening out the contours of Nietzsche's thinking. Much of the contemporary attitude towards his passionate insights is summed up by that cartoon in which a question-master is addressing a panel of depressingly dim-looking clergymen: 'Next question, please. Now this one is for the chairman of our God-is-dead department.'

Friedrich Nietzsche was born in 1844 in Röcken, a small town not far from Leipzig, into a family which on both sides came from Lutheran clerical stock. The background is characteristic; from Handel through Lessing and Wieland to Hermann Hesse, German culture owes to the Lutheran parsonage a special debt which, as often as not, takes the form of a reaction against its spiritual ethos. His father died when Nietzsche was five years old, probably of a mental malady; at all events, the boy's attacks of migraine were taken to be hereditary. At the age of fourteen Nietzsche became a pupil at the famous school of Pforta (where Klopstock, Lessing and Fichte had been), destined by his mother for a clerical career; at Pforta he discovered the poetry of Hölderlin, at that time almost unknown. At the University of Bonn, which he entered in 1864, he attended lectures in classical archaeology and philology, and history of art. His later criticisms of the onesidedness of the German educational ethos must not obscure the fact that to the German universities of his time we owe the finest achievements and most important discoveries of modern classical scholarship – achievements moreover, to which he contributed and for which he retained an ambivalent admiration. A year later Nietzsche followed his teacher, F. Ritschl, to Leipzig. His studies were interrupted by a few months' service as a stretcher-bearer in an artillery regiment at Naumburg, from which he was discharged after an injury. In February 1869, even before he had submitted his doctoral dissertation, he was called to the University of Basle where, in the following year, he was given the Chair of Classical Philology. Volunteering as a medical orderly in the Franco-Prussian war of 1870, he was discharged after a month's service with grave gastric troubles. On his return to Basle severe attacks of migraine increasingly affected his eyesight; he resigned his teaching post, after prolonged periods of leave of absence, some six years later. From 1877 to the end of his conscious life in 1888 he lived mainly on a small university pension, in various parts of Switzerland, Northern Italy and Southern France, his threatened energies entirely devoted to his philosophical undertaking; only occasionally – as in the course of his friendship and break with Richard Wagner, whom he first met in 1868 – did he engage in polemical encounter.

Nietzsche's life is like an image of the life of the intellectual refugee of the 1930s. With a small case of books and a paraffin stove he moved from Alpine boarding-houses to modest rooms in Nice, Venice and Genoa, restless and almost entirely solitary. Hardly any friendships endured the strain of his exacting personality for long, again and again his relations founder on his refusal to compromise with those from whom he demanded absolute allegiance, regarding them at the same time as intellectually uninspiring. From this charge perhaps only his Basle colleague, the historian Jakob Burckhardt, for whom he retained an admiration tinged with irony, is ultimately exempt.[6] Burckhardt, he felt, had chosen to remain within the comforting precincts of scholarship – a refuge Nietzsche himself had rejected; but for all that it was Burckhardt who knew the full extent of his philosophical venture and who understood what forces had determined Nietzsche's choice.

The all but absolute solitude of Nietzsche's creative life is the setting as it is a major determining factor of his all but absolute individualism. For whom did he write? For the best among his contemporaries? For the future? The changes of tone, the varieties of rhetorical devices, all issue from soliloquy. His most 'popular' work, *Zarathustra*, its style leaning on Luther's Bible but also on

Heine's *Atta Troll* (without any of Heine's humour), is dedicated 'to None and All', meaning presumably a public of his own creation. In due course that public came into being – but what its qualities were I have already described.

The writings Nietzsche himself published span the astonishingly short period of sixteen years. Beginning with *The Birth of Tragedy* of 1872 and ending with the autobiographical *Ecce Homo* of 1888, he wrote some fourteen major works, which are followed by a convolute of more than a thousand notes intended for a final systematic résumé of his life's work. The heroic quality of this achievement in the face of increasing odds may well be without parallel; only rarely (in *Morgenröte, Aurora*, of 1881, his own favourite book, and its sequel, *Die fröhliche Wissenschaft, The Gay Science*, of 1882) is the intellectual pace of his writing anything but the most exacting.

Early in January 1889, in a street in Turin, he suffered a physical and mental collapse from which he never recovered. His disease, paralysis of the insane, is thought to have been syphilitic in origin. He endured it, with intermittent periods of sanity, in the hideous care of his sister. Surrounded by the 'Nietzsche-Archiv' through which this self-important lady was cashing in on his growing fame, he died at Weimar in 1900.

. . . schauen zu müssen und zugleich über das Schauen hinaus sich zu sehnen . . .[7]

In his second work, *Unzeitgemässe Betrachtungen* (*Thoughts out of Season*, 1873–6), in the section entitled 'On the Uses and Abuses of History in Life' (1874), Nietzsche assails the 'disinterested' study of the past and the untrammelled pursuit of knowledge generally. Such pursuits, he writes, are the subterfuge of those who are morally and existentially incapable of fulfilling, let alone determining, the demands of their own age or the course of history. His first work, *The Birth of Tragedy from the Spirit of Music* (on which I shall here concentrate), is the brilliant masterpiece of his classical apprenticeship; it exemplifies what Nietzsche means by an authentic use of scholarship. His manner of exposition implicitly refutes the time-honoured distinction between creative and learned prose – he convinces as much by apocryphal anecdote and telling story as he does by discursive argument. In his account of the history of Greek drama and thought there is no difference of status between 'the god Silenus' and 'the demon Socrates', between 'was' and 'was believed to be'. Like most nineteenth-century writers he sees the origin of Greek drama in the chorus. *Its* origin, however, lies not in prayer or orderly ritual; least of all is it a manifestation of the city-state's democratic will. Its origin lies in music. The chorus is for him, quite literally, the assembly of satyrs as they accompany Dionysus on his drunken revels in the forest. In their ecstasy ('Rausch') and in their dirge, they and their god are one. What they express in their music and song is the oneness of all things, the absence of individuation in their world. (This idea points back to Schopenhauer's world of the Cosmic Will, and forward to Freud's 'oceanic feeling' as well as to Heidegger's concept of *Angst*.) Intuitively, as yet unbeknown to them (for to know would be to be distinct and separate from the object of knowledge), their song expresses the desolateness and impermanence of all things and of life itself. This desolateness is for Nietzsche the fundamental disposition of man ('das menschliche Urgefühl'). In their wake King Midas roams through the woods, seeking Dionysus's companion, Silenus, who is hiding from him. And when at last the mortal Midas finds and catches him and forces him to speak, the devastating truth Silenus discloses brings him self-consciousness, reflectiveness, and tragic apprehension:

> You want to know what life is about [Silenus asks]? The best is out of your reach, for the best of all things is not to have been born, not to be, to be nothing. (section 3)

Faced with this knowledge men become sober, reflective, they are no longer at one with themselves (we think of Schiller's 'sentimentalisch' poet, but also of Rilke's Fourth Duino Elegy). Their task is now to hide this terrible knowledge from themselves and, eventually, from those who watch their revels. This they do by making an image of it, an ecstatic show, a story, an action. It is of the essence of that action that it should *both* preserve the tragic nature of the knowledge they now possess *and* make it bearable. And the god who helps them to fashion this story, who helps them to organise this knowledge in a bearable, that is beautiful form, is the image-making god Apollo.

At this point (section 4) we have reached the two fundamental modes of knowledge-and-life which encompass Nietzsche's view of tragedy (and a good deal more besides): its Dionysian foundation

('Urgrund') and the Apolline order superimposed upon it. The distinction has its roots in Schopenhauer's dichotomy of the world as Will and Idea; comprehends but goes beyond Aristotle's distinction of matter and form; and it belongs among the three or four memorable arguments in the history of modern European aesthetics. When the Dionysian element rules, ecstatic chaos threatens; when the Apolline predominates, the tragic feeling recedes. Of the two, the Dionysian remains the fundamental, but the balance in the great works of tragic art is of the subtlest and most precarious. It is achieved in Aeschylus, reaches its finest form in Sophocles; and where – as in the work of Euripides – the Dionysian is attenuated and finally suppressed, there tragedy dies and the thwarted god (in *The Bacchae*) takes his revenge.

The predominance of the Dionysian in Greek tragedy at its finest implies intuition and ecstasy as the only authentic mode of artistic creation; it implies, more specifically, an unreflective belief in the germinal myths from which tragedy is fashioned, a belief the Greek poets share with their public. What these myths represent is not a mimetic *action* but the articulation of a *mood*, 'eine Grundstimmung', which we have called a style of life. This conception of a 'mood' is, throughout Nietzsche's writings, more fundamental than rational argument, of which it is the source. The decline of tragedy begins where creative ecstasy gives way to cold calculation; now the old myths become objects of analysis, and the gods are judged according to the prosy maxims of reasoned justice. Man's unreflective exposure to the tragic spectacle Nietzsche had identified with aesthetic delight. Now tragedy is expected to yield a didactic, moral message. Thought takes over from art, the reign of Socrates begins. Socrates is the ugly, inartistic man *par excellence*. His emphasis on conviction through cleverness in rational argument is the refuge of one who has no understanding of the ecstatic mystery of art, no fervour of belief in the gods. In *Jenseits von Gut und Böse* (*Beyond Good and Evil*, 1886) Nietzsche will continue the polemic by describing the cause of Socrates' impiety and dialectical skill as a vital deprivation, a lack of natural gifts and powers; the cause is, finally, Socrates' defective and thwarted will to power, which triumphs over 'life' (represented by the gifted and handsome Alcibiades) by means as clever as they are ignoble. The 'blackmail' of Socrates' sacrificial death is the final sanction and triumph of his rationality; the connection between it and the triumph of the 'otherworldly' and 'hinterweltlich' morality of the Christian religion with *its* sacrificial death is elaborated in *Zur Genealogie der Moral* (*The Genealogy of Morals*, 1887).

In *The Birth of Tragedy* a different aspect of the same story is told. The death of tragedy in the new reign of rationalism is followed by the emergence of new genres – the Aesopian fable and the Platonic dialogue. The latter especially is a debasement of the ancient form, its real though unacknowledged aim is the destruction of the ancient myths and natural pieties. Tragic man is superseded by rational, scientific man, the creative pessimism of those who were initiated into Silenus's mystery gives way to the flat optimism of the Socratic paradox, which Nietzsche presents as the basic dogma of Socratic morality (in other words, he does to the Socratic paradox what the Nietzscheans did to *his* paradoxes). In the identification of knowledge with virtue, of the clever and well-informed man with the good, Nietzsche sees the crowning folly of Socrates' impious conviction that reason and science can reach to the ground of man's being. There is perhaps no need to labour the obvious: Nietzsche's account of the death of tragedy and his critique of Socratic rationality is a critique of contemporary scientism and of its shallow optimism.

What we have followed up to this point (the end of section 16) is, roughly, the historical and critical argument of Nietzsche's *Birth of Tragedy*. Before turning to its constructive part it may be useful to consider three main objections that are likely to arise in the reader's mind. First, and most obviously, scholars are likely to impugn many of his sources, especially in the polemic against Socrates, as suspect in their authenticity; it takes no great classical learning to see that some of these sources are hardly more than time-hallowed gossip. There is, secondly, Nietzsche's peculiarly mixed manner of seeking to convince: a compound of rhetoric, anecdotes, sorties into 'straight' scholarship, appeals to the authorities of Kant and (in the passages on music) Schopenhauer, and imposed on these the penetrating psychological insights and inferences.[8] And there are, thirdly, occasional distortions, or at least suppressions, of evidence pointing to different conclusions. Some of these objections, it may be added, are likely to be raised against his later works also. Little is gained, I think, by defending *The Birth of Tragedy* against these charges. All one can do is point to the profound insights into the psychology of art that the essay affords, and to ask what other work that sails under the flag of 'classical scholarship' affords a comparable illumination. The attempt to explain (rather than defend) these flaws is likely to be more fruitful.

What Nietzsche has undertaken is not primarily a piece of scholarship but a critique of the modern mind in its exaltation of reason over music and art, of rational morality against myth. Moreover (we now move into the 'constructive' part of the argument), the essay aspires to being not only a critique of but a contribution to the new myth of which modern Europe – or rather Germany – is said to be in such dire need. For at this point a peculiar causality is introduced. Once we have accepted the account of the decline of Greek drama as caused by the demise of the life-giving myths, it follows that a re-birth of tragedy and of the arts, indeed of *the tragic sense of life*, can only come about through the birth, or rather the creation, of new myths. Music is not only the source of tragedy, it is also (here Nietzsche takes up Schopenhauer's argument in book iii of *The World as Will and Idea*) the one art above all others which encompasses and most directly retraces the whole world of men, 'its weal and woe'; it does this in a medium to which considerations of morality, utility and survival itself are irrelevant. 'Only as an aesthetic pheno-menon' – as music or as a tragic spectacle – 'is the being of man justified.' Three times the thought is repeated in Nietzsche's essay, each time its ostensible aim is to free the aesthetic from importuning moral considerations, from rationality itself. Yet behind this osten-sible aim lies the belief with which Nietzsche's historical account began. Ultimately the function of music and of tragedy is not so much to justify the world as rather to make it bearable. And – this is Nietzsche's grand finale – it is in the music of Richard Wagner, in the third act of *Tristan und Isolde*, that the new German myth is born.

Has the need for new myths been really proved? Can the creation of new myths ever be part of a deliberate programme? Why Germany, why Richard Wagner? Instead of launching on the contingent indictment of Nietzsche as an irrationalist, proto-fascist and nationalist, it may be better to attempt answers to these three interconnected questions.

Chief among the omissions of Nietzsche's historical argument is any mention of the political aspect of Greek tragedy. The conflict of laws that informs *Antigone* has no place in his account. Oedipus is for him, as he is for Freud, not a ruler at all but a single heroic man in agony. Were Nietzsche to take issue with the apotheosis of the rule of law and the inception of representative democratic government as we find them at the end of *The Cupbearers* (the second part of Sophocles' *Oresteia*), he could not reject the interpretation of the chorus as 'a constitutional representation of the people' out of hand, adding for good measure that 'one hopes the Greeks in their tragedies had not even an inkling of such a blasphemy'. In brief, Nietzsche bypasses Hegel's entire undertaking – unique among German theories of tragedy – to secure a political dimension for our under-standing of Greek tragedy. It is Hegel, not Nietzsche, who cultivates our sense for its otherness, and shows how irrelevant nineteenth-century individualism is to the political aspect, and thus also to the total character, of classical tragedy. Nietzsche's sole emphasis is on the metaphysical 'Urgrund', for him there is only the prepolitical collective of the ecstatic chorus on the one hand, and the alienated individual of the Socratic ideology on the other. The city state (we read in an earlier essay)[9] is the embodiment of the heroic will to power. As such (the argument is taken up in *The Birth of Tragedy*) it is again a creation of the image-making faculty of Apollo; for, like all life, it becomes meaningful 'only as an aesthetic phenomenon'. Political and social activity is secondary and derivative, the primacy of the mythopoeic is never questioned. The state is the creation of the Apolline 'will to form'. The next step in Nietzsche's argument[10] is to present its ruler as an artist at work in the medium of society, creating 'aesthetic' forms out of the human material of the body politic: imprinting on it his untrammelled will, indifferent to ques-tions of guilt and responsibility, informed by 'the terrible egoism of the artistic genius'. And the next step after that. . . .

But we had better return to *The Birth of Tragedy*. To be meaning-ful, Nietzsche's formulation has to be tied to a sequential argument: human existence is what it is *before* it ever receives its 'justification'. Is it the function of 'the aesthetic' simply to portray that existence or to change it? To encompass all life or to improve it? Such a justi-fication, if it is to be total, a set of brackets outside, cannot change anything inside the world; it can only make the world appear in a different light, under a different mode; inside, it must leave every-thing as it is. Yet Nietzsche's concern is also with the consequences of the aesthetic 'justification' as a regeneration of the national life, with a change inside the brackets: and this, whether or not he acknowledges it, is a political concern. What was true for the beginning of Greek tragedy is equally true for its end. We find Nietzsche asserting a causal sequence from the destruction of the myths to the death of tragedy: is it not (we may ask) just as convincing[11] to see the death of the myths as a consequence of the political decay of Greece? And if so, can the creation of new myths ever bring about a national rebirth – a rebirth, that is, of the tragic sense of life *in the nation*? Above all, if we consider a nation not as a cultural but as a political unit, in what sense can a nation ever be said to have 'a tragic sense of life'?

In the pious hope that new aesthetic myths will bring about a national rebirth, Nietzsche's thinking is not as unseasonable ('unzeitgemäß') as he fancies. This, after all, is the wish-fulfilment of the many deprivations voiced by German poets throughout the century, and exploited by the nationalists of the Second Reich. The hope that a cultural and aesthetic rebirth would lead to a new national unity had been expressed in similar terms by Novalis and Hölderlin; and some of Nietzsche's own formulations are surprisingly close to Heine's,[12] albeit without Heine's caustic *cavete canem*. This hope is the inspiration of Jacob Grimm, father of German literary and linguistic scholarship,[13] as it is an essential part of the 'nonpolitical' ambience that made possible, even if it was not the cause of, the power politics of Bismarck and his successors. Nietzsche too shares 'the German ideology', the belief in the priority of spiritual causation over material,[14] and the belief in the non-political, otherworldly character of the 'true' Germany, when he writes in section 23:

> The value of a nation – and also, incidentally, of a man – is equal to its capacity to inform its living experiences [seine Erlebnisse] with the stamp of the Eternal; for in this way the nation is as it were made unworldly [entweltlicht], and shows its unconscious inner conviction regarding the relative nature of time and the true, that is metaphysical, meaning of life.

But why should a 'nation' behave in the same way as a man? Why should it have the same or an analogous capacity for 'experience'? What nation has ever opted out of the world? Why, conversely, should 'the world' be something different from the nations that

compose it? It is difficult to think of these hypostatisations as anything but primitive, and one wishes Nietzsche's contempt for 'the
English political economists' had been less absolute.

Again and again throughout Nietzsche's work we find the most
penetrating critical insights capped by most dubious 'constructive'
proposals: 'Without a myth every culture loses its healthy, creative
natural power. Only a horizon enclosed by myths gives unity to a
whole cultural movement.' Nietzsche's critical observation, we feel,
is no less relevant to the condition of our culture than it was to his.
But the truth of this insight doesn't make his plea for 'the birth' of a
new mythology less preposterous. In the second of his *Thoughts out of
Season* he will enlarge on his psychological idea of 'the human horizon', arguing that it is the necessary limiting condition of a man's
vital and intellectual powers alike. In *The Birth of Tragedy* only its
aesthetic and spiritual functions are discussed. The rebirth he has
in mind refers, as I have said, to the tragic feeling of life, not to
power-politics, yet the falsification of his thought is entailed by the
thought itself. Myths *can* be made up, and they can be effective. The
Wilhelminian idea of 'das Volk' was just such a synthetic myth. It
had its roots in Romantic theorising, as 'an imaginary national
whole, . . . which so far admittedly exists only imperfectly, and only
in the longing of the best Germans.'[15] Even when it became a major
factor in the German politics of the era, the myth retained its
peculiarly literary and aesthetic quality. But it was hardly what
Nietzsche had in mind when (at the end of *The Birth of Tragedy*) he
apostrophised Richard Wagner as the white hope of German culture
and when, in 1878, finding that the Wagnerian myth had taken root
among the German 'Kulturphilister', he broke with Wagner and his
work.

'Not this', he is in effect saying to each reconciliation of metaphysics with reality as it comes into view, 'Not this . . . and not that
either.' Contemptuous of jingoism, of the German aspirations in
Europe, of his sister's odious circle of anti-Semites, contemptuous
of the socialist ideology, and eventually of the scientific attitude too—
what concrete form did he expect the new myth to take?

Coming to the last sections of *The Birth of Tragedy*, a reader
unacquainted with the temper of the age is bound to rub his eyes in
puzzlement. After this *tour de force* through classical antiquity, why

Wagner, why Germany? We might also ask, why 'the Superman', why the paradox of 'the Eternal Recurrence?' The questions take us back to the 'style' of Nietzsche's philosophical venture, to the fact that he never reconciled himself to its being 'merely' a philosophical and reflective undertaking. The very violence of his notorious metaphors, especially in *Zarathustra*, points to the dissatisfaction with his rôle as 'only a thinker'; so do Nietzsche's poems; so do his various rhetorical styles and parables and his mixing of literary genres. A philosopher of life? To Nietzsche this was apt to be a contradiction in terms, for 'life' as he saw it was the *ground* of all thought,* and could therefore not be defined, let alone determined, by philosophical thought. He counters the dogma of rationalism by subordinating thought to 'life', 'nature', 'instinct', 'good taste', and other such professedly non-rational criteria; and in so doing rebuts all rational criticism *ex hypothesi*. From this contradiction springs the breathtaking energy of his thinking, and his ever-present need for concreteness, for a *grounding* of his thought in the world. In *The Birth of Tragedy* 'Wagner' and 'Germany' fulfil, or are meant to fulfil, this need. But this early work already foreshadows the way Nietzsche's ethical programme – his project to create a new, finer style of life – will merge with his epistemological programme – his attempt to close the gap between world and interpreted world.

How is this concreteness to be achieved? The fantastic racial notions of Nietzsche's later work and some of his remarks about national character, which bring the blush of embarrassment to his reader's cheek, derive from his brief and superficial acquaintance with the contemporary biological sciences; so do the 'Supermen's' most rebarbative qualities. Science, in the early 1880s, seems to

---

* This is the logical conundrum to which I referred on p. 184 above. It is handed down from Schopenhauer to Nietzsche and from Nietzsche to Alfred Rosenberg, Ernst Jünger *et alia*; this is its form: *If* you take X to be the Will; or the Will to Power; or blood; or race; or 'die Gestalt des Arbeiters', etc.; *if* you take Y to be reason; or analytical reason; or criticism; or the pallid/degenerate critical/hypercritical faculty, etc., *then*: any attempt to define X by Y must fail, *because* X is the basis, or root, or ground (= Urgrund) of Y, and how can you expect to define or explain the fundamental by means of its derivate, the primary by means of the secondary?

o

offer him the firm ground he seeks for his philosophy. The doctrine of the 'Eternal Recurrence', that proving-stone of the Superman's worth, is a part of this search. 'To be compelled to look and at the same time to yearn beyond the looking.' The paradoxical doctrine of an everlasting repetition of the here-and-now is to supply man's need for a metaphysics, but this metaphysics is to be concrete and 'immanent' because in it life, *this* life, is to be made eternal:

> I shall return [Zarathustra proclaims] with this sun, with this earth, with this eagle, with this snake – *not* to a new life, or a better life, or a similar life:
> – I shall return always to this self-same life, in the greatest and in the smallest things, that I may again teach the recurrence of all things, – that I may speak again the Word of the great noon of earth and of man, that I may again herald the Superman to all men.[16]

And to this recurrence the Superman is to give his absolute assent. So great is to be his love of life that even when life is to be perpetuated in all its greatness and triviality *ad infinitum* and *ad nauseam*, without change or added meaning, he will assent to it. Then indeed he will have proved himself, then he will have fully exposed himself to the merciless rays of the midday sun, the sun that sheds its harsh light into every nook and cranny of experience, leaving no comfort in the dark caves and picturesque grottoes of ancient comforts and religions. This is the most difficult faith – likely to make our vital powers shrivel up in horror – that the Superman's creator has been able to devise for him: this, ultimately, is the new myth that Wagner has failed to create.

An early poem of Friedrich Hölderlin's, to which I have already referred (see p. 152), is entitled 'Mein Eigentum' ('My Possessions'). In it, he evokes the necessaries of a man's life: orchard and field, vineyard, house and hearth.

> Es leuchtet über festem Boden
> Schöner dem sicheren Mann sein Himmel.

> Above firm ground the sky gleams
> More beautifully to the safe man.

Without these things a man's body and soul are dispossessed and unaccommodated. So much so, Rilke takes up the thought, a hundred years later, that

> . . . die findigen Tiere merken es schon,
> dass wir nicht sehr verlässlich zu Haus sind
> > in der gedeuteten Welt.

> even the canny animals notice
> that we are not very reliably at home
> > in the interpreted world.[17]

The poet (Hölderlin continues) has no such possessions, yet he too needs such a sheet anchor, 'lest homeless my soul should yearn/on and beyond life.' And he finds it in his song, his friendly refuge: 'dass . . . heimathlos meine Seele mir nicht/Über das Leben hinweg sich sehne/Sei du, Gesang! mein freundlich Asyl! . . .'

The philosopher Nietzsche faces a predicament at once similar and more radical. The man *he* finds is not 'safe', but 'gemütlich', gross and comfortable; his 'possessions' are contemptible; gone, too, is the sky's beautiful gleam, a dark wintry sky broods over him. And the philosopher-poet's song – where shall he find substance for it? Another of Hölderlin's poems[18] takes up the central question of Nietzsche's philosophy, his and his century's search for a reality – or at least the fragments of a reality – that would not turn to dross:

> Weh mir, wo nehm ich, wenn
> Es Winter ist, die Blumen, und wo
> Den Sonnenschein
> Und Schatten der Erde?

> Alas, where shall I find when
> Winter comes, flowers, and where
> Sunshine
> And the shadows of earth?

References

CHAPTER I

1 *Re-Interpretations. Seven Studies in Nineteenth-Century German Literature* (London 1964).
2 See Nietzsche's second Introduction to 'Die Philosophie im tragischen Zeitalter der Griechen', in *Werke* (ed. Karl Schlechta, vol. iii, München n.d., 352).
3 Marx-Engels, *Gesamtausgabe* I/vol. v (Berlin 1932), 18–19. I shall return to the 'sensuous assurance' ('sinnliche Gewissheit'), a quotation from Hegel, below, pp. 210–11.
4 *Die politischen Reden des Fürsten Bismarck*, ed. H. Kohl, vol. xiii (Stuttgart 1905), 361.
5 Jacob Grimm, *Kleinere Schriften*, vol. viii (Berlin 1864), 304.
6 This testament was first published in Alfred Heuss's *Theodor Mommsen und das neunzehnte Jahrhundert* (Kiel 1956), 282.
7 Bertolt Brecht, *Kleines Organon für das Theater*, §75.
8 *Die Poggenpuhls* (1896), chapter 4.
9 G. Roethe, *Deutsche Dichter des 18. und 19. Jahrhunderts und ihre Politik* (Berlin 1919), 5; my italics.
10 *Wissenschaft als Beruf* of 1919 and *Politik als Beruf*, 1921; reprinted in Max Weber, *Schriften zur theoretischen Soziologie*, ed. Graf zu Solms (Frankfurt/M. 1947).
11 Erich Auerbach, *Mimesis*, transl. by W. R. Trask (New York 1953), 433–4.

CHAPTER 2

1 The following plays of Grillparzer have been translated by

Arthur Burkhard (all published at Yarmouth Port, Mass.): *The Guest-Friend – The Argonauts* (1942, revised 1947); *Medea* (1941, 1947); *Sappho* (1953); *Esther – The Jewess of Toledo* (1953); *Family Strife in Hapsburg* (1940, 1949); *A Faithful Servant of His Master* (1941); *King Ottocar, his Rise and Fall* (1962); *Hero and Leander (The Waves of the Sea and of Love)* 1962. *Medea* has also been translated by F. J. Lamport (Penguin Classics, 1969).

2 Act i, last scene. I follow, with some changes, Arthur Burkhard's translation, *Family Strife in Hapsburg* (1949), 29.

3 I shall quote from the fourth Insel edition, *Georg Büchners Werke und Briefe*, ed. F. Bergemann (Leipzig 1949).

4 Thomas Paine in *Dantons Tod*, Act II, scene I.

5 I here choose Miss Margaret Jacobs's text, *Georg Büchner: Dantons Tod and Woyzeck* (Manchester 1954).

6 *Judith and Holofernes* (1849), scene 24.

7 *Der Zerrissene* is taken from the vaudeville *L'homme blasé* by Duvert and Lanzaune (1843); an English version, *Used Up* (1844) was produced by the actor, John Thomas Matthew (1805–1889). Occasionally this process has been reversed, as when Thornton Wilder adapted *Einen Jux will er sich machen* for *The Matchmaker*. English versions are to be found in *Johann Nestroy: Three Comedies*, transl. M. Knight and J. Fabry (New York 1967).

CHAPTER 3

1 My only excuse for these translations is that I haven't found better ones.

2 In the poem 'Zu Heinrich Heines Gedächtnis', beginning 'Zerrissnen Tones, überlauter Rede/Verfänglich Blendwerk muss vergessen sein. . . .'

3 I have quoted the famous prophetic passage from Heine's *History of Religion and Philosophy in Germany* of 1852 in *Re-Interpretations*, 221.

4 T. W. Adorno, 'Die Wunde Heine', in *Noten zur Literatur*, I (Frankfurt/M. 1958), 144 ff.

5 See W. Victor, *Marx und Heine* (Berlin 1953); Barker Fairley (see his ed. of *Heinrich Heine: Atta Troll, ein Sommernachtstraum – Deutschland, ein Wintermärchen*, Oxford 1966) offers a soberer account of the relationship (33–4).

6 Quoted in the postscript to Barker Fairley, ibid., 207.

7 Barker Fairley, ibid., 209.

8 Karl Kraus in *Die Fackel* of November 1920, reprinted in *Widerschein der Fackel*, vol. iv of *Werke* (München 1956), 281.

9 Friedrich Engels's translation of the poem from *The New Moral World*, no. 25, of 13 December 1844 (quoted from the facsimile in *Marx-Engels: Werke*, vol. ii, Berlin 1962, 512).

10 See S. S. Prawer, *German Lyric Poetry* (London 1952), 146.

11 See Walther Killy, *Wandlungen des lyrischen Bildes* (Göttingen 1961), 103 ff.; predictably, the social and critical direction of Heine's clichés is ignored.

12 See Barker Fairley, *Heinrich Heine, an Interpretation* (Oxford 1954).

13 'There are clear indications [in the Harvard manuscript] that the colloquy between two strange lovers (which is now, in every sense, the centre of the poem), was an afterthought.' (S. S. Prawer, *Heine, the Tragic Satirist*, Cambridge 1961, 259.)

CHAPTER 4

1 Benno von Wiese, *Eduard Mörike* (Tübingen 1950).

2 H.-E. Holthusen, 'Eduard Mörike', *Merkur* 237, xxi. Jahrgang, Heft 12 (December 1967), 1122–1140.

3 S. S. Prawer, *Mörike und seine Leser* (Würzburg 1960), which also contains a list of the many musical settings of his poems.

4 Romano Guardini, *Gegenwart und Geheimnis; eine Auslegung von fünf Gedichten Mörikes* (Stuttgart 1957).

5 Most directly Emil Staiger, *Grundbegriffe der Poetik* (Zürich 1946).

6 A critical edition of Mörike's work (*Werke und Briefe: historisch-kritische Gesamtausgabe*, ed. H.-H. Krummacher, etc., Stuttgart 1967) is in progress but unfortunately begins (vol. iii, 1967) with his prose writings; my quotations come from *Sämtliche Werke*, ed. H. G. Göpfert (München 1964).

7 For a sympathetic English biography see M. L. Mare, *Eduard Mörike: the Man and the Poet* (London 1957).

8 Romano Guardini, op. cit.

9 My translation owes much to N. K. Cruickshank's; see *Poems of Mörike*, transl. N. K. Cruickshank and G. F. Cunningham (London 1959), 76.

CHAPTER 5

1 *The Blue and Brown Books*, 1933–4 (Oxford 1964), 17–18.
2 Jean-Paul Sartre, *La Nausée* (Paris 1938), 146.
3 *Abdias* (1843), opening section.
4 *Der Kuss von Sentze*, 1869.
5 '. . . wenn sich anders etwas so wenig Gegliedertes darstellen lässt, das eher durch sein einfaches Dasein als durch seine Erregung wirket.' *Erzählungen*, vol. iv, *Sämtliche Werke*, ed. L. Müller (Prague 1911), 218, my italics. I shall quote from this edition.
6 *Sonette an Orpheus*, ii, II.
7 See the opening of Stifter's *Abdias* (1842); 'Dieses war den Alten Fatum, furchtbar letzter starrer Grund des Geschehenden . . . letzte Unvernunft des Seins. . . .'
8 It is, however, a pleasure to record the perceptiveness of Victorian criticism. The following passage is taken from an anonymous review of the first four volumes of *Studien* (1844, 1847) in *The Athenaeum* of 26 August 1848 (pp. 851–3): 'Stifter appears to be most at home among the forests and in the ravines of that lonely mountainous tract, – where the high pine-clad ridges that separate Austria from Bohemia part some of the great waters of Germany; on the one hand, sending down the Moldau and Löschnitz from its rocky bosom northward to join the Elbe beyond the walls of Prague, – and on the other, overhanging with masses of primeval shade the valley of the Danube between Passau and Linz. This range, known by the name of the Boehmerwald, where it turns in a north-westerly direction to mark the frontier of Bavaria, is still in parts a solitude as virgin from the touch of man as in the days when the whole region around was dark with the great Hercynian forest. The high valleys only that run up amidst the spurs of the mountains, scantily tilled, support a few robust and simple men, half foresters, half peasants, little changed in speech or habits from the rudeness of ancient times, and still living with undisturbed faith in the customs and traditions of the past. They seldom wander beyond the limits of this secluded region, and know little of strangers from the busier world beyond it. Here, then, may still be found in undisturbed

power the awfulness as well as the beauty of forest and mountain scenery; the deep impressiveness of which is to the German what the ocean influences are to the English poet. . . . It is one of the few districts now remaining in the heart of modern Europe where Nature may still be found slumbering in majestic proportions, unchanged by the quick industry of man; where a sensitive, dreamy lover of her looks and voices may still busy himself, and for a time forget the restless work, of human energies and human wants, that has nearly effaced her original features from the Europe of our day.' On *Abdias*: 'The story . . . is ill proportioned, – and the close so abrupt, after a most elaborate beginning, that the effect is like that of a highly finished doorway leading into mere vacant space.' (Quoted from M. Enzinger, *Adalbert Stifter im Urteil seiner Zeit*, Wien 1968, pp. 128–32.) It seems probable (at least, on the evidence of a note about his 'literary earnings for 1848' and his interest in German literature) that the review was by G. H. Lewes (see *The George Eliot Letters*, ed. G. S. Haight, London, 1956, vol. vii, p. 369).

9 Max Stefl, *Adalbert Stifter: Erzählungen in der Urfassung*, 3 vols. (Augsburg 1952).

10 E.g. 'die *obenerwähnten* Bäume'; elsewhere Stifter uses emphatic pronouns like '*derselbe*' where they are grammatically redundant; inexorably elaborated subjunctives, and the heaviest of compound tenses; heavy final '-e's, etc.

11 These are reprinted in *Die Schulakten Adalbert Stifters*, ed. K. Vancsa (Nürnberg 1955) which records, in full detail, the unbelievably tedious administrative work Stifter had to undertake until at last his request for a pension was granted – two years before his death.

12 *Der Hochwald* (1842), section 2, both versions, my italics.

13 *A. Stifters kulturpolitische Aufsätze*, ed. W. Reich (Einsiedeln 1948).

14 *St Augustine's Exposition on the Book of Psalms* (Oxford 1857), vol. vi, 327 ff., my italics.

15 *Der Nachsommer*, chapter 2; I have kept to Stifter's punctuation but added my italics.

16 See *Briefwechsel*, ed. A. Sauer, etc., vol. iv (Prague 1925) 45, Stifter's italics; cf. also K. G. Fischer, *Adalbert Stifter: psychologische Beiträge zur Biographie* (Linz 1961), 93.

17 C. E. Schorske, 'The Transformation of the Garden: Ideal and Society in Austrian Literature' in *Transactions of the Twelfth International Congress of the Historical Sciences* (Vienna 1965), 1283–1320.

CHAPTER 6

1 R. Pascal, *The German Novel* (Manchester 1957), 35.
2 Georg Lukács, *Gottfried Keller* (Berlin 1947).
3 '. . . wir sind allzumal dualistische Tröpfe.' The remark is made by one of Heinrich Lee's friends at Munich.
4 See, e.g., H. S. Hughes, *Consciousness and Society* (London 1958).
5 E. H. Carr, *What is History?* (London 1964), 31.
6 *Der Fall Wagner*, ed. Kröner, vol. v (Leipzig 1930), 42.
7 *Menschliches, Allzumenschliches*, ed. cit., vol. ii, 227.
8 *Faust* I, last scene.
9 Theodor Fontane, *Schriften zur Literatur*, ed. H.-H. Reuter (Berlin 1960), 63.
10 'Frau Regel Amrain und ihr Jüngster', end.
11 In 'Romeo und Julia auf dem Dorfe'.

CHAPTER 7

1 Barker Fairley, *Wilhelm Raabe: an Introduction to his Novels* (Oxford 1961), 266.
2 Quoted ibid., 267–8, from *Alte Nester* (1879).
3 Georg Weerth, *Fragment eines Romans*, ed. B. Kaiser, in *Georg Weerth: Sämtliche Werke*, vol. ii (Berlin 1956), 147–484.
4 See H. Meyer, *The Poetics of Quotation in the European Novel*, transl. by T. and Y. Ziolkowski (Princeton 1968).
5 See H. Meyer, *Der Sonderling in der deutschen Literatur* (München 1963).
6 See J. P. Stern, *Thomas Mann* (Columbia Series on Modern Writers, New York 1967).
7 G. Steiner, *Tolstoy or Dostoevsky* (London 1960).
8 However, both Barker Fairley and Romano Guardini regard it as Raabe's greatest work.
9 'Epilog zu Essex.'

P

10 Cf. J. P. Stern, 'The Dear Purchase', in *German Quarterly*, xli, May 1968, 317–37.

11 We shall probably never know whether Thomas Mann, who mentions Raabe only in the most perfunctory manner, ever read *Die Akten*.

CHAPTER 8

1 See *Beyond Recall* (i.e. *Unwiederbringlich*), Oxford 1964, and *Effi Briest* (Penguin Books 1967), introduced and translated by Douglas Parmée.

2 *Die Poggenpuhls* (1896), chapter iv.

3 *Betrachtungen eines Unpolitischen, 1914–1919.*

4 See M.-E. Gilbert, *Das Gespräch in Fontanes Gesellschaftsromanen* (Leipzig 1930) and P. Demetz, *Formen des Realismus: Theodor Fontane* (München 1964).

5 *Morgenröte* (1886), book iv, para. 244.

6 *Effi Briest* (1895), chapters 19–21; there is a nostalgic echo of this scene in Samuel Beckett's *Molloy*, and also in *Krapp's Last Tape*.

7 *Vor dem Sturm*, chapter 79.

8 P. Demetz, op. cit., 59 f. compares and contrasts Lewin with Sir Walter Scott's Edward Waverley; he also (p. 75) quotes a particularly glaring example of what I have called the intellectual bad manners of the unregenerated nationalistic 'critics'.

9 Fontane has interpolated the passage that follows in Fichte's lecture course, *Die Staatslehre, oder über das Verhältnis des Urstaates zum Vernunftreich* held at the University of Berlin in the summer of 1813 (see J. G. Fichte's *Sämtliche Werke*, iv, Berlin 1945, 369–600). It was Fichte's habit (see ibid., 603–10) to interrupt his lectures with an excursus in which he proceeded to apply his theoretical deliberations to questions of the day. Fontane places the tirade at the beginning of the second section of *Die Staatslehre*, entitled 'Über den Begriff des wahrhaften Krieges' (ibid., 401). The mimesis is perfect – a reader of the lectures who is familiar with Fichte's style may well need reminding that Fontane's interpolation is indeed a fiction.

10 The phrase is Ian Watt's in *The Rise of the Novel* (London 1957). See also his 'Second Thoughts . . .' in *Novel*, i, Spring 1968, 205–18.

CHAPTER 9

1 See T. J. Rogers, *Techniques of Solipsism: a Study of Theodor Storm's Narrative Fiction* (Cambridge 1970).

2 In the volume *Fünf Schlösser* (1888, a continuation of *Wanderungen durch die Mark Brandenburg*) Fontane shows considerable familiarity with Schopenhauer's life and letters (see his *Sämtliche Werke*, vol. xiii, München 1960, 125–32), but on a much later occasion (in a letter to the philosopher, Friedrich Paulsen, 1 June 1898) he confesses to his complete lack of philosophical training (and, one feels, interest).

3 This observation would of course not have pleased Schopenhauer, who regarded 'the Charlatan' ('Windbeutel') Hegel as his direst enemy.

4 Its connection with Calvinism is established in Max Weber's famous essays in *Die protestantische Ethik und der Geist des Kapitalismus* of 1904–5.

5 Paul de Lagarde in 1886; quoted from H. Pross, *Die Zerstörung der deutschen Politik: Dokumente 1870–1933* (Frankfurt 1959), 278.

6 i.e. The Hon. Mrs Skewton of *Dombey and Son*.

7 I quote from D. Parmée's translation, *Beyond Recall* (Oxford 1964), 222–3; my italics.

8 Ibid., 113.

9 *Beyond Recall*, ed. cit., 269–70.

CHAPTER 10

1 *Also sprach Zarathustra* (*Thus Spake Zarathustra*, *1883*), book ii, chapter 2.

2 Ibid., book i, chapter 20.

3 Ibid., Introduction, para. 2.

4 *Unzeitgemässe Betrachtungen* (*Thoughts out of Season*, 1874), book ii, para. 10.

5 *Morgenröte* (*Aurora*), para. 326 *et passim*.

6 See Erich Heller, 'Burckhardt and Nietzsche', chapter 3 in *The Disinherited Mind* (New York, 1957).

7 '. . . to be compelled to look and at the same time to yearn beyond the looking . . .' (*The Birth of Tragedy*, section 24).

8 Nietzsche himself raises these objections in the dithyrambic 'Versuch einer Selbstkritik' ('Essay in Self-Criticism') of 1886.

9 *Der griechische Staat* (*The Greek State*), written before *The Birth of Tragedy* but published posthumously.

10 *Zur Genealogie der Moral* (*The Genealogy of Morals*, 1887), ii, section 17.

11 I assume that no 'evidence' satisfactory to a historian is likely to decide the issue.

12 Section 23 of *The Birth of Tragedy*; see also the peroration of Heine's *History of Religion and Philosophy in Germany*.

13 See the 1852 introduction to his famous *Dictionary*.

14 This is the burden of Marx's polemic in the *German Ideology* of 1843.

15 '. . . in der Sehnsucht der Besten'. H. A. Korff, quoted from W. Emmerich, *Germanistische Volkstumsideologie* (Tübingen 1968).

16 *Also sprach Zarathustra*, book iii, chapter 13.

17 First Duino Elegy.

18 Second stanza of 'Hälfte des Lebens', 'Middle of Life', in Michael Hamburger's translation.

Select Reading List

HISTORY

Eyck, Erich, *Bismarck and the German Empire*, London 1960. (This is a one-volume abridgement of Eyck's *Bismarck*, 3 vols., Zürich 1941–4).

Heuss, Theodor, *Ein Vermächtnis: Werk und Erbe von 1848*, Stuttgart 1948.

Menzel, Karl Adolf, *Neuere Geschichte der Deutschen, seit der Reformation*, Breslau ²1854–5.

New Cambridge Modern History, The, vol. 10 (1960), *The Zenith of European Power*, 1830–70, ed. J. P. T. Bury; see especially chapter vii, 'Imaginative Literature' by Erich Heller.

Obermann, Karl (ed.), *Einheit und Freiheit: die deutsche Geschichte von 1815 bis 1849, in zeitgenössischen Dokumenten dargestellt und eingeleitet*, Berlin 1950.

Pflanze, Otto, *Bismarck and the Development of Germany . . . 1815–1871*, Princeton 1963.

Schnabel, Franz, *Deutsche Geschichte im neunzehnten Jahrhundert*, Freiburg/B, 4 vols., ²1948–55.

Taylor, A. J. P., *Bismarck, the Man and the Statesman*, London 1955.

—— *The Course of German History: a Survey of the Development of Germany since 1815*, New York ²1962 (paperback).

—— *The Habsburg Monarchy, 1809–1918: a History of the Austrian Empire and Austria–Hungary*, London ²1964.

SOCIAL AND INTELLECTUAL HISTORY

Bramsted, Ernest Kohn, *Aristocracy and the Middle Classes in Germany; Social Types in German Literature, 1830–1900*, Chicago ²1964.

Chamberlain, H. S., *The Foundations of the Nineteenth Century*, New York 1912.

Dahrendorf, Ralf, *Gesellschaft und Demokratie in Deutschland*, München 1965.

Engels, Friedrich, *Germany: Revolution and Counter-Revolution* (articles, in collaboration with Karl Marx, from the *New York Daily Tribune*, 1851–2), New York 1933.

Heuss, Alfred, *Theodor Mommsen und das neunzehnte Jahrhundert*, Kiel 1956.

Hughes, H. S., *Consciousness and Society*, New York 1961, London 1958.

Kohn, Hans, *The Mind of Germany: the Education of a Nation*, New York 1960.

Marx, Karl and Engels, Friedrich, *The German Ideology*, parts I and III, ed. R. Pascal, New York 1947.

REALISM AND NINETEENTH-CENTURY GERMAN LITERATURE

Adorno, Theodor Wiesengrund, *Noten zur Literatur*, 3 vols., Berlin 1958–66.

Auerbach, Erich, *Mimesis; the Representation of Reality in Western Literature* (trsl. W. R. Trask), Princeton 1953 etc.

Bennett, E. H., *A History of the German Novelle from Goethe to Thomas Mann*[2], revised &c. by H. M. Waidson, Cambridge 1961.

Brinkmann, Richard, *Wirklichkeit und Illusion*, Tübingen [2]1966.

Gray, R. D., *The German Tradition in Literature, 1871–1945*, Cambridge 1965.

Hamburger, Michael, *From Prophecy to Exorcism: the Premises of Modern German Literature*, London 1965.

Heller, Erich, *The Artist's Journey into the Interior, and other essays*, New York 1965.

—— *The Disinherited Mind: Essays in Modern German Literature*, New York 1957.

Höllerer, Walter, *Zwischen Klassik und Moderne: Lachen und Weinen in der Dichtung einer Übergangszeit*, Stuttgart 1953.

Killy, Walther, *Wirklichkeit und Kunstcharakter: neun Romane des 19. Jahrhunderts*, München 1963.

Levin, Harry, 'A Symposium on Realism', arranged by Harry Levin, in *Comparative Literature*, III/3, Oregon 1951.

Lukács, Georg, *Die Theorie des Romans*, Neuwied [2]1963.
—— *Historical Novel, The* (trsl. H. and S. Mitchell), New York 1965.
—— *Studies in European Realism* (trsl. E. Bone), New York, 1964.
—— *Deutsche Realisten des neunzehnten Jahrhunderts*, Bern 1951.
Martini, Fritz, *Deutsche Literatur im bürgerlichen Realismus 1848–1898*, Stuttgart [2]1964.
Mayer, Hans, *Von Lessing bis Thomas Mann. Wandlungen der bürgerlichen Literatur in Deutschland*, Pfullingen 1959.
Muschg, Walter, *Tragische Literaturgeschichte*, Bern 1948.
Pascal, R., *The German Novel*, Manchester 1957.
Pongs, H., 'Ein Beitrag zum Dämonischen im Biedermeier', in *Dichtung und Volkstum*, xxxvi, 1935, pp. 235–60.
Ritchie, J. M., 'The Ambivalence of "Realism" in German Literature, 1830–1880', in *Orbis Litterarum*, xv, 1960, pp. 200–17.
Roethe, G., *Deutsche Dichter des 18. und 19. Jahrhunderts und ihre Politik*, Berlin 1919.
Silz, Walter, *Realism and Reality: Studies in the German Novelle of Poetic Realism*, Chapel Hill 1954.
Staiger, Emil, *Die Kunst der Interpretation*, Zürich [2]1963; esp. chapter 2 on Mörike and chapter 12 on C. F. Meyer.
Stern, J. P., *Re-Interpretations: Seven Studies in Nineteenth-Century German Literature*, London 1964.
Weigel, Hans, *Flucht vor der Grösse: Beitrag zur Erkenntnis und Selbsterkenntnis Österreichs*, Wien 1960. (Essays on Grillparzer, Nestroy, Stifter etc.)
Wellek, René, 'The Concept of Realism in Literary Scholarship', in *Neophilologus*, xxxv, 1961, pp. 1–20.

GRILLPARZER

Baumann, Gerhart, *Franz Grillparzer. Sein Werk und das österreichische Wesen*, Wien 1954.
Fülleborn, Ulrich, *Das dramatische Geschehen im Werk Franz Grillparzers*, München 1966.
Müller, Joachim, *Franz Grillparzer*, Stuttgart 1963 (ed. *Metzlers Realienbücher für Germanisten*).
Nadler, Josef, *Franz Grillparzer*, Wien n.d. [1948?].
Naumann, Walter, *Grillparzer: das dichterische Werk*, Stuttgart 1955.

Politzer, Heinz, *Franz Grillparzers 'Der arme Spielmann'*, Stuttgart 1967.

Strich, Fritz, *Franz Grillparzers Aesthetik*, Berlin 1905.

Volkelt, Johannes Immanuel, two essays on Grillparzer in *Zwischen Dichtung und Philosophie*, München 1908.

Yates, Douglas, *Franz Grillparzer, A Critical Biography*, vol. i (the only vol. published), Oxford, 1946.

NESTROY

Forst-Battaglia, Otto, *Johann Nestroy*, München [1962].

Kraus, Karl, *Nestroy und die Nachwelt. Zum 50. Todestage gesprochen . . .*, Wien 1912.

Rommel, Otto, *Johann Nestroy: der Satiriker auf der Altwiener Komödien-bühne*, Wien 1948.

HEBBEL

Kreuzer, Helmut, *Hebbel in neuer Sicht*, Stuttgart 1963.

Liepe, Wolfgang, essays on Hebbel in *Beiträge zur Literatur – und Geistesgeschichte*, ed. E. Schulz, Neumünster 1963.

Meetz, Anni, *Friedrich Hebbel*, Stuttgart 1962 (ed. *Metzlers Realien-bücher . . .*).

Purdie, Edna, *Friedrich Hebbel, A Study of His Life and Work*, London 1932.

Walzel, Oskar Franz, *Hebbelprobleme: Studien*, Leipzig 1909.

BÜCHNER

Johann, E., *Georg Büchner in Selbstzeugnissen und Bilddokumenten*, Hamburg 1956.

Knight, A. H. J., *Georg Büchner*, Oxford 1951.

Mayer, Hans, *Georg Büchner und seine Zeit*, Wiesbaden [2]1960.

Mayer, Hans, 'Georg Büchners aesthetische Anschauungen', in *Zeitschrift für deutsche Philologie*, lxxiii, Berlin 1954, pp. 129–60.

Schmid, Peter, *Georg Büchner, Versuch über die tragische Existenz*, Bern 1940.

Viëtor, Karl, *Georg Büchner: Politik, Dichtung, Wissenschaft*, Bern 1949.

White, J. S., 'Georg Büchner, or the Suffering through the Father', in *The American Image*, ix, Boston 1952, pp. 365–427.

HEINE

Butler, E. M., *Heinrich Heine: a biography*, London 1956.

Fairley, Barker, *Heinrich Heine, an Interpretation*, Oxford 1954.

Galley, Eberhard, *Heinrich Heine*, Stuttgart 1963 (*Metzlers Realienbücher* . . .).

Marcuse, Ludwig, *Heinrich Heine in Selbstzeugnissen und Bilddokumenten*, Hamburg 1960.

Kraus, Karl, 'Heine und die Folgen', in *Die Fackel*, vol. xiii, Wien 1911, nos. 329/330, pp. 1–33.

Prawer, S. S., *Heine: Buch der Lieder*, London 1960.

—— *Heine, the Tragic Satirist; a Study of his Later Poetry, 1827–1856*, Cambridge 1961.

Rose, William, *Heinrich Heine: Two Studies of His Thought and Feeling*, Oxford 1956.

Spann, Meno, *Heine*, London 1966 (in *Studies in Modern European Literature and Thought*).

Vermeil, Edmond, *Henri Heine, ses vues sur l'Allemagne et les révolutions européennes*, Paris 1939.

MÖRIKE

Goes, Albrecht, *Mörike*, Stuttgart ²1954.

Guardini, Romano, *Gegenwart und Geheimnis: eine Auslegung von fünf Gedichten Eduard Mörikes*, Würzburg 1957.

Gundolf, Friedrich, *Romantiker* (Neue Folge), Berlin 1931, chapter 5.

Mare, M. L., *Eduard Mörike, the Man and the Poet*, London, 1957.

Meyer, Herbert, *Eduard Mörike*, Stuttgart 1961 (*Metzlers Realienbücher* . . .).

Prawer, S. S., *Mörike und seine Leser: Versuch einer Wirkungsgeschichte*, Stuttgart 1960.

Wiese, Benno von, *Eduard Mörike*, Tübingen 1950.

STIFTER

Aprent, Johannes, *Adalbert Stifter, eine biographische Skizze*, Nürnberg 1955.

Bertram, Ernst, *Georg Christoph Lichtenberg. Adalbert Stifter: Zwei Vorträge*, Bonn 1919.

Blackall, E. A., *Adalbert Stifter, A Critical Study*, Cambridge 1948.

Fischer, K. G., *Adalbert Stifter, psychologische Beiträge zur Biographie*, Linz 1961.

Hein, A. R., *Adalbert Stifter, sein Leben und seine Werke*, Wien[2] 1952.

Hohoff, Kurt, *Adalbert Stifter: seine dichterischen Mittel und die Prosa des neunzehnten Jahrhunderts*, Düsseldorf 1919.

Lunding, E. P., *Adalbert Stifter. Mit einem Anhang über Kierkegaard und die existentielle Literaturwissenschaft*, Kjøbenhavn 1946.

Roedl, Urban, *Adalbert Stifter: Geschichte seines Lebens*, Bern[2] 1958.

Staiger, Emil, *Adalbert Stifter als Dichter der Ehrfurcht*, Zürich 1952.

KELLER

Böschenstein, Hermann, *Gottfried Keller: Grundzüge seines Lebens und Werkes*, Bern 1948.

Fränkel, Jonas, *Gottfried Kellers politische Sendung*, Zürich 1939.

Lukács, Georg, *Gottfried Keller*, Berlin 1947.

Rowley, B. A., *Keller: Kleider machen Leute*, London 1960.

Ziegler, Leopold, *Dreiflügelbild: Gottfried Keller, Heinrich Pestalozzi, Adalbert Stifter*, München 1961.

MEYER

Faesi, Robert, *Conrad Ferdinand Meyer*, Frauenfeld [2]1948.

Henel, Heinrich, *The Poetry of Conrad Ferdinand Meyer*, Madison 1954.

Williams, W. D., *The Stories of C. F. Meyer*, Oxford 1962.

STORM

Bonwit, Marianne, *Der leidende Dritte: das Problem der Entsagung in bürgerlichen Dramen und Novellen, besonders bei Theodor Storm*, Berkeley 1952.

McCormick, E. A., *Theodor Storm's Novellen: Essays on Literary Technique*, Chapel Hill 1964.

Rogers, T. J., *Techniques of Solipsism: a Study of Theodor Storm's Narrative Fiction* (Cambridge 1970).

Wedberg, Lloyd Warren, *The Theme of Loneliness in Theodor Storm's Novellen*, The Hague 1964.

FONTANE

Demetz, Peter, *Formen des Realismus: Theodor Fontane*, München 1964.
Gilbert, Mary-Enole, *Das Gespräch in Fontanes Gesellschaftsromanen*, Leipzig 1930.
Mann, Thomas, 'Anzeige eines Fontane-Buches' (1919) in *Reden und Aufsätze*, Oldenburg, 1, 1965, pp. 294–304.
Mann, Thomas, 'Der alte Fontane', in *Adel des Geistes*, Oldenburg 1959, pp. 448–69.
Schillemeit, Jost, *Theodor Fontane: Geist und Kunst seines Alterswerks*, Zürich 1961.
Wandrey, K., *Theodor Fontane*, München 1919.

SCHOPENHAUER

Copleston, F. C., *Arthur Schopenhauer, Philosopher of Pessimism*, London 1946.
Fischer, Kuno, *Schopenhauers Leben, Werke und Lehre*, Heidelberg ³1934.
Keyserling, Hermann Alexander Graf von, *Schopenhauer als Verbilder*, München 1910.
Simmel, Georg, *Schopenhauer und Nietzsche*, Leipzig 1907.
Wolff, Hans Matthias, *Arthur Schopenhauer hundert Jahre später*, Bern n.d. [1960].

NIETZSCHE

Andler, C. P. T., *Nietzsche, sa vie et sa pensée*, Paris ⁶1958.
Bertram, Ernst, *Nietzsche: Versuch einer Mythologie*, Bonn ⁸1965.
Brock, Werner, *Nietzsches Idee der Kultur*, Bonn 1930.
Copleston, F. C., *Friedrich Nietzsche, philosopher of culture*, London 1942.
Heidegger, Martin, *Nietzsche*, Pfullingen 1961.
Heller, Erich, *The Modern German Mind: the Legacy of Nietzsche in French and German Letters Today* (Library of Congress Lectures), Washington 1960.
Jaspers, Karl, *Nietzsche: an Introduction to the Understanding of His*

Philosophical Activity (trsl. C. F. Wallraff and F. J. Schmitz), Tucson 1965.

Jaspers, Karl, *Nietzsche and Christianity* (trsl. E. B. Ashton), Chicago 1961.

Knight, A. H. J., *Some Aspects of the Life and Work of Nietzsche . . .* , Cambridge 1933.

Mann, Thomas, *Nietzsche's Philosophy in the Light of Contemporary Events* (Library of Congress Lectures), Washington 1947.

Podach, E. F., *The Madness of Nietzsche* (trsl. F. A. Voigt), New York 1931.

Salin, Edgar, *Jakob Burckhardt und Nietzsche*, Heidelberg ²1948.

Schlechta, Karl, *Nietzsches grosser Mittag*, Frankfurt 1954.

Wolff, H. M., *Friedrich Nietzsche, der Weg zum Nichts*, Bern n.d.

Würzbach, F. (ed.), *Nietzsche: sein Leben in Selbstzeugnissen, Briefen und Berichten*, Berlin 1943.

Index

Note: Page references in italic indicate extensive treatment.